Editor
Lori Kamola, M.S. Ed.

Managing Editor
Karen Goldfluss, M.S. Ed.

Editor-in-Chief
Sharon Coan, M.S. Ed.

Illustrator
Ken Tunell

Cover Artist
Denise Bauer

Art Coordinator
Denice Adorno

Imaging
James Edward Grace

Product Manager
Phil Garcia

Many pages taken from
Extension Activity Book Series,
Teaching Spice, and *Thinking*
Skills Series
Publisher:
Blake Education

Publishers
Rachelle Cracchiolo, M.S. Ed.
Mary Dupuy Smith, M.S. Ed.
Americanized Edition

Brain Games
for Kids

Contributing Authors

Rosalind Curtis, Maiya Edwards,
Jean Haack, Fay Holbert,
Sharon Shapiro, Timothy Tuck

Introduction

Today's children are the problem solvers of the future. Children need many opportunities to explore creative solutions to problems, and unfortunately, many activity books for children ask questions with only one right answer or that can be answered without much thought put into the process. This book is a compilation of creative, fun, and unique activities for children to complete independently. This book is divided into two units, each containing three sections: *Brain Warm-ups, Brain Workouts,* and *Brain Challenges.* The sections progress from easier activities to more challenging ones. Within each section are four categories: Math, Word Activities, Writing, and Creative Thinking. While the first three of these categories are often thought of as basic skills, in this book, the activities all emphasize creative-thinking strategies. Some of the activity pages are word puzzles with a twist: each asks a question that is solved with the help of a clue or some scrambled letters after the rest of the activity has been completed. Other activities include math word problems that encourage drawing pictures to help solve the question. On other pages, children are given a creative writing prompt and encouraged to write and illustrate a story. Many pages are fun thinking skills activities asking children to create new objects or change and improve objects and explain their thinking. All children can learn to think more critically and creatively. A foundation in creative thinking skills will enable children to pursue lifelong learning.

••••••••••••••••••••••••••• What is a Thinking Skill? •••••••••••••••••••••••••••

In addition to helping us think clearly, thinking skills help us critically and creatively collect information to effectively solve problems. As a result of learning thinking skills, children will also become more aware of decision-making processes.

Improved thinking encourages children to look at a variety of ideas, search to greater depth, practice more critical decision making, challenge accepted ideas, approach tasks in decisive ways, and search for misunderstandings, while keeping the aims of the task clearly in mind.

The end results will be decisions that are more reliable, deeper understanding of concepts, contributions that are more creative, content that is examined more critically, and products that are more carefully created.

••••••••••••••• Why do Children Need to Develop Thinking Skills? •••••••••••••••

Children need to develop the abilities to judge, analyze, and think critically in order to function in a democratic and technological society. A family should value the development of thinking skills and provide opportunities for these processes to be modeled and developed. Thinking skills can be taught, and all students can improve their thinking abilities. Creativity is present in children regardless of age, race, socioeconomic status, or different learning modes.

The basic skills are generally thought of as reading, writing, spelling, and math. These processes involve computation, recall of facts, and the basic mechanics of writing. Of course, parents should want their children to master basic skills, but the learning process should not stop there. Frequently, children are faced with tasks that expect them to demonstrate their ability to use higher level thinking without having had the opportunities to develop their abilities with these thinking processes.

Introduction *(cont.)*

Thinking Domains

It is desirable to develop different thinking domains, as they have different aims and develop different skills:

♦ *Critical thinking* examines, clarifies, and evaluates an idea, belief, or action's reasonableness. Students need to *infer*, *generalize*, take a *point of view*, *hypothesize*, and find *temporary solutions*.

♦ *Brainstorming*, *linking ideas*, *using analogies*, *creating original ideas*, *organizing information*, and looking at a problem from *different perspectives* will lead to alternative solutions useful in decision making and problem solving.

♦ The *collection*, *retention*, *recall*, and *use of information* when needed is another vital skill.

♦ *Creative thinking* develops original ideas.

Thinking Processes

Eight processes, categorized into cognitive and affective abilities, have been identified as being important in fostering thinking skills:

Cognitive (thinking) Abilities

Fluency allows as many ideas as possible to be thought of by children.

Flexibility helps children look at problems from different perspectives and think of ways to combine unusual ideas into something new and different. At times, objects may have to be grouped according to different criteria.

Originality involves producing unusual or unique ideas.

Elaboration involves adding or further developing ideas.

Affective (feeling) Abilities

Curiosity involves working out an idea by instinctively following a pathway.

Complexity involves thinking of more complex ways of approaching a task. This may involve searching for links, looking for missing sections, or restructuring ideas.

Risk-taking is seen in children who guess and defend their ideas without fear that others will make fun of their thoughts.

Imaginative children can picture and instinctively create what has never occurred and imagine themselves in other times and places.

Introduction *(cont.)*

Parents can help their children learn thinking skills in a variety of ways. There are many questions that parents can ask of themselves:

☆ Do our children have opportunities to work on problems where creative thinking is valued?

☆ Are they encouraged to apply history's lessons to today's problems?

☆ Are they involved in planning family outings that will satisfy the needs of all family members?

☆ Are they allowed to participate in family projects such as redesigning rooms?

☆ Most importantly, are children allowed to be different?

☆ Are they listened to, even if their ideas are unusual or impractical?

☆ Are they reassured that, even if they are disagreed with, their ideas and input are valuable?

☆ In terms of the family as a whole, are they encouraged to be part of an environment where it is acceptable to make mistakes?

☆ Is the focus on learning from our children?

Introduction (cont.)

Computer skills can be integrated into many aspects of the learning experience. Computer technology is useful for programming and problem solving. Spreadsheets and databases can develop higher order thinking skills and lateral thinking. They will also develop spacial orientation. Computer games can be used to motivate students and encourage task commitment. When software is carefully selected, it can be used to develop higher-order thinking skills. Simulation or strategy software is motivational and open-ended and involves players in critical thinking, risk taking, and real-life problem solving.

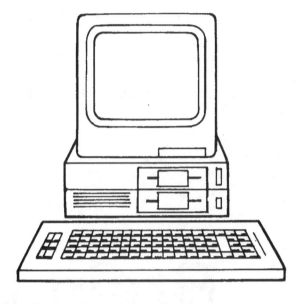

·························· Assessment ·······························

Many pages in this book have open-ended answers; no one correct answer is required. For the pages with concrete answers, an answer key is provided at the back of Part 1 and Part 2 of this book. These pages are not meant to be graded; the answer key is provided for self-checking of answers. Many of the pages in this book ask thought-provoking questions, stimulating the children to think creatively and use their imaginations. Children can work on the activities at their own rate; progress charts are included for children who like to keep track of the activities they have completed. A parent or other adult might choose to mark the progress chart swith a sticker or a stamp after the activities have been completed to reward the child for a job well done. There are many options of stickers that can be purchased through Teacher Created Materials; some that might work well are TCM#1929, TCM#1990, TCM#1989, and TCM#1982. Also provided are some awards in the back of the book that parents can fill out and give when their children complete several of the activity pages. Children often enjoy devising their own problem-solving techniques; space is provided on the activity pages for children to explain how they arrived at their answers.

Brain Games
for Kids
Part 1

6

Table of Contents
Part 1

Brain Warm-ups

Math

Word Activities

Part 1 Table of Contents *(cont.)*

Part 1 Table of Contents *(cont.)*

Brain Workouts

Math

Part 1 Table of Contents *(cont.)*

Part 1 Table of Contents *(cont.)*

Part 1 Table of Contents *(cont.)*

Brain Challenges

Math

Part 1 Table of Contents *(cont.)*

Word Activities

Writing

Part 1 Table of Contents

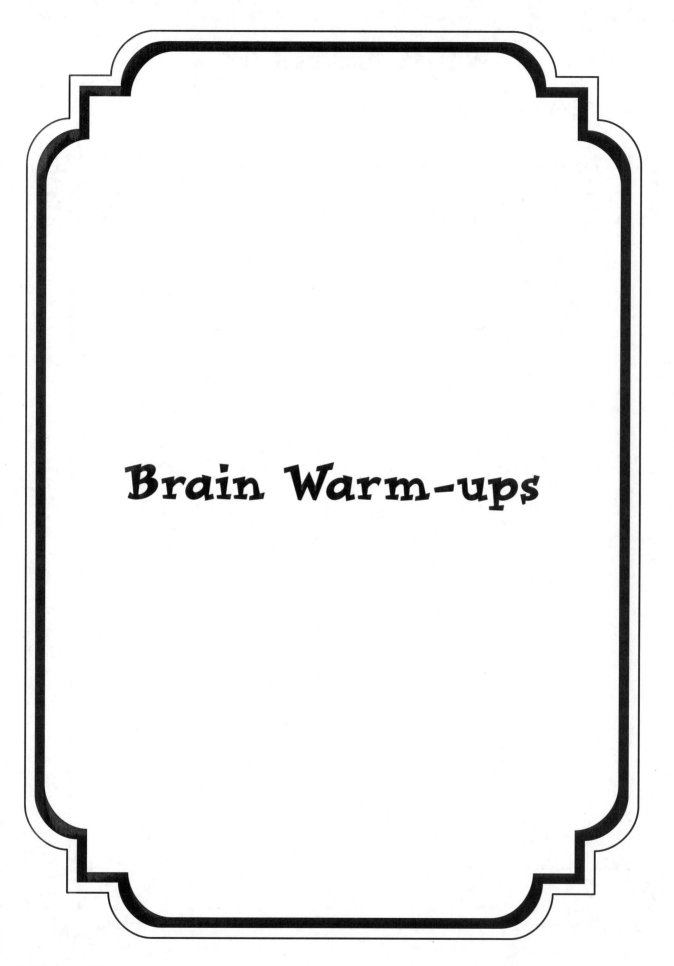

Brain Warm-ups

What Makes 4?

2 x 2 = 4. Think of 8 different ways to arrive at the number 4.

How Many?

1. A farmer has 12 sheep and 15 cows. How many animals does the farmer have altogether?

2. If a school has 12 classes and there are 25 students in each class, how many students are there altogether?

3. How many different ways can you show the number 285? Show 10 ways.

Representing Numbers

We can represent the number 12 using pictures and number sentences.

12 ✪✪✪✪✪✪✪✪✪✪ ✪✪	12 ✳✳✳✳ ☆☆☆☆ ✳✳✳✳
10 + 2	4 + 4 + 4

Think of two more ways to represent the number 12.

12	12

Use pictures and numbers to represent the numbers 11,15, and 18 in as many different ways as you can.

11	15	18

Train Games

Draw a train like the one shown using cylinders of different sizes.

How many cylinders make up your train?

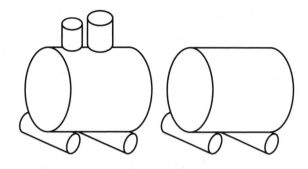

On the Beat

Out on the beat at 7 A.M., Police Officers Betty and Bernice pick up a trail. A brazen thief has stolen multiples of seven! Fortunately, the thief has dropped some along the way. So follow the trail until you exit the city block— and catch the thief!

	↓							49	
	7	21	49	70	77	50	14	56	
49	15			28				70	
	35	84	42	48	35	70	84	23	77
				20			21		70
49	14	63	56	42			14		56
	17			35	29	22	35	42	55
	77			56		48		49	70
	35	27	35	77	35	28			77
			48			14	7	14	28

20

Figure-Eights

Complete the figure-eight circuit by solving the problems below.

Across

1. 43 − 15

2. 9 x 2

3. 39 + 26 + 20

Down

1. 76 ÷ 2

2. 11 x 8

3. 100 − 11

4. 21 + 27

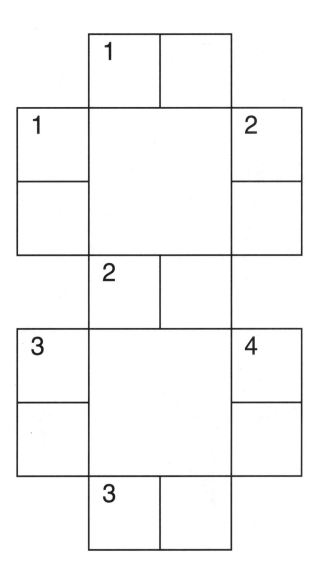

　　　　　　　　　　　　　　　　　　　　　　#8122 Brain Games for Kids

Travel Around the Island

Juan flew around the island in 95 hours. But which route did he take? Start from 'M' on the map and fly west to "A", then continue around the island. Your flight must take exactly 95 hours.

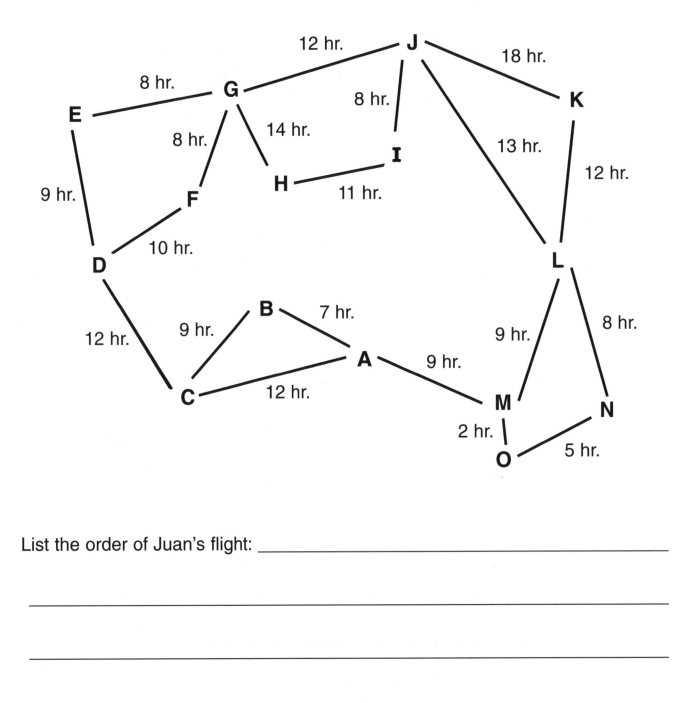

List the order of Juan's flight: _____

_____

_____

_____

A Grave Set of Sums

Starting with 12, write the answer to each math problem in the next circle. If you return to the top with the answer of 12, you've worked them all correctly!

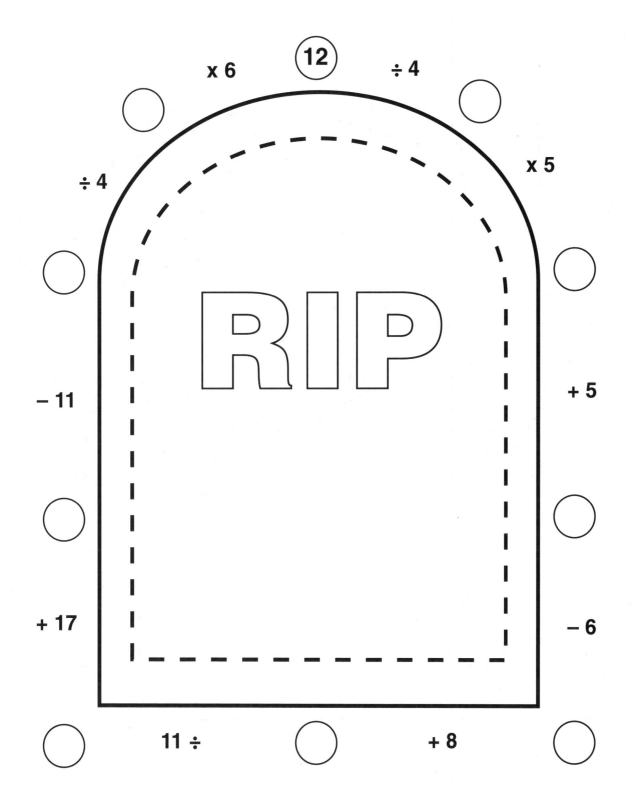

Tunnel Vision

George is stuck in another tunnel. The best way out is the one where he passes the smallest total, adding up the numbers as he goes. Can you find the best way for George to get out of the tunnel? Show your work.

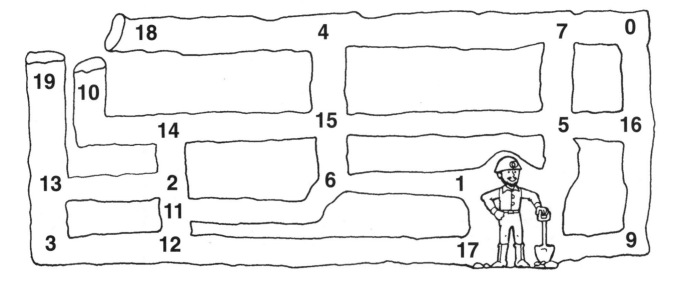

Roll 'em, Roll 'em, Roll 'em

The early stagecoach drivers were not very accurate when they were drawing their maps. This one certainly was not drawn to scale! The stagecoach needs to figure out how to get to town using the shortest route. The driver cannot tell which route is the shortest by looking at the map. Add up the miles between the towns to figure out which of the three routes (A, B, or C) is the shortest.

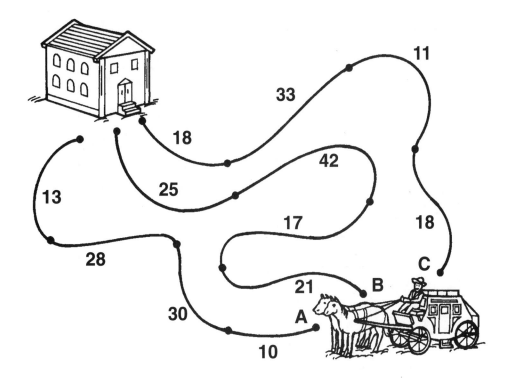

Which route should the stagecoach take? _____

What Comes Next?

Draw the next shape in each series.

1.	○ □ □ ○ □ □ ○ □	
2.	♡ △ △ ♡ △ △ ♡ △	
3.	○ ☆ ○ ☆ ○ ☆ ○ ☆	
4.	□ □ □ D D D ♡ ♡	
5.	○ △ ○ ▽ ○ △ ○ ▽	
6.	≡ ☆ □ ≡ ☆ □ ≡ ☆	
7.	□ △ △ ♡ ♡ ♡ D D D	
8.	△ △ ○ ○ △ △ □ □ △	
9.	♡ ♡ ☆ ♡ ♡ □ ♡ ♡ ☆ ♡	
10.	□ ▭ □ ▬ □ ▭ □ ▬ □	

Picture Shapes

Find the triangles and circles in the picture. Color the picture.

These things have △s:	These things have ◯s:

How Many Triangles?

How many triangles are in the picture? Count them and then color the picture.

There are _____ triangles.

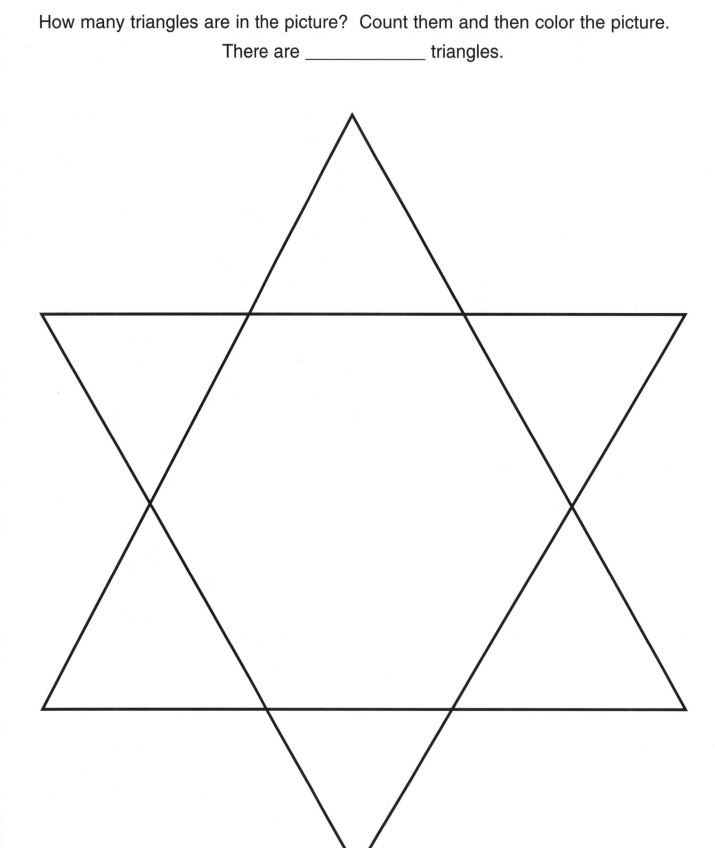

Color This Design

Color this design so that no shapes of the same color touch one another. You may use only three colors. (*Hint:* Think about the design before you begin to color.)

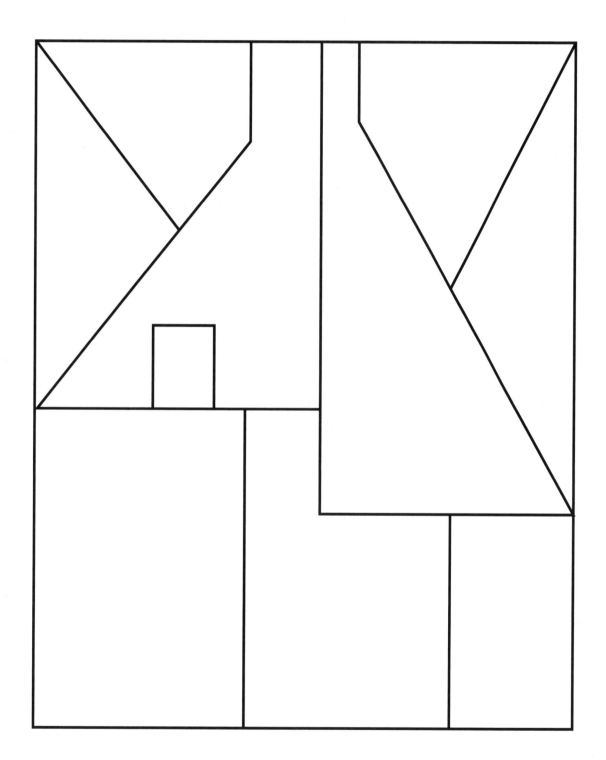

Addition and Subtraction Word Problems

Read the following problems. Circle the important facts you need to solve them. Use the space provided to find the solution to each problem.

1. There were 76 students in a school jog-a-thon. Twenty-six of them were in 3rd grade, 28 of them were in 4th grade, and 22 of them were in 5th grade.

   a. How many 4th and 5th-grade students were in the jog-a-thon?

   _____

   b. Which grade had the most students in the jog-a-thon? _____

2. The jog-a-thon route covered 150 kilometers. There were four rest stops for the runners. Niki ran 52 kilometers and stopped at the second rest stop.

   a. How much further does Niki have to run to complete the route?

   _____

   b. Has she gone at least half the distance? _____

Addition and Subtraction
Word Problems *(cont.)*

Read the following problems. Circle the important facts you need to solve them.
Use the space provided to find the solution to each problem.

3. Melita's team wanted to collect a total of $325.00. They collected
$208.75 from the jog-a-thon and $76.20 from a candy sale.

 a. How much money did they collect? _____

 b. Would they collect more money from three candy sales than from
 one jog-a-thon? _____

4. Twenty team members had lunch together at the third rest stop.
They had traveled 70 kilometers. Thirteen team members drank milk
with their lunches and the rest drank grape juice.

 a. How many team members drank grape juice? _____

 b. How many students did not drink milk or grape juice? _____

Addition and Subtraction
Word Problems *(cont.)*

Read the following problems. Circle the important facts you need to solve them. Use the space provided to find the solution to each problem.

5. Bill, Holly, and Katie collected contributions from their neighbors. Bill collected $13.78, Holly collected $16.85, and Katie collected $12.34.

   a. How much more did Holly collect than Bill? _____

   b. How much did Holly and Katie collect together? _____

6. To get ready, Carol bought new shoes for $36.00 and a new water bottle for $1.36. Her mom gave her $47.00 to spend.

   a. How much did she spend for the shoes and water bottle?

   _____

   b. How much more were the shoes than the water bottle? _____

Who's Who?

Mr. Fitzpatrick has three boys in his class who go by variations of the name Robert. From the statements below, determine each boy's full name and age. Mark an "**O**" in each correct box and an "**X**" in the boxes that are not correct.

1. Wilson is younger than Robert but older than Johnson.

2. Bobby is not the youngest.

3. None of the boys are the same age.

4. Anderson is the oldest.

	Johnson	Wilson	Anderson	7	8	9
Bob						
Bobby						
Robert						

Change for Fifty Cents

There are over 75 ways to make change for 50 cents. Work with a friend to list as many ways as you can. List the coins in order on each line, from largest to smallest. (*Hint:* Working from large to small coins will also help you find more ways to make change.) The list has been started for you.

Use the following abbreviations:

hd (half dollar)　　q (quarter)　　d (dime)　　n (nickel)　　p (penny)

1. 1 hd

2. 2 q

3. _____

4. _____

5. _____

6. _____

7. _____

8. _____

9. _____

10. _____

11. _____

12. _____

13. _____

14. _____

15. _____

16. _____

17. _____

18. _____

19. _____

20. _____

More Who's Who?

Mr. Martin has three boys in his science class who each go by a variation of the name Theodore. From the statements below, discover each boy's full name and age. Mark the correct boxes with an "**O**" and the incorrect boxes with an "**X**".

1. Agee is younger than Dalton but older than Chin.

2. Ted is not the youngest or the oldest.

3. Theodore's last name is Chin.

4. None of the boys are the same age.

	Agee	Chin	Dalton	8	9	10
Ted						
Theodore						
Teddy						

Shapes

The four shapes shown below are:

_____   _____

_____   _____

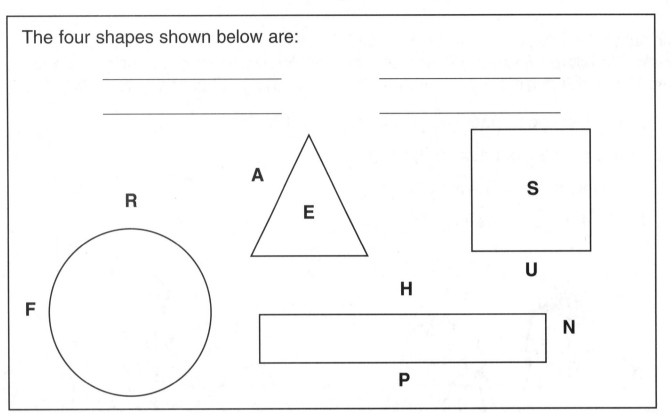

Directions: Answer the questions in the correct box to discover the hidden message.

Write the letter to the right of the rectangle in box 12.

Write the letter to the left of the triangle in boxes 3 and 7.

Write the letter under the rectangle in box 4.

Write the letter above the rectangle in box 2.

Write the letter inside the triangle in boxes 5 and 9.

Write the letter under the square in box 11.

Write the letter inside the square in boxes 1 and 6.

Write the letter above the circle in box 8.

Write the letter to the left of the circle in box 10.

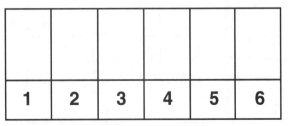
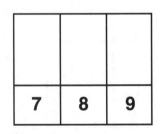
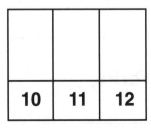

1	2	3	4	5	6

7	8	9

10	11	12

Escape the Volcano

Complete each math problem. Eight answers have the number 4 in them; they show the only safe way across the island to avoid the lava. Draw a line to show the way across.

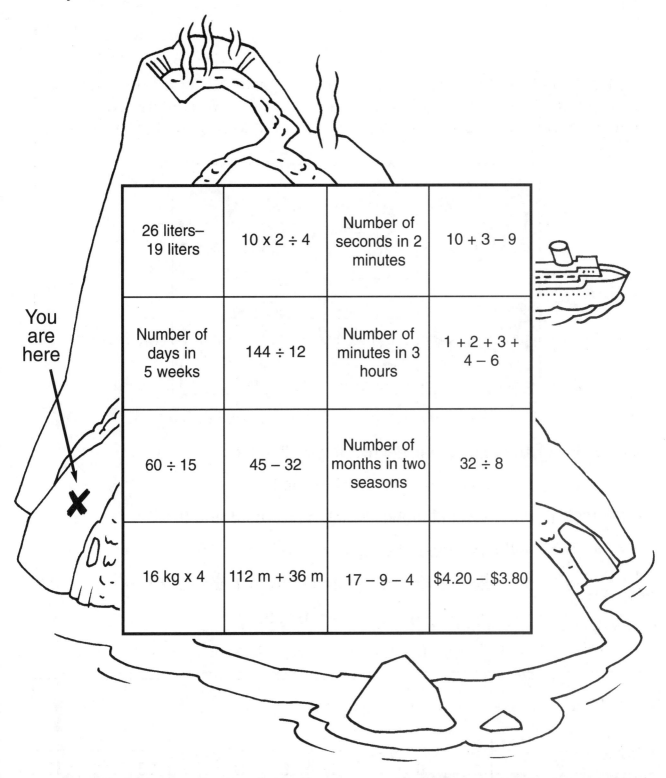

You are here

26 liters– 19 liters	10 x 2 ÷ 4	Number of seconds in 2 minutes	10 + 3 – 9
Number of days in 5 weeks	144 ÷ 12	Number of minutes in 3 hours	1 + 2 + 3 + 4 – 6
60 ÷ 15	45 – 32	Number of months in two seasons	32 ÷ 8
16 kg x 4	112 m + 36 m	17 – 9 – 4	$4.20 – $3.80

Math Puzzles

1. Two jugs are marked 5 L and 3 L. Show how they can be used to measure exactly 7 liters of water.

2. Until last week, all the dogs at Bob's Kennels (pictured below) had their own enclosures. Three more dogs will arrive this week. What is the fewest number of new walls Bob will have to build to make sure each dog will have its own enclosure?

3. A new clock has been invented which looks like this:

- 2 + 2 means start at 2 and move clockwise 2 numbers. (2 + 2 = 4)
- 0 − 1 means start at 0 and move counter-clockwise 1 number. (0 − 1 = 4)
- 4 x 2 means start at 0 and make 4 moves of 2 numbers clockwise. (4 x 2 = 3)

What times are represented here?

1 + 2 = _____	1 x 3 = _____	3 + 3 = _____
3 x 2 = _____	4 − 3 = _____	2 − 3 = _____

Alphabet Animals

Find names of animals for each letter of the alphabet. Write as many as you can think of for each letter. For example, for the letter "**D**" you could write: dog, duck, dinosaur, deer, etc.

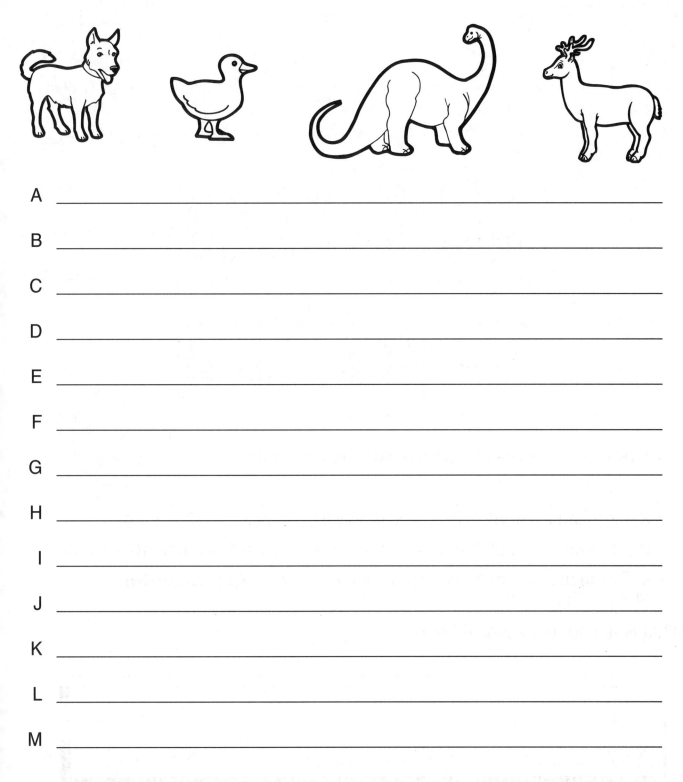

A _____

B _____

C _____

D _____

E _____

F _____

G _____

H _____

I _____

J _____

K _____

L _____

M _____

Alphabet Animals *(cont.)*

N   _____

O   _____

P   _____

Q   _____

R   _____

S   _____

T   _____

U   _____

V   _____

W   _____

X   _____

Y   _____

Z   _____

Alphabet Shapes

Print the alphabet using capital letters in three groups of shapes.

letters with all straight lines

letters with all curved lines

letters with both straight and curved lines

Treasure Island Word Hunt

There are lots of words in the book *Treasure Island*—and there are lots of words hidden in the words "Treasure Island," too. Because there are so many, we're making it easier for you—you only have to find five-letter words—and they can't be plurals ending in "S." List all the words you find.

TREASURE ISLAND

Riddle

Riddle: What do dentists in court trials have to swear?

1. Assemble the three-letter groups into one long line following the order of the spiral (starting from DYU).

2. Add 12 letter "O"s.

3. Answer the riddle!

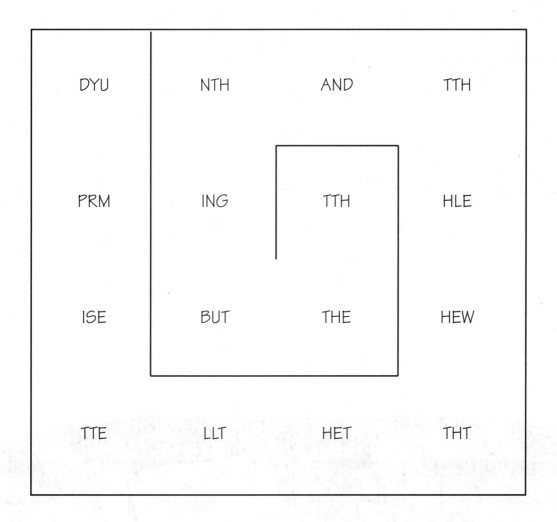

DYU	NTH	AND	TTH
PRM	ING	TTH	HLE
ISE	BUT	THE	HEW
TTE	LLT	HET	THT

And the answer is . . . _____

Sally in Space

It took Sally a long time to get into space. How long will it take you to change STARS into SPACE? Use each clue to form a new word, but you can only change one letter at a time.

S	T	A	R	S	
					fights
					extra
S	P	A	C	E	

What's in a Word: Napoleon

How many four (or more) letter words can you make from the word *Napoleon*?

Keeping a Tab on Things

Steph is learning how to play the guitar using tablature, a music reading system where numbers are used to represent the notes on the different strings. After playing a few tunes, she discovered she could make words from the different notes. Can you discover what each word is?

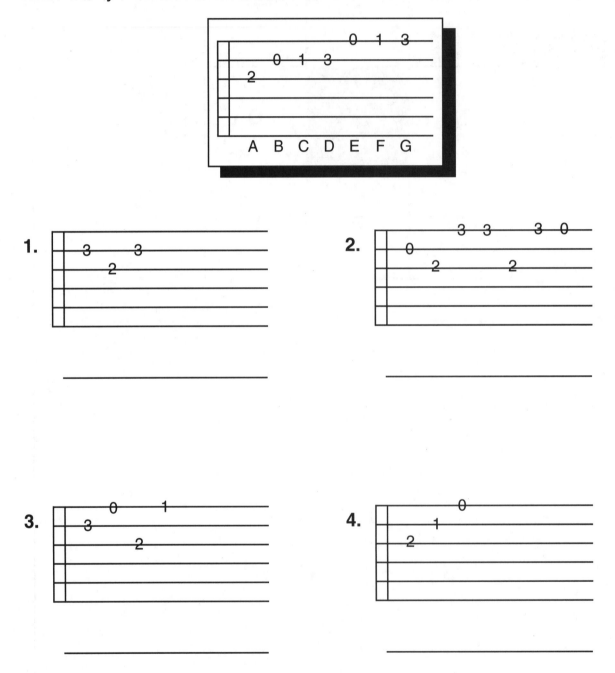

Spic-and-Span Spinach

Spinach the vegetable—full of vitamins and minerals! Spinach the word—full of other words! How many three- (or more) letter words can you find in spinach? You may not use plurals. (*Hint:* There are two words in the title!)

SPINACH

Alliteration Challenge

Peter Pan's name is alliterative; it has the same consonant (P) at the beginning of each word. Can you match up these other alliterative characters?

Black	**Tucker**
Doctor	**Duck**
Donald	**Doolittle**
Goosey	**Beauty**
Maid	**Mouse**
Mickey	**Rabbit**
Miss	**Marion**
Mister	**Gander**
Peter	**McGregor**
Roger	**Pan**
Tommy	**Muffet**

Weather Report

The weather forecast is in. But the words (which should be in the middle row of each grid) are missing. Find them by completing each of the three-letter words going down the grid.

C	S	B	A
Y	D	D	Y

S	P	W	O
E	T	T	D

A	I	P	S	O
E	L	T	M	D

O	H	A
F	G	E

Secret Code

Crack the code to figure out the message.

A	B	C	D	E	F	G	H	I	J	K	L	M
○	□	♥	✳	▲	❄	✦	→	☆	★	⇨	♣	▼

N	O	P	Q	R	S	T	U	V	W	X	Y	Z
🐦	☛	✂	✈	❖	◗	■	✏	✍	✚	☆	◉	✿

___ ___ ___ ___ ___ ___ ___
❖ ▲ ○ ✳ ☆ 🐦 ✦

___ ___   ___ ___ ___ ___   ___ ___
☆ ◗   ♣ ☛ ■ ◗   ☛ ❄

___ ___ ___ !
❄ ✏ 🐦

Rhyming Word Pairs

Find two words that rhyme and have about the same meaning as the phrase that is given. An example has been done for you.

bashful insect = shy fly

1. chicken yard _____

2. distant sun _____

3. warm pan _____

4. rabbit stool _____

5. boat journey _____

6. runaway fowl _____

7. good sleep _____

8. angry father _____

9. large fake hair _____

10. reading area _____

11. not fast bird _____

12. a group of noon eaters _____

13. damp plane _____

14. sweet rodents _____

15. kitty cap _____

                        #8122 Brain Games for Kids

Three-Letter Words

Each of the following words has a synonym that contains three letters. Write them on the lines.

1. work   ___ ___ ___

2. crazy   ___ ___ ___

3. fresh   ___ ___ ___

4. ancient   ___ ___ ___

5. sick   ___ ___ ___

6. every   ___ ___ ___

7. auto   ___ ___ ___

8. repair   ___ ___ ___

9. consume   ___ ___ ___

10. plump   ___ ___ ___

11. finish   ___ ___ ___

12. lad   ___ ___ ___

13. feline   ___ ___ ___

14. remark   ___ ___ ___

15. attempt   ___ ___ ___

Rhyming Word Pairs

Find an adjective that rhymes with a noun so that together the two words have about the same meaning as the phrase that is given. An example has been done for you.

soaked dog = soggy doggy

1. heavy slumber   _____

2. second male sibling   _____

3. able Daniel   _____

4. big flat boat   _____

5. naked bunny   _____

6. high shopping center   _____

7. crazy kid   _____

8. wooden lower limb   _____

9. igloo   _____

10. tuna dinner   _____

11. consume beef   _____

12. funny William   _____

13. heavy feline   _____

14. impolite man   _____

15. extra bus money   _____

16. short cry   _____

17. extra points   _____

18. aging green stuff   _____

19. downcast father   _____

20. loafing flower   _____

What Can You Make from Celluloid?

Celluloid was used for manufacturing a huge variety of items. Can you manufacture a huge variety of words? List all the words you can find using the letters in celluloid.

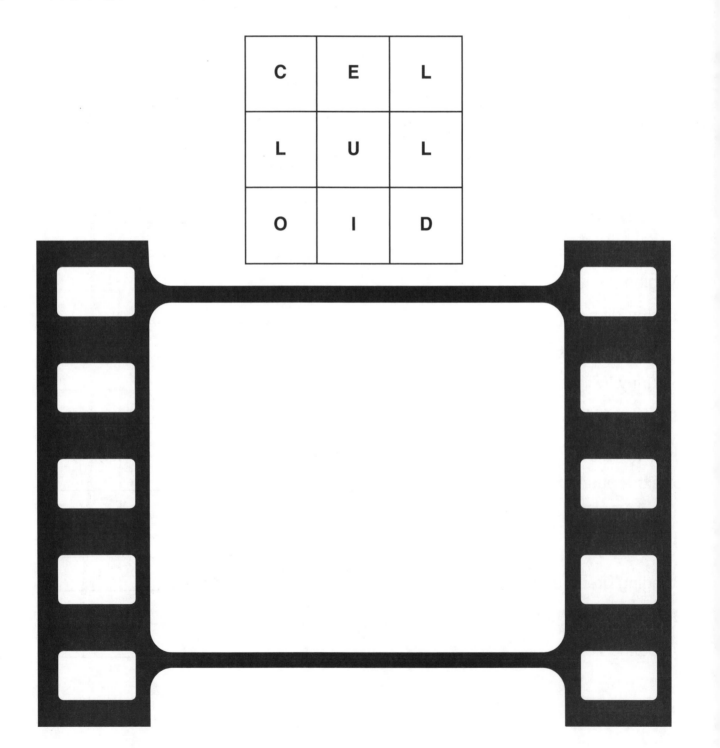

C	E	L
L	U	L
O	I	D

Only in America...

How many words of three letters or more can you make from the word AMERICA?

What Could It Be?

1. List some things that are smaller than your hand. Draw some of the items from your list in the box on the right.

   _____

   _____

   _____

   _____

   _____

2. What can be hidden under your shoe? Draw some of the items from your list in the box on the right.

   _____

   _____

   _____

   _____

   _____

3. What can you balance on your hand? Draw some the items from your list in the box on the right.

The Trancapar

Draw a trancapar. (There is no such thing as a trancapar, so it can be anything you like.)

Write a story about what happened to the trancapar last Tuesday.

_____

_____

_____

_____

_____

_____

What a Tale!

Write a story about the toaster and the cat. You can add other things to your story as you write it.

Any Animal

If you could be any animal in the world, which animal would you choose? Give at least five reasons for your choice. Draw a picture of your animal.

The Circus #1

Write a story about "My First Circus" from the point of view of a clown who is performing in one of the acts.

_____

_____

_____

_____

_____

_____

_____

_____

_____

_____

_____

The Circus #2

Start a story with this beginning: It was my first visit to the circus. I was very excited. Suddenly, the crowd went quiet. I looked up and could not believe my eyes. . .

You Won!

You have just won $50. You have to spend it all on your dog. Describe how you would spend your money.

Imagine . . .

Imagine you are only 6 inches (15 centimeters) tall. How would the world be different?

Promoting Your Least Favorite Subject

Be a copywriter and write a radio commercial for your least favorite school subject. (That's hard since you don't like the subject, but hey, advertising agencies have to do it all the time!)

Magic and Make-believe

What if Cinderella's Fairy Godmother could perform some magic for the Three Little Pigs and the Big Bad Wolf? What do you think they would ask for?

_____

_____

_____

_____

_____

_____

_____

_____

_____

_____

_____

_____

Life in a Goldfish Bowl

Pretend you are a goldfish. Think of a name for yourself and fill in the information below.

My name is _____.

I am a_____.

I eat _____.

Good things about living in a goldfish bowl.

Bad things about living in a goldfish bowl.

_____   _____

_____   _____

_____   _____

_____   _____

_____   _____

One day something terrible happened to me . . .

_____

_____

_____

_____

Clever Categories

Create categories for the following words and then divide the words into those groups. Put the words into their categories in the space below.

girl	chair	sock
butter	unicorn	egg
castle	cat	tree
apple	fairy	waterfall
forest	train	bicycle
cake	frog	fire engine

How Could You . . . ?

List all the different ways you could travel to school tomorrow:

_____

_____

_____

_____

_____

List how you could make people laugh:

_____

_____

_____

_____

_____

List other ways to use a magazine besides reading it:

_____

_____

_____

_____

List different uses for a spoonful of peanut butter:

_____

_____

_____

_____

More How Could You . . . ?

Think of ways that you could

. . . brush your hair without a hairbrush or comb.

. . . write a story without pencil or paper.

. . . get dressed without using clothes.

What If?

What if your friends all grew three feet taller in one night?

What if it rained milk?

What if people were born old and became younger?

Make a Picture

Choose a shape and change it into . . .

a car	a house	an imaginary friend	a dog

Jack and the Beanstalk

Imagine that Jack is climbing up the beanstalk. Draw four different pictures of what he might have seen as he climbed higher and higher.

Change the Chair

Redesign the chair using the BAR system. Explain your reasons for making the changes.

B = make it Bigger or smaller

A = Add something

R = Remove something and Replace it with something else

B

Reasons _____

_____

A

Reasons _____

_____

R

Reasons _____

_____

What Are These?

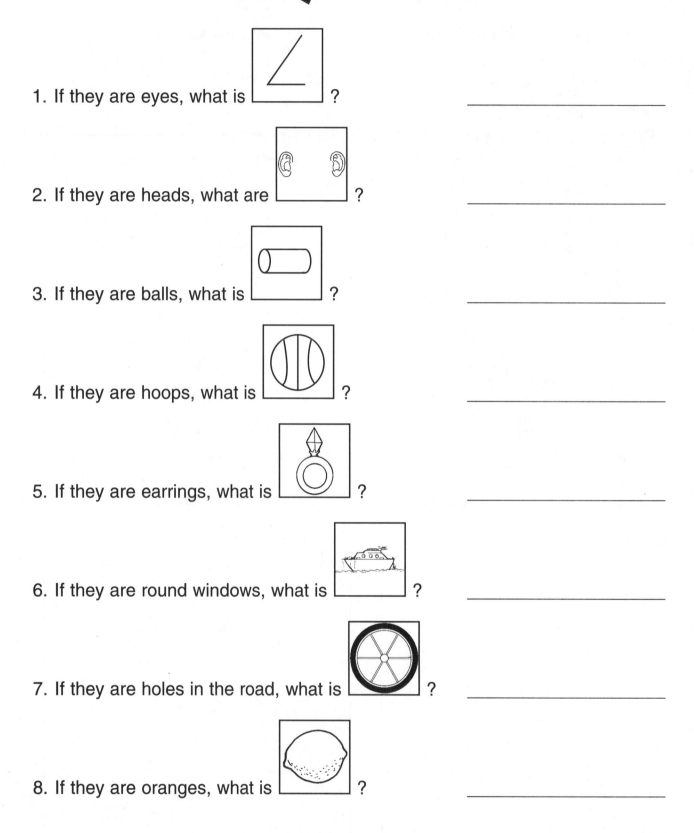

1. If they are eyes, what is [   ] ?   _____

2. If they are heads, what are [   ] ?   _____

3. If they are balls, what is [   ] ?   _____

4. If they are hoops, what is [   ] ?   _____

5. If they are earrings, what is [   ] ?   _____

6. If they are round windows, what is [   ] ?   _____

7. If they are holes in the road, what is [   ] ?   _____

8. If they are oranges, what is [   ] ?   _____

What is the Same?
What is Different?

Use the acronym SCUMPS to compare the two objects. List everything that you can think of about the objects that is the same or different.

S = Size   Same: _____

                Different: _____

C = Color   Same: _____

                Different: _____

U = Use   Same: _____

                Different: _____

M = Materials   Same: _____

                Different: _____

P = Parts   Same: _____

                Different: _____

S = Shape   Same: _____

                Different: _____

What Are These Splotches?

This is a baby bird with its beak open. It is crying for food.

Write in the space what each splotch could be.

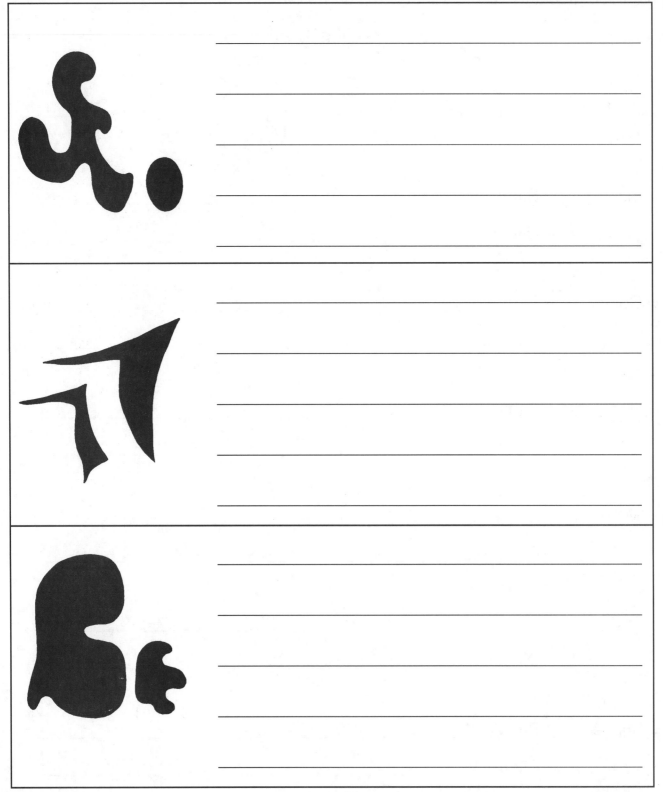

The Future

Design new tools and vehicles that community helpers (examples: firefighters, policemen, nurses might be able to use in the future.

Draw diagrams of your inventions with labels for their parts. Explain how your inventions would work.

_____

_____

_____

_____

People Who Help in the Community

1. Draw some of the equipment these community helpers use.

Fire Fighters	Police Officers	Ambulance Drivers

2. Draw an emergency where all three of the above community helpers have been called upon to work together.

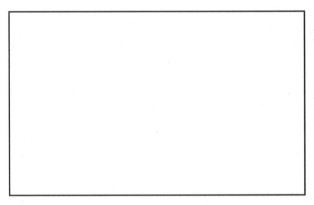

3. Describe what happened.

_____

_____

_____

_____

_____

A Different School

Design a new school. You can decide what the school will be called and what type of lessons are to be taught.

My new school will be called _____.

This is what my new school will look like.	
Lessons to be taught	**When**

I would like these lessons because _____

_____

_____

_____

Three important school rules will be:

1. _____

2. _____

3. _____

A New Toy

Develop a new toy that has wheels, wings, feet, and springs.

In the spaces below, write how many of each item your toy will have and draw what each part will look like.

Wheels	Wings	Feet	Springs

My toy will be called:_____

This is what my toy can do: _____

_____

_____

Draw how you and your friends could use this toy.

The best thing about this toy is: _____

Famous Sports People

1. Draw a picture of a famous sports person. Write some facts about this person.

   Name: _____

   Sport: _____

   Sport equipment used:

   _____

   _____

2. If you were to meet this person, what two questions would you like to ask him or her?

   a. _____

   b. _____

3. List four skills you would need to be good at this sport.

   Draw pictures of yourself practicing these skills.

Skill:	**Skill:**
Skill:	**Skill:**

Food

1. Draw a picture of each food.

| apple | potato | carrot | banana | orange |

| cake | sausages | ice cream | tomato | biscuits |

2. Sort these foods into different groups. For example, an apple is a healthy food.

Healthy Food	Unhealthy Food

Eating

Which of these foods would you like to eat for lunch?

Answer **Yes** or **No**

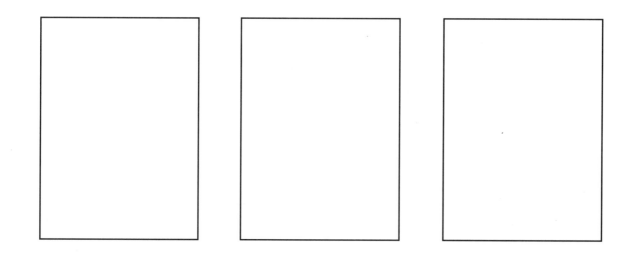

1. a cheese sandwich   _____

2. a bucket of nails   _____

3. leaves   _____

4. an apple   _____

5. yogurt   _____

6. snail sausages   _____

7. grapes   _____

8. a chocolate worm   _____

9. a banana   _____

10. spider jelly   _____

Imagine that you can eat anything you want for breakfast. List the items below and then draw a picture of what you would eat.

I would eat the following items:

1. _____   2. _____   3. _____

Environment Watch

1. What kind of damage has been done to the environment by modern methods of transportation?

_____

_____

_____

_____

_____

_____

2. Draw a picture of some of the damage that has been caused by the various types of transportation.

[ ]

3. Can anything be done to improve this, or is it too late?

Write your thoughts here: _____

_____

_____

_____

School Travel

Invent a new way you could travel to school. Draw a picture of your invented vehicle.

Patch the Balloon

The Montgolfier brothers' balloon was made up of two different colored stripes. Soon it got a few holes in it and had to be patched. The brothers didn't want any patch to touch a stripe of the same color, or another patch of the same color. What is the least number of colors they could use?

Taxi Ride

You've been lecturing on transportation systems at the city museum but it's time to return home. So, you call for a taxi.

1. Turn left onto East Terrace.

2. Take the second right.

3. Take the next right and then left.

4. Turn at the next right and pick up a passenger.

5. Turn right, cross the intersection, and stop. Pick up more passengers.

6. Turn right, then left.

7. Turn right, then right again. Cross the next intersection and stop. Get out of the taxi and leave town.

Questions:

1. How many people are in the taxi altogether? _____

2. How did you leave town? _____

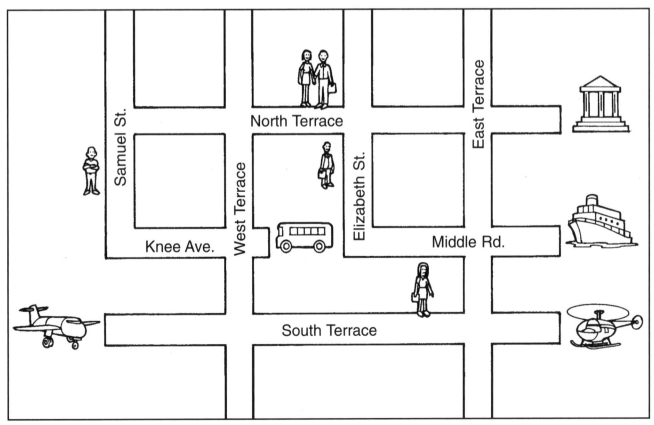

Stamp Forgery

List as many differences as you can find between the original stamp and the fake stamp below.

Original   **Fake**

_____

_____

_____

_____

_____

_____

_____

_____

_____

Postcard Rebus

Your lucky friend is on a round-the-world trip. You've received lots of postcards but sometimes it's tricky finding out just where in the world they've come from. Can you decode these countries' names?

Spot the Difference

Two landscape artists drew the same landscape, but on different days and at different times. Can you spot the ten differences?

_____   _____

_____   _____

_____   _____

_____   _____

A Light Humor

Match up the joke and the correct answer for a chuckle. Match up the joke and the incorrect answer for a real laugh.

Joke

| 1. Why was the lighthouse keeper fired? |
| 2. Why did the overweight captain change jobs? |
| 3. How do you know the sea is friendly? |
| 4. Did you hear about the red ship and the blue ship that collided? |
| 5. Why do shipments go in cars? |
| 6. Why did the lighthouse keeper go crazy? |
| 7. How can you tell lighthouses are happy? |
| 8. What lies on the bottom of the ocean and shivers? |

Answer

| a nervous wreck |
| and cargoes go in ships? |
| Both crews were marooned. |
| He couldn't sleep with the light on. |
| It's always waving. |
| The spiral staircase drove him around the bend. |
| They beam all the time. |
| to become a light housekeeper |

Plastic Memory Game

Look carefully at the picture below. It shows 12 different objects. Each object is made completely out of plastic or plastic parts. Looked long enough? On the following page, write a list of as many items as you can remember.

Plastic Memory Game *(cont.)*

How many objects can you remember? List them below.

_____

_____

_____

_____

_____

_____

_____

_____

_____

_____

_____

The Limbo of the Lost Yachts!

The Bermuda Triangle strikes again, snaring five yachts in its mysterious maze-like currents. Fortunately, four of the yachts can escape.

Which is the unlucky one? __B_____

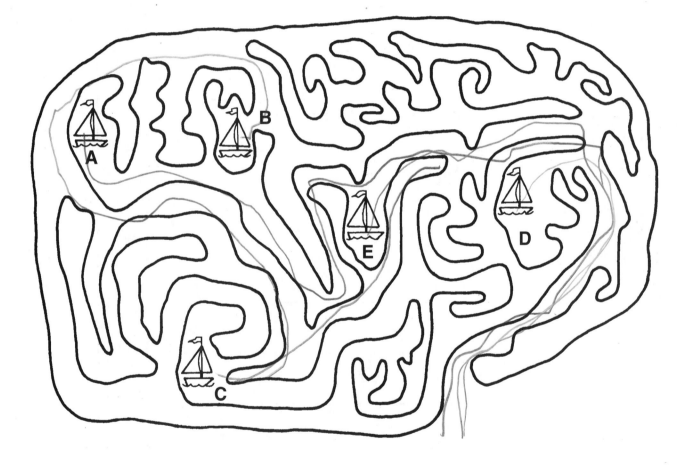

In My School Room

Draw a picture of a school room with the following items in it.

1 chalkboard   1 picture   4 books   3 chairs   3 tables

Equations

Each equation below contains the initials of words that will make it complete. Find the missing words. An example has been done for you.

9 P in the S S = 9 Planets in the Solar System

1. 26 L in the A = _____

2. 52 C in a D = _____

3. 88 P K = _____

4. 3 B M (S H T R) = _____

5. 4 Q in a G = _____

6. 11 P on a F T = _____

7. 7 C on the E = _____

8. 50 S in the U S = _____

9. 6 P for a T = _____

10. 20,000 L U the S = _____

11. 1,001 A N = _____

12. 5 D in a Z C = _____

13. 5 F on the R or L H = _____

14. 4 S in the Y = _____

15. 8 S on a S S = _____

School of the Future

Design a school of the future that would really appeal to children. Sketch and label some of your ideas below.

Elephant Jokes

Match these elephant jokes to the funniest answer.

Questions	Answers
How do you get an elephant out of the water?	A pachydermatologist
What do you call any elephant that is an expert on skin disorders?	An elephant rolling down a hill with a daisy in its mouth
What has two tails, two trunks, and five feet?	An elephant with spare parts
What is beautiful, gray, and wears very big glass slippers?	An inside-out elephant
What's gray on the inside and pink and white on the outside?	Take away its credit card
What's gray, yellow, gray, yellow . . .?	Cinderelephant
Why do elephants wear sandals?	Have you ever tried to iron one?
Why are elephants wrinkled?	So that they don't sink in the sand
How do you stop an elephant from charging?	wet

What a Racket!

1. Glasses

2. Make lenses bigger so frames don't interfere with vision.

3. Add sunshades, so sun doesn't get in the eyes.

4. Replace earpieces with elastic, so glasses stay on when playing sports.

Design a new and improved tennis racket using **BAR** to help you. Draw and explain each change.	**B** Make it **B**igger.
A **A**dd something.	**R** **R**eplace, change or **R**earrange.

Fairy Tale Designer

Design a business card for the Big Bad Wolf.

Create a different outfit for Little Red Riding Hood.

Crazy Combinations

Brainstorm a list of different fruit and follow this with a list of different animals. Draw an **anifruit** by combining features of one of the animals and one of the fruits. Give your **anifruit** a name. For example, a combination of an apricot and a cat could be an apricat or invent any name that feels appropriate. Describe what your anifruit does, what it likes, and what it doesn't like.

What Can it Be?

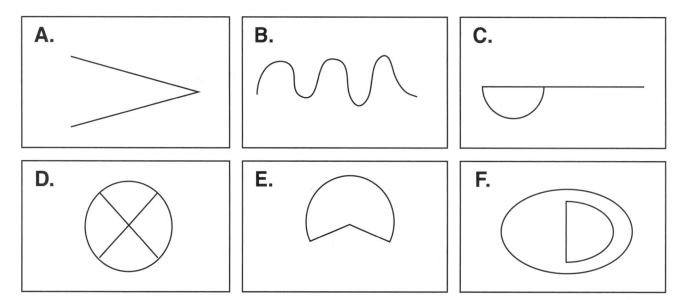

Look at the pictures and write what you think they could be. You can look at them in any way—sideways, backwards, right side up, or upside-down.

It's something to do with school. What is it?	It's something to do with the holidays. What is it?
A _____	A _____
B _____	B _____
C _____	C _____
D _____	D _____
E _____	E _____
F _____	F _____

An Ideal Pet

Create an animal that can fly, swim, walk, climb, carry you for long distances, and would make an ideal pet. Draw a picture of your pet and tell about it.

_____

_____

_____

_____

_____

Brain Workouts

Multiplication and Division Word Problems

Read each problem and then answer the questions.

The Bailey family runs a small market that not only sells but also grows fresh fruit and vegetables. They sell gardening tools, seeds, and plants. They help their customers with questions about picking which plants to grow and how to best care for them.

1. Two hundred fifteen watermelon seeds were planted in the ground. Five seeds were planted in each small hole. How many small holes were there?

2. The gardeners at Bailey's Market planted 48 onions in each of 12 rows. How many onions were planted?

3. A clerk sold Garrett a rake for $7.75 and a shovel for $13.77. He paid half and had his brother pay the other half. How much did each pay?

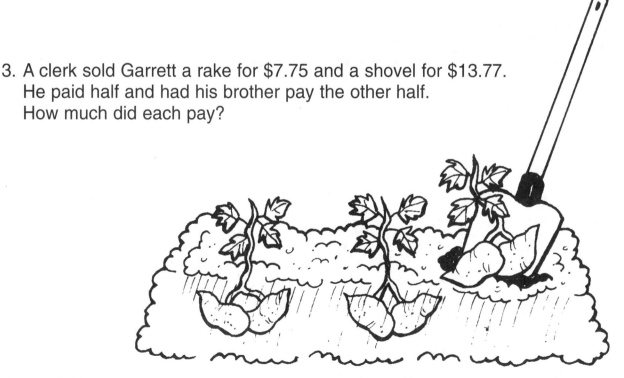

Multiplication and Division
Word Problems *(cont.)*

Read each problem and then answer the questions.

4. Tim bought 2,000 carrot seeds on Monday and 3,985 seeds on Tuesday.
   He needs to plant all of the seeds. He plants seven seeds in each hole.
   How many holes will he have when he is finished?

5. Randy planted seven rows of corn and each row had eight plants in it. He
   needed to wrap them into bundles of four. How many bundles would he
   have?

6. Two customers each bought 25 potatoes for a pot luck supper.
   They made 10 pots of stew and used all of the potatoes.
   How many potatoes did they use in each stew?

Multiplication and Division
Word Problems *(cont.)*

Read each problem and then answer the questions.

7. Each seed packet costs $.79. Robyn bought nine of them. How much did she spend?

8. Each seed packet has 135 seeds in it. Robyn will need to plant 15 seeds in a row. How many rows will she plant?

9. What will be the total cost of two bags of grapes at $2.00 each, one bag of potatoes at $1.99 each, and four baskets of strawberries at $3.46 each?

10. The workers need to move the display case that has the apples in it. There are six bins with different kinds of apples. Each bin has 44 apples in it. How many apples are there in the display case?

                           #8122 Brain Games for Kids

Change These Shapes

Create interesting objects from these shapes. Under each drawing explain what you have drawn.

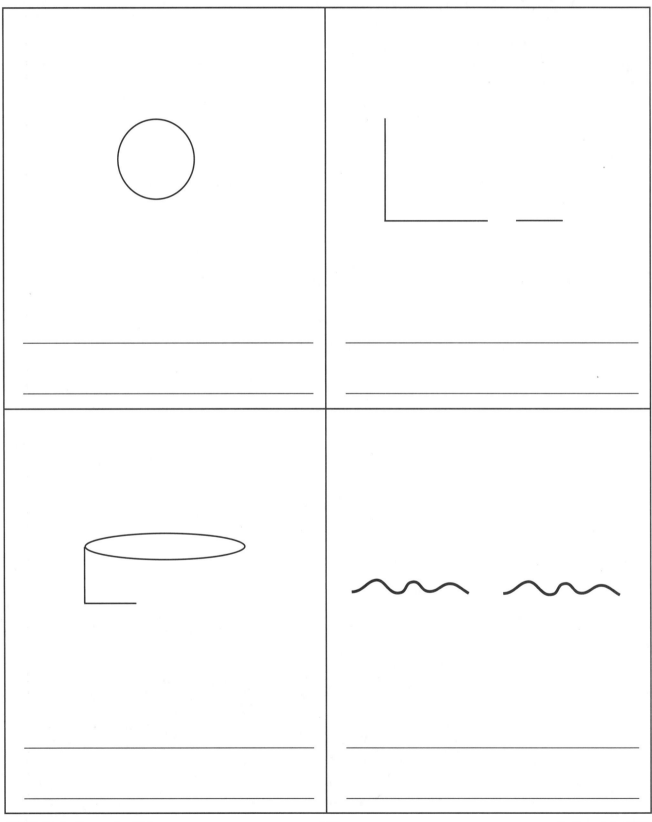

My Perfect Day

Write out a timetable for your perfect day.

For example: 8:00 A.M.—wake up and eat *ice cream* for breakfast.

Time	Event
_____	_____
_____	_____
_____	_____
_____	_____
_____	_____
_____	_____
_____	_____
_____	_____
_____	_____
_____	_____

What's the Question?

The answer is 50. What are 15 questions?

1. _____

2. _____

3. _____

4. _____

5. _____

6. _____

7. _____

8. _____

9. _____

10. _____

11. _____

12. _____

13. _____

14. _____

15. _____

Audition for Trivia Show

You have been asked to audition for a television quiz show called *Number Trivia.*
The television producer asks you to solve the following problem:

- Circle sets of three numbers that add up to eight.

- You can only circle each number once.

- When circling numbers you may not cross another line.

- You must use all of the numbers.

2	0	8	0	1
1	5	4	7	0
3	1	3	5	1
4	1	1	5	2
7	0	0	2	0
1	8	0	7	1

Audition for Trivia Show (cont.)

Imagine you have been hired as assistant television producer. Design a problem similar to the previous problem for another contestant to solve.

Measurement Mysteries

Solve this mystery.

a. Fred sells flour and potatoes in the market. In this market, a bucket filled with sand—a "sacket"—is the accepted measure of weight. Fred sells his flour for $1.79 per sacket and his potatoes for $2.47 per sacket. Frieda is a customer who buys seven sackets of flour and three sackets of potatoes. How much change will she receive if she pays with a $20 bill?

b. After receiving her change, Frieda finds a $5 bill in her purse. She doesn't like change and wants to spend as much of this money as she can. What can she buy from Fred that will leave her with the least amount of change?

A New Jail

The Police Commissioner of Toothpick City designed a brand new jail with 13 toothpicks. This jail had six cells for the prisoners. When he showed the design to the mayor, the mayor said he didn't like the shape. The mayor said, "If you used 12 toothpicks instead, you could have a much more interesting looking jail with the same number of cells."

Task: Use 12 toothpicks to build the new jail.

Old Jail

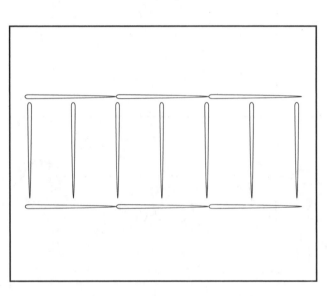

New Jail

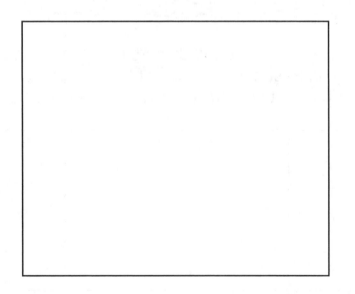

A New Jail *(cont.)*

Now try these!

   1 Start with 12 toothpicks in square 1.

   2. In square 2 move two toothpicks and make 2 squares.

   3. In square 3 move three toothpicks and leave only 3 squares.

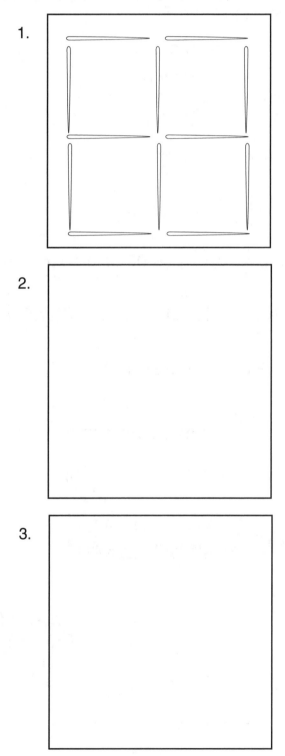

1.

2.

3.

Speeding Along

To calculate the average speed of a moving object, divide the distance traveled by the time taken. For example, a car travels 44 km in two hours. Its average speed is 44 ÷ 2 km/hour, i.e. 22 km/hour

Calculate the average speed of each of these moving objects.

1. A plane travels 1,470 km in three hours.   _____

2. A snail travels 55 cm in 11 minutes.   _____

3. A cyclist travels 95 km in five hours.   _____

4. A racing car travels 320 km in two hours.   _____

5. A dad with a baby carriage travels 2,000 m in 40 minutes.   _____

6. The space shuttle travels five km in 10 hours. (Careful!)   _____

   Why did the space shuttle travel so slowly? _____

   _____

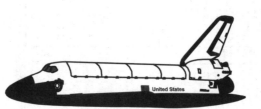

Recording Time Line

The past 100 years has seen sound recording progress from the wax cylinders of Edison's original phonograph through to the DVDs being installed in many computers. Use the clues to place all these recording inventions on the circular time line.

Cassette: Invented just in time to record the Beatles.

CD: Wow! They're about 20 years old!

DAT: Digital Audio Tape. Mainly found in videos, invented 93 years after the phonograph.

DVD: The latest and greatest!

Gramophone: The first flat record.

LP: Long-playing record. Invented 50 years after the tape recorder.

Phonograph: The first sound recording device.

Tape recorder: Invented in the 19th century.

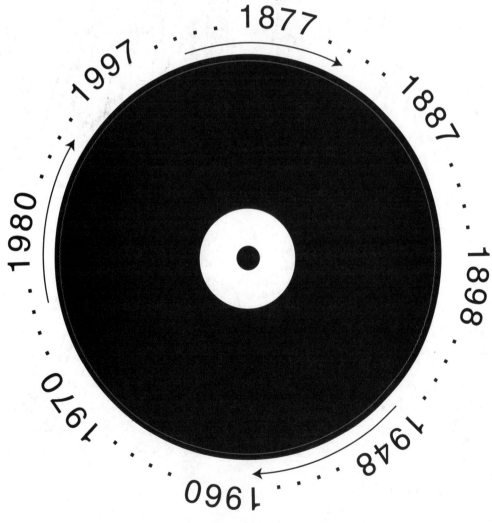

Island Math

The navigator on the Santa Maria has an unusual way of recording the year in which the expedition lands on each island. Can you figure out which were discovered in the same year as Columbus set sail?

373 x 4

186 x 8

1492 x 1

165 x 9

213 x 7

298 x 5

248 x 6

497 x 3

746 x 2

I've Been Framed!

Each number in the boxes below is written within a different shape or frame. Using this as a guide, write the correct number in each shape below and solve each problem.

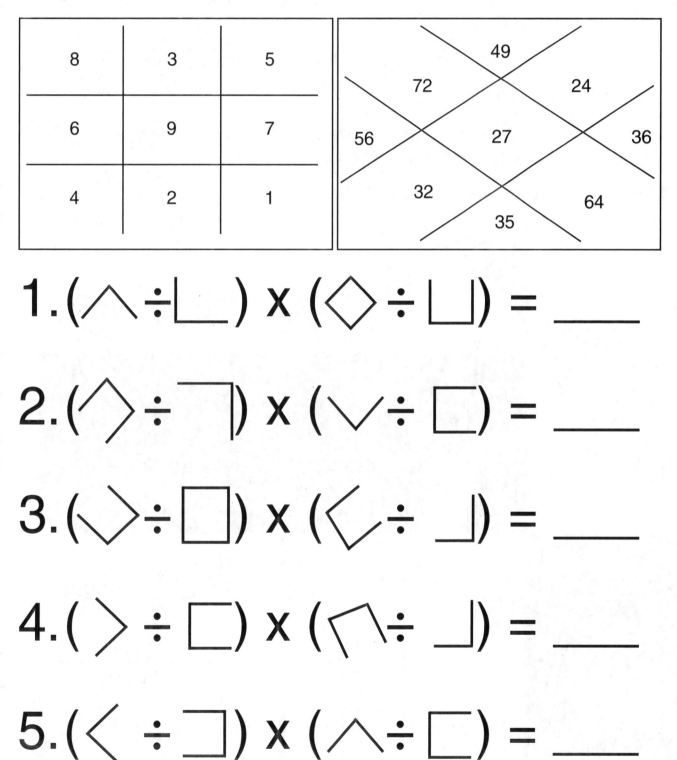

1.$(\wedge \div \sqcup) \times (\diamondsuit \div \sqcup) = \underline{\quad}$

2.$(\diamondsuit \div \daleth) \times (\vee \div \square) = \underline{\quad}$

3.$(\vee \div \square) \times (\swarrow \div \lrcorner) = \underline{\quad}$

4.$(> \div \square) \times (\wedge \div \lrcorner) = \underline{\quad}$

5.$(< \div \daleth) \times (\wedge \div \square) = \underline{\quad}$

At the Zoo

Melanie, Jessica, Sarah, and Rachael went to the zoo last Saturday. Each girl saw her favorite animal and ate her favorite food. From the clues given, determine each girl's favorite animal and food. (*Hint:* No two girls have the same favorite food or animal.)

1. Melanie loves the wolves but does not like lollipops or chocolate bars.

2. Sarah is afraid of the jaguars.

3. The girl who loves jaguars does not eat chocolate bars or potato chips, but the girl who eats hot dogs loves the gorillas.

4. Jessica enjoys any kind of chocolate bar.

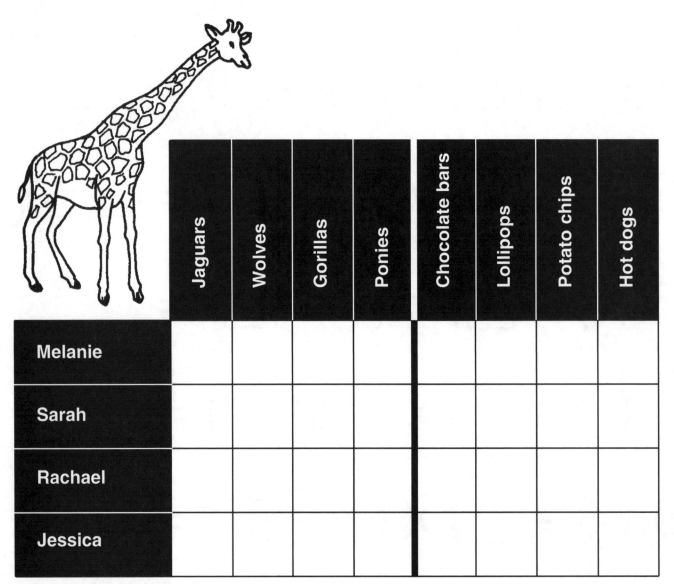

	Jaguars	Wolves	Gorillas	Ponies	Chocolate bars	Lollipops	Potato chips	Hot dogs
Melanie								
Sarah								
Rachael								
Jessica								

Number System

Invent a new number system. Write five problems and answers using any new symbols.

Example: ▲ + ★ = ✹

---

1. _____

2. _____

3. _____

4. _____

5. _____

The Decimal Fraction Derby

And they're off! There's No Chance in the outside lane, Fat Chance in the middle lane, and Slim Chance in the inside lane. Who will win the derby? Add each number each horse crosses—the horse with the lowest total at the end wins!

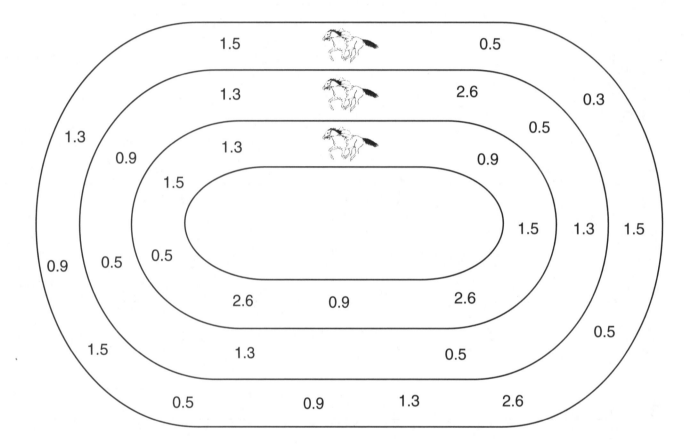

Final Count

No Chance   _____

Fat Chance   _____

Slim Chance   _____

Lucky Three-Leaf Clovers

What a shame! All these leaves and not one of them a lucky four-leaf clover.
Ah, but ONE of them is lucky; three times luckier than all the others! Can you
figure out which one it is?

17 x 8

37 x 9

9 x 15

22 x 6

11 x 21

17 x 18

27 x 5

Mail Muddle-up

Andre, Ben, Cindy, and Daphne's mail is in the mailbox. There is a parcel, a postcard, a bill, and a letter (not necessarily in order). They have been sent by a mom, a dad, a baker, and an aunt (also not necessarily in order). Three items have stamps: flowers, pets, and a building. One item has no stamp. Use the information below to discover who got what from which sender and with what stamp.

1. Andre's mail was not a postcard, didn't come from his mom, and had no stamp.

2. Cindy passed on the parcel with the flower stamp to the correct person.

3. One person was jealous because they only got a postcard, while her sister got a parcel.

4. The dad put the wrong child's name on his mail.

5. One person's mail, sender, and stamp were alliterative with that person's name!

Birthday Cake

Can you cut a birthday cake into eight pieces, using only three cuts?

Show how you would do this.

Who Won the Race?

Seven snails competed in the inaugural Compost Heap to the Vegetable Garden Race. Use the information below to learn who came in where:

1. Edward finished before Francis, but after Denise.

2. Bernard could only see Abigail in front of him at the finish.

3. Gabby got fed up seeing Francis' shell for the whole race.

4. Cathryn finished before Denise.

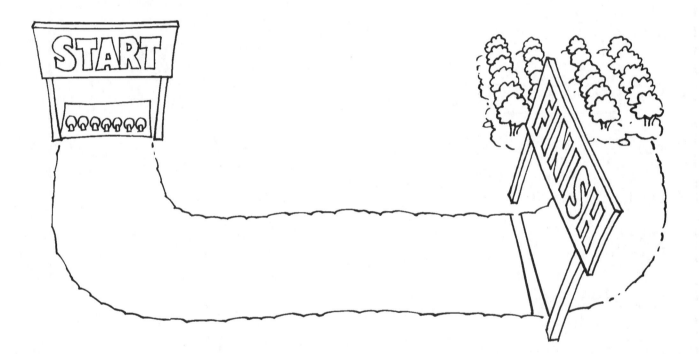

Draw a picture of the seven snails, showing who won, and what place the other snails finished. Explain how you solved the problem.

_____

_____

_____

Spot the Water Bird

Water birds are often well camouflaged to protect them from predators and there are ten well-hidden in the words below. To find them, complete these word problems by 'subtracting' letters from the main word or words and unscrambling the remaining letters.

1. SUN DECK – ENS = _____

2. GENUINE PART – TARE = _____

3. APPLIANCE – AP = _____

4. NEWS CAST – TECS = _____

5. GLUE BOTTLE – EETTBO = _____

6. LOOKS GREAT– RATLK = _____

7. LONG BOOK – OKBG = _____

8. FRANCE – F = _____

9. REGRET – R = _____

10. STRIPED PANTS – TST = _____

What's in the Bag? #1

Read the words on the next page. Then match the letters with the correct synonyms in the clues. (You will not use all of the letters.) Put the five clues together and discover what's in the bag!

A = stake	N = banner
B = soup	O = sew
C = enemy	P = refund
D = dock	Q = sled
E = stable	R = colonist
F = shaggy	S = slope
G = squirt	T = grasp
H = trench	U = image
I = serpent	V = ooze
J = doze	W = contest
K = spark	X = king
L = invent	Y = cowboy
M = guide	Z = elect

What's in the Bag? #1 (cont.)

Clue 1:

___ ___ ___ ___ ___

slant   seize   barn   barn   create

Clue 2:

___ ___ ___ ___ ___

slant   ditch   post   settler   repay

Clue 3:

___ ___ ___ ___ ___

nap   stitch   snake   flag   slant

Clue 4:

___ ___ ___ ___

race   stitch   stitch   pier

Clue 5:

___ ___ ___ ___ ___ ___

ditch   post   leader   leader   barn   settler

What's in the bag? _____

What's in the Bag? #2

Read the words on the next page. Then match the letters with the correct synonyms in the clues. (You will not use all of the letters.) Put the five clues together and discover what's in the bag!

A = anger

B = purchase

C = sorcerer

D = timid

E = calm

F = grief

G = rule

H = canine

I = feline

J = ache

K = misty

L = dense

M = sincere

N = late

O = peppy

P = mix

Q = thump

R = lanky

S = lather

T = grass

U = riddle

V = nation

W = power

Y = grease

Z = wind

What's in the Bag? #2 *(cont.)*

Clue 1:

_____   _____   _____   _____   _____   _____

suds   witch   rage   thick   quiet   suds

Clue 2:

_____   _____   _____   _____   _____   _____   _____

suds   thick   cat   lawn   dog   quiet   tall

Clue 3:

_____   _____   _____   _____   _____

witch   spry   cat   thick   suds

Clue 4:

_____   _____   _____   _____

thick   spry   tardy   govern

Clue 5:

_____   _____   _____   _____

honest   spry   thick   lawn

What's in the bag? _____

What's in the Bag? #3

Read the words on the next page. Then match the letters with the correct synonyms in the clues. (You will not use all the letters.) Put the five clues together and discover what's in the bag!

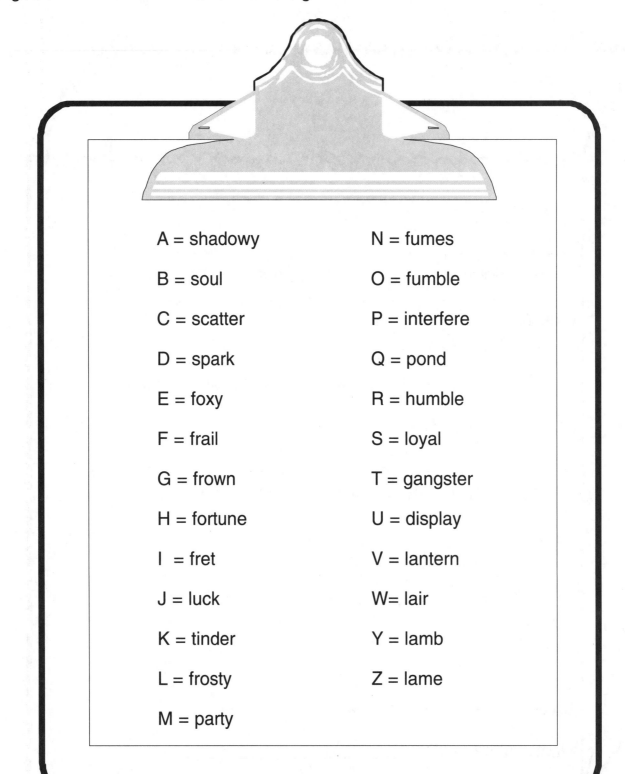

A = shadowy

B = soul

C = scatter

D = spark

E = foxy

F = frail

G = frown

H = fortune

I = fret

J = luck

K = tinder

L = frosty

M = party

N = fumes

O = fumble

P = interfere

Q = pond

R = humble

S = loyal

T = gangster

U = display

V = lantern

W = lair

Y = lamb

Z = lame

What's in the Bag? #3 *(cont.)*

Clue 1:

_____   _____   _____   _____   _____   _____   _____

faithful   outlaw   poor   dark   gases   scowl   crafty

Clue 2:

_____ _____ _____ _____ _____ _____ _____ _____ _____

faithful   meddle   dark   disperse   crafty   faithful   riches   worry   meddle

Clue 3:

_____   _____   _____   _____   _____   _____

riches   mistake   lamp   crafty   poor   faithful

Clue 4:

_____   _____   _____   _____   _____   _____

dark   freezing   worry   crafty   gases   faithful

Clue 5:

_____   _____   _____   _____   _____

freezing   worry   scowl   riches   outlaw

What's in the bag? _____

What's in the Bag? #4

Read the words on the next page. Then match the letters with the correct synonyms in the clues. (You will not use all the letters.) Put the five clues together and discover what's in the bag!

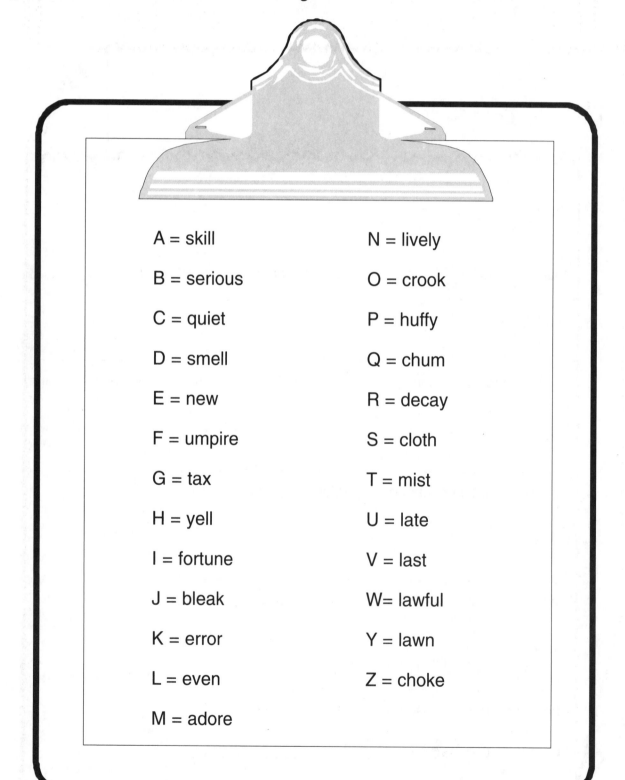

A = skill

B = serious

C = quiet

D = smell

E = new

F = umpire

G = tax

H = yell

I = fortune

J = bleak

K = error

L = even

M = adore

N = lively

O = crook

P = huffy

Q = chum

R = decay

S = cloth

T = mist

U = late

V = last

W = lawful

Y = lawn

Z = choke

134

What's in the Bag? #4 *(cont.)*

Clue 1:

_____

calm   shout   novel   legal   grass

Clue 2:

_____

odor   thief   tardy   toll   shout

Clue 3:

_____

grave   art   mistake   novel   odor

Clue 4:

_____

fabric   tardy   toll   art   rot   grass

Clue 5:

_____

odor   thief   gag   novel   spry   fabric

What's in the bag? _____

Banana Split

Split the banana by removing the given letters. Then add the extra letter in and unscramble the word using the clue.

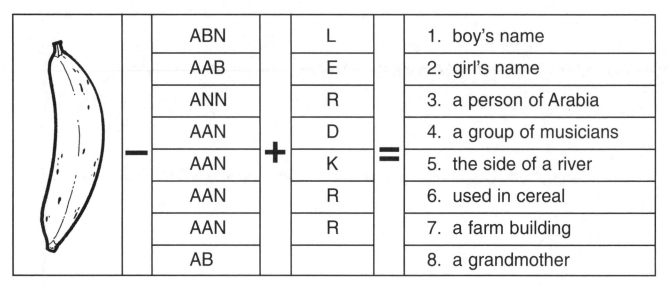

	ABN	L	1. boy's name	
	AAB	E	2. girl's name	
	ANN	R	3. a person of Arabia	
−	AAN +	D =	4. a group of musicians	
	AAN	K	5. the side of a river	
	AAN	R	6. used in cereal	
	AAN	R	7. a farm building	
	AB		8. a grandmother	

1. ` _____

2. _____

3. _____

4. _____

5. _____

6. _____

7. _____

8. _____

Extra Points: BANANA + D = an item of headwear

Bicycle Word Search

Lots of bits make up a bike—and they're hidden "wheely well" . . .
Find the following words:

air, bell, bicycle, BMX, chain, gears, light, handlebar, mirror, mudguard, oil, pedal, pump, seat, spoke, sprocket, tube, tire, valve, wheel

Japanese Words

Find these Japanese words in the puzzle below. The left-over letters spell the special name given to Japanese written characters.

The word is: _____

BAMBOO	NOH (theater)
BUNRAKU (form of puppetry)	ORIGAMI
CHIN (small dog)	SAMISEN (musical instrument)
HAIKU (poem)	SAMPAN (boat)
HARI-KARI (a form of ritual suicide)	SHINTO (religion)
HIROSHIMA	SHO (musical instrument)
JUDO	SUSHI
KABUKI (theater)	TSUNAMI (tidal wave)
KOTO (musical instrument)	YEN (currency)
NIPPON (name for Japan)	

O	R	I	G	A	M	I	N	O	H
T	H	I	R	O	S	H	I	M	A
S	A	M	I	S	E	N	P	I	I
U	R	S	U	S	H	I	P	S	K
N	I	S	D	E	H	X	O	H	U
A	K	A	B	U	K	I	N	O	J
M	A	M	G	C	H	I	N	R	U
I	R	P	K	O	T	O	A	T	D
P	I	A	H	B	A	M	B	O	O
B	U	N	R	A	K	U	Y	E	N

Pair the Pairs

It takes two to duel, or at least a couple, or a twosome. Match up these definitions with their correct pair.

DEFINITIONS

_____ 1. a pair of performers

_____ 2. a performance by two musicians

_____ 3. double

_____ 4. two people closely associated

_____ 5. two rhyming lines of verse

_____ 6. a set of two objects used together

_____ 7. one more than one

_____ 8. two people together

_____ 9. the two on a dice or a playing card

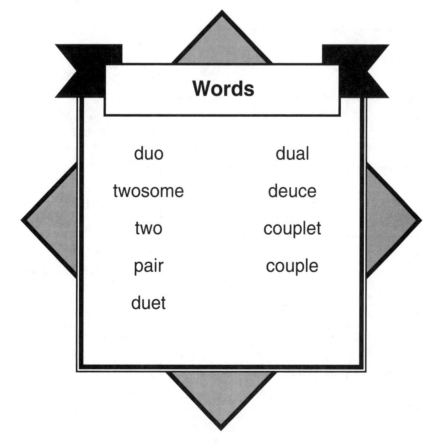

Words

duo	dual
twosome	deuce
two	couplet
pair	couple
duet	

Mars Plus

The Martian moons might have been hard to find, but Mars isn't. It's everywhere. It's hidden in tRAMS and SwARM and MAReS. It's also in every word of today's puzzle!

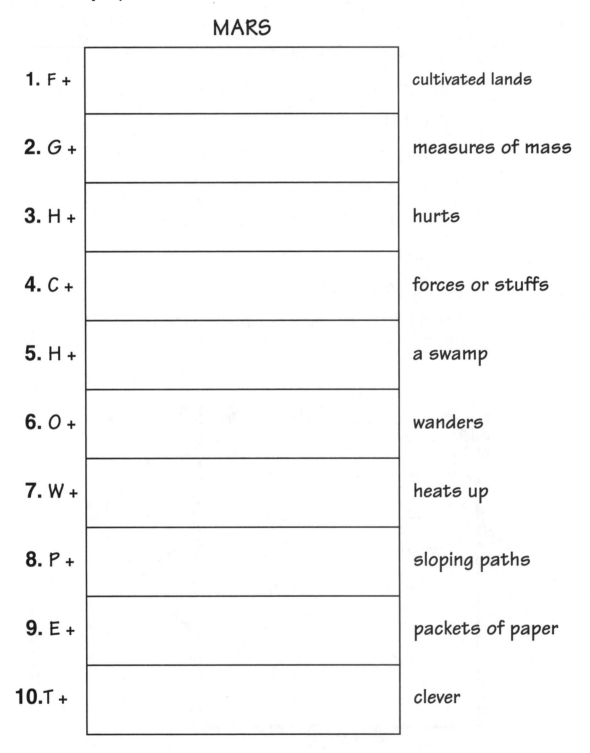

MARS

1. F + ___ cultivated lands

2. G + ___ measures of mass

3. H + ___ hurts

4. C + ___ forces or stuffs

5. H + ___ a swamp

6. O + ___ wanders

7. W + ___ heats up

8. P + ___ sloping paths

9. E + ___ packets of paper

10. T + ___ clever

Angling Find-a-Word

Locate the words listed below. The letters left over spell the name of an important fishing manual from the 15th century.

Angle (v): to fish with a hook and line

angle, cast, fly, freshwater, hook, lakes, line, lure, ponds, reel, river, rod, trout, worm

The name of the fishing manual is:

_____

Solve It!

Read the clues and complete the words. Each word only contains letters from the word STRAWBERRY.

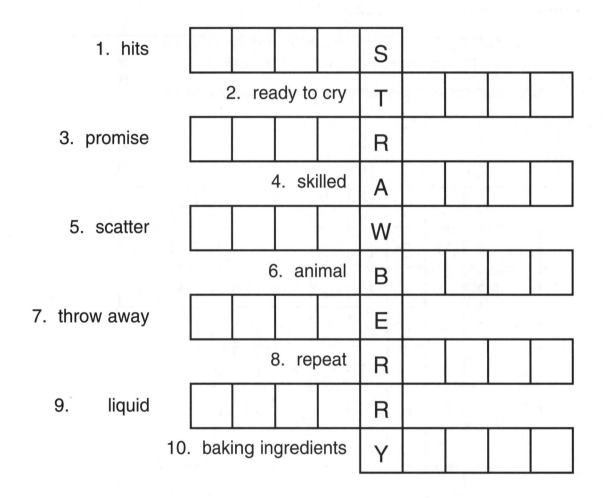

1. hits

2. ready to cry

3. promise

4. skilled

5. scatter

6. animal

7. throw away

8. repeat

9.   liquid

10. baking ingredients

Fruit and Vegetable Circular Puzzle

Here are clues to eight unusual vegetables and fruits. The first word begins with a "T." Each answer begins with the last letter of the preceding word. The last word ends in "T."

1. mildly acid red fruit eaten as a vegetable

2. small oval-shaped European fruit important for food and oil

3. berry-like fruit of the elder shrub

4. the edible root of a tropical vine

5. large, oval, smooth-skinned tropical fruit

6. edible bulb, which causes eyes to sting when peeled

7. smooth-skinned variety of the peach

8. egg-shaped vegetable with a shiny, dark purple skin

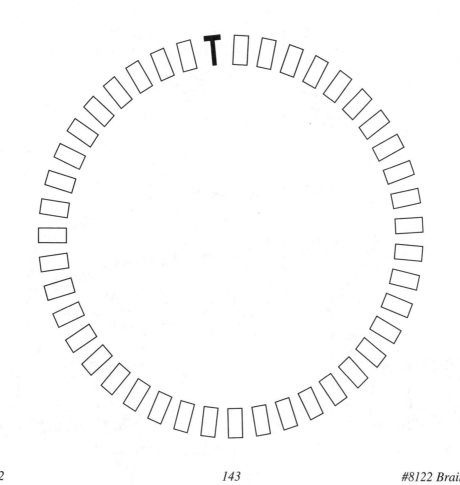

Drive Into This Puzzle!

Cars and films seem to go together so well, but can you turn cars into a film?
Use the clues to help—but you're only allowed to change one letter at a time.

C	A	R	S	
				Rowing implements
				Belonging to us
				Pelts
				Trees
				Combustion
				A steel hand tool
F	I	L	M	

Birds of a Feather

Oh boy! There are bits of birds everywhere! Each bird's name has been split in two—and separated. Join them back to see what's in this flock. P.S. One bird (poor thing) got split into three.

ARD	CO	EON	OST	EN	TURE
PIG	CORM	VUL	PAR	EAG	INAL
CARD	ROT	LE	PECK	ROW	WOOD
CHICK	RICH	ORANT	BUZZ	SPAR	ER

_____

_____

_____

_____

_____

_____

_____

_____

_____

Solar System Word Search

The solar system is a busy place, with planets, the sun, space probes, and satellites. But it's a big place, and sometimes even a planet can be hard to find. Start with a search for these words. The leftover letters will spell out the name of what some scientists believe will be our tenth planet, if we ever find it!

asteroid	gas	meteor	Pluto	Sun
comet	Jupiter	moon	rocket	Uranus
dust	Mars	Neptune	satellite	vacuum
Earth	Mercury	orbit	Saturn	Venus

```
U  E  M  A  R  S  Y  A  P  E  R
R  A  S  E  S  R  S  T  S  U  D
A  R  P  U  U  T  T  I  B  R  O
N  T  N  C  E  N  R  U  T  A  S
U  H  R  R  J  U  P  I  T  E  R
S  E  O  M  E  T  E  O  R  O  V
M  I  T  E  K  C  O  R  H  T  A
D  V  E  N  U  S  O  N  E  U  C
S  A  T  E  L  L  I  T  E  L  U
C  O  M  E  T  N  O  O  M  P  U
G  A  S  E  N  U  T  P  E  N  M
```

Some scientists believe our tenth planet will be called _____.

Henry's Six Wives

Henry's six wives are lost in the spiral! Can you find them all? (*Hint:* He married three Catherines, two Annes, and a Jane.)

_____   _____

_____   _____

_____   _____

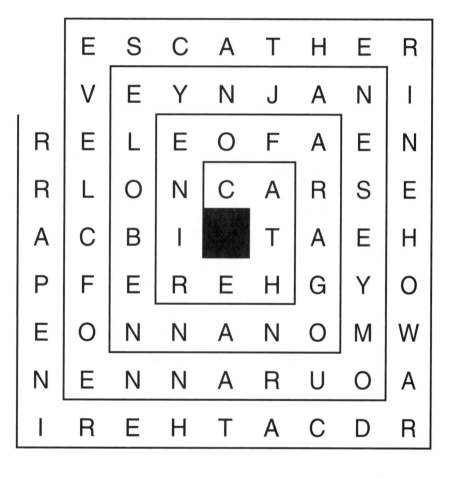

A Colonial Word Search

Test your knowledge of daily life in the 13 colonies. Use these clues to find the
20 words in the word search on page 149.

1. the only sport in which women could participate _____

2. metal from which some plates and cups were made _____

3. the only utensil used for eating _____

4. common method of punishment for criminals _____

5. type of home built by early Dutch settlers _____

6. plant used in making candles _____

7. girls embroidered these _____

8. they sold wares and spread news _____

9. cloth spun from the flax plant_____

10. dish made from wood or stale bread_____

11. children ages six to eight attended these _____

12. plant grown for its blue dye _____

13. windows were made by soaking cloth in this oil _____

14. a basic ingredient of soap _____

15. game in which metal rings were tossed at an iron stake_____

16. one page of letters fastened to a wooden frame_____

17. waist-length jacket worn by men _____

18. fried cornmeal bread _____

19. type of house with sloping roof _____

20. day of worship _____

A Colonial Word Search *(cont.)*

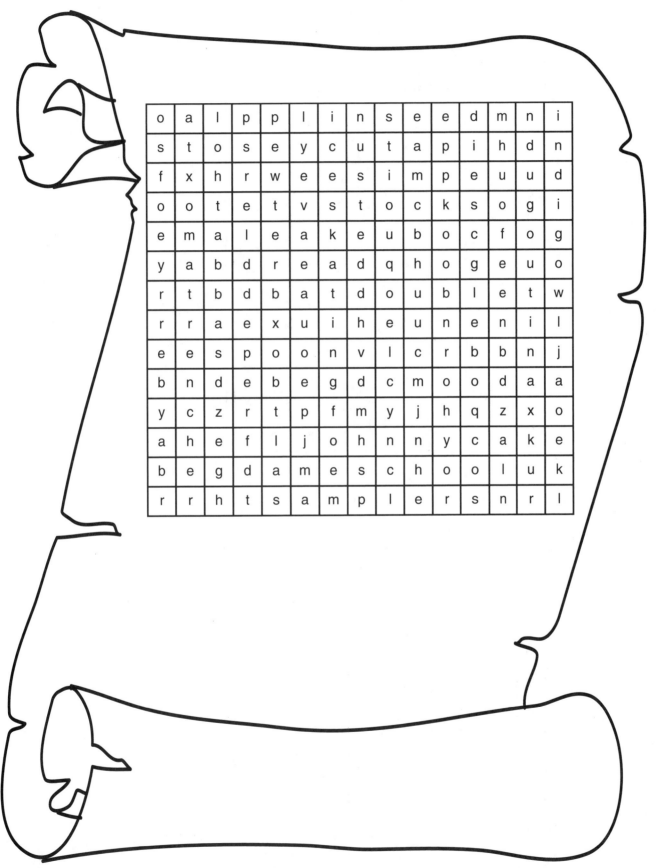

o	a	l	p	p	l	i	n	s	e	e	d	m	n	i
s	t	o	s	e	y	c	u	t	a	p	i	h	d	n
f	x	h	r	w	e	e	s	i	m	p	e	u	u	d
o	o	t	e	t	v	s	t	o	c	k	s	o	g	i
e	m	a	l	e	a	k	e	u	b	o	c	f	o	g
y	a	b	d	r	e	a	d	q	h	o	g	e	u	o
r	t	b	d	b	a	t	d	o	u	b	l	e	t	w
r	r	a	e	x	u	i	h	e	u	n	e	n	i	l
e	e	s	p	o	o	n	v	l	c	r	b	b	n	j
b	n	d	e	b	e	g	d	c	m	o	o	d	a	a
y	c	z	r	t	p	f	m	y	j	h	q	z	x	o
a	h	e	f	l	j	o	h	n	n	y	c	a	k	e
b	e	g	d	a	m	e	s	c	h	o	o	l	u	k
r	r	h	t	s	a	m	p	l	e	r	s	n	r	l

Sand Dune Word Puzzle

Can you make sand into a dune and back into sand by changing one letter at a time?

S	A	N	D
D	U	N	E

D	U	N	E
S	A	N	D

Catch the Elephant

List ways you can think of to catch an elephant that has escaped from the zoo. Try to think of as many creative and unusual ways as you can.

Pin the Tail on the Words

You'll need to be sharp to work out all these clues—although every answer does begin with a pin.

1. a squeeze with
   the fingers   _____

2. a color   _____

3. liquid
   measurement   _____

4. an arcade game   _____

5. alternative
   name for table
   tennis   _____

6. a lofty peak   _____

7. large sweet
   tropical fruit   _____

8. to locate exactly   _____

9. a small cushion
   into which pins
   are stuck   _____

A Sweet Puzzle

Here are 13 words. Just place them correctly in the squares below and you will have nine types of treats.

AND	IN	POP
BUT	LATE	RICE
CHEW	MALL	SCOT
CORN	MARS	
GUM	OFF	

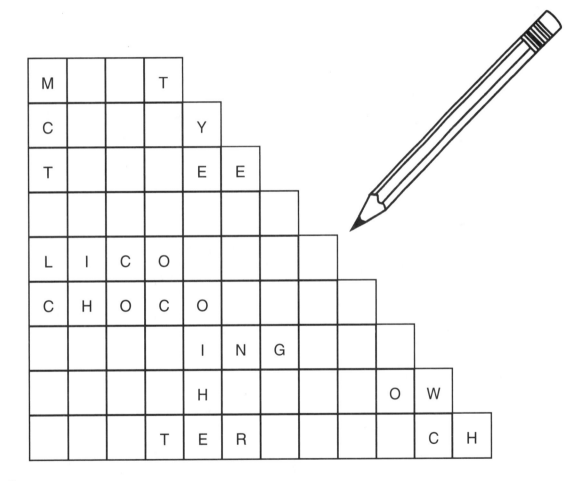

The Big, Bad Wolf

Imagine that the big, bad wolf wants to reform. What advice would you give to help him turn over a new leaf?

_____

_____

_____

_____

_____

_____

_____

_____

_____

_____

_____

_____

Rip Returns!

Imagine that you are a modern-day Rip Van Winkle and go to sleep for 100 years. Describe the world you will find when you awake.

_____

_____

_____

_____

_____

_____

_____

_____

_____

_____

_____

_____

_____

_____

_____

Fantasy Character Conversation

Work with a partner to make up a play about a conversation between different fantasy characters such as Jack from *Jack and the Beanstalk* and Ariel from the *Little Mermaid*.

Now What Happens?

Devise a different ending to *Little Red Riding Hood*.

_____

_____

_____

_____

_____

_____

_____

_____

_____

_____

_____

_____

_____

_____

To the Rescue

Imagine you are living in the magical kingdom of Goth. Your best friend has been captured by a fire-breathing dragon. Write the story of how you rescue him or her. You can use three of the following:

- a flute
- a pair of roller blades
- a magnifying glass
- a packet of bubble gum
- a dog
- a baseball bat

_____

_____

_____

_____

_____

_____

_____

_____

_____

_____

_____

_____

_____

_____

_____

Consequences

What if dinosaurs had not become extinct? Give ten different consequences.

1. _____

2. _____

3. _____

4. _____

5. _____

6. _____

7. _____

8. _____

9. _____

10. _____

Sea Creatures

What kind of sea creature is this?

It has _____ tentacles.

Is it a fish?   Yes / No

Can it breathe underwater? Yes / No

Write a true story about yourself at the beach.

_____

_____

_____

_____

_____

_____

_____

_____

_____

_____

_____

Land With No Gravity

Focus on an imaginary land where there is no gravity. Picture the people; the colors, shapes, sounds and smells; the homes, landscape, buildings, traffic, etc.

What are the people doing? Where are they going?

_____

_____

_____

_____

_____

_____

_____

_____

_____

_____

_____

_____

Ice Cream Poem

Imagine you have been asked to write a poem about ice cream.

Think about the following:

- *The form*—Will it be a limerick, rap, nursery rhyme, prose, chant, or free verse?
- *The structure*—Will it contain similes and metaphors?
- *Visual impact*—Will it be a shape poem or a haiku?

Write the poem.

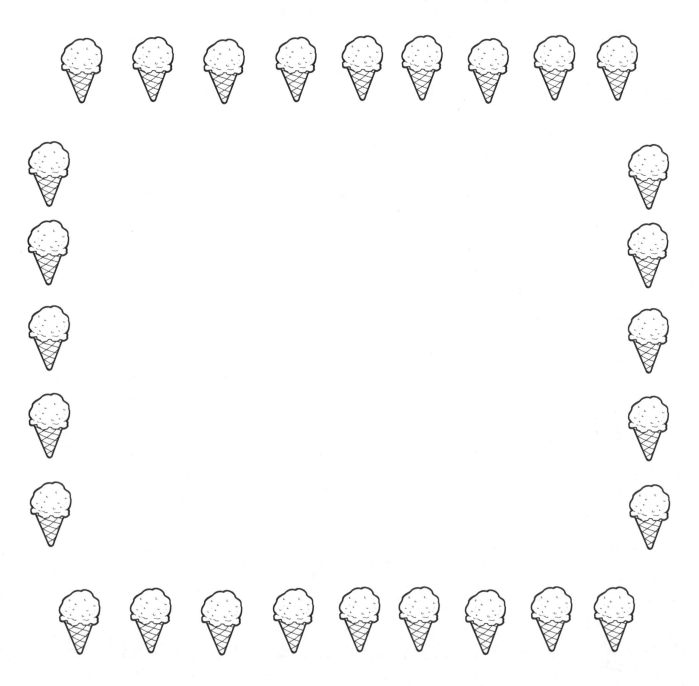

Brainstorm!

Brainstorm the sorts of things that make you laugh.

Brainstorm a list of crazy or far-out things to sell. Examples could be thigs like: birthday parties on the moon, ice cream pizzas, or back-to-front shoes. Challenge yourself to write an advertisement for the product.

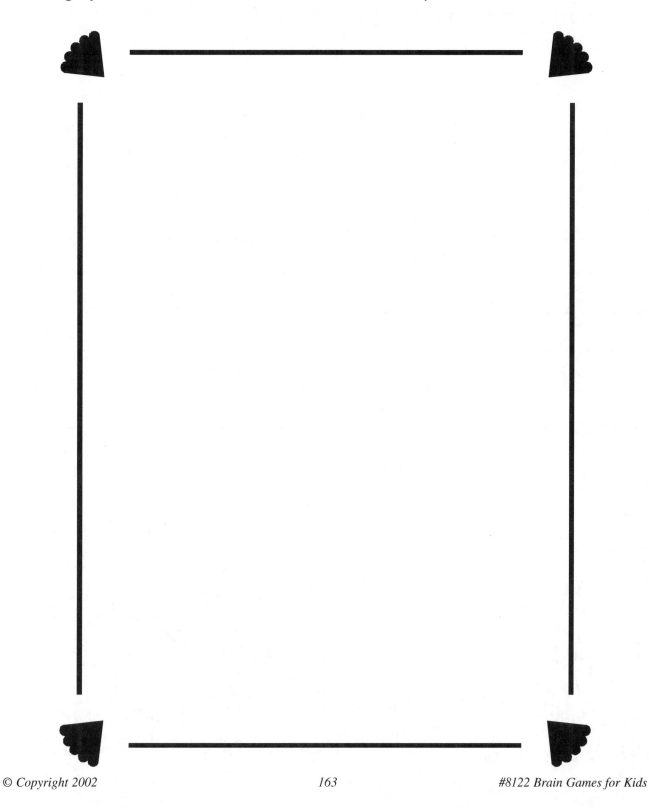

Treasure

This treasure chest contains something amazing that has never been seen before on Earth.

What do you imagine it could be? Draw a picture of the treasure and write about it.

What a Question!

This is a happy line leaping and bounding along!

Draw a silly line.

Draw a sad line.

The answer is "no." Write three questions. _____

_____

_____

List reasons why the people were laughing and shouting. _____

_____

You cannot see out of the windows. List the possible reasons why this is so.

_____

_____

_____

Why can't you open the door? Think of possible reasons.

_____

_____

_____

Street Safety

Think of different ways to make your street safer by making cars and other traffic travel more slowly and cautiously. Explain and draw your suggestions.

How Can You Use It?

List possible uses for a milk carton.

_____

_____

_____

_____

_____

_____

_____

_____

_____

How can a piece of string be used for each of these activities or functions?

To play a sport?	To play a game?	An item . . . .

What Can It Be?

This food is shaped like a soccer ball._____

This food is two colors, one outside and the other inside. _____

This food comes in a bag. _____

You cannot eat this food with a fork. _____

This food makes a noise when it is cooked. _____

List three things that you could never touch.

_____

_____

_____

List three things that you could never wash.

_____

_____

_____

List three things that you could never see at the zoo.

_____

_____

_____

What If?

Explore alternatives by imagining you have the ability to change three things in your life.

What three things would you change?

_____

_____

_____

How would you change them?

_____

_____

_____

_____

How would this affect your life?

_____

_____

_____

_____

_____

My Fun Park

Design and name your own fun park. Write the rules and regulations you feel are important for running the park, and explain why these are necessary. What rides would you have? How would your fun park be different from parks that already exist? What improvements could you make to the existing parks?

My Fun Park *(cont.)*

_____

_____

_____

_____

_____

_____

_____

_____

_____

_____

_____

Inventing a Robot

Design a robot that will be able to meet your needs in the future. The robot does not have to resemble a person, so you can be very creative. Write a user's manual for your robot, explaining the function or task that each feature of the robot will perform.

_____

_____

_____

_____

_____

_____

_____

Stranded

Imagine that all means of transport other than walking are no longer available. Invent new ways of traveling, using items you would be able to find at home or school.

Is That Red?

List or draw all the red objects that you can think of. To be more creative, try to think about the color from a different point of view or as a result of an action, for example: a face blushing or the sun setting.

Finding Categories

Divide these objects into groups with at least two items per group. Label each group with a description, for example, "articles of clothing."

rice	smile	envelope	hat
eggs	cheese	pilot	folder
coin	eyebrows	frown	teacher
scratch	scissors	itch	soldier
wink	legs	box	ears
donut	nail	tin	stamp
toaster	sun	nurse	
beans	rub	rose	

Groups

Recruitment Ad

Imagine you are the most famous artist in the mythical kingdom of Tarambala and you have been asked by your king to design a recruitment ad. The ad is for brave adventurers who are willing to retrieve the precious Golden Orb that has been stolen by fierce pirates.

Design your ad so that all the best and bravest people in the kingdom apply.

Hobbies

List five hobbies for which you would require the following skills:

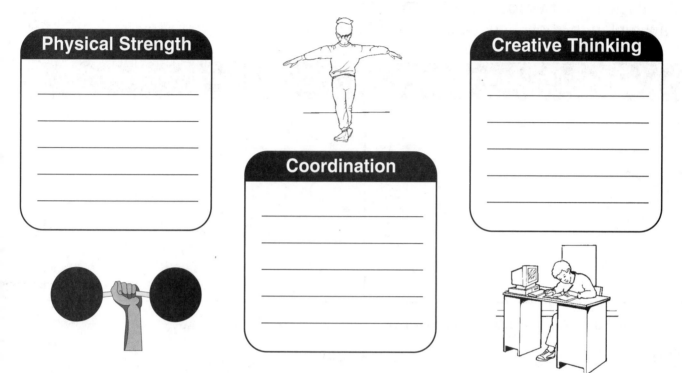

Physical Strength

Coordination

Creative Thinking

Can you recommend a hobby for these students?

Type of Student	Recommended Hobby	Why Recommended
physically impaired		
visually impaired		
hearing impaired		
inner city dweller		
rural country dweller		
extremely shy person		

Describe the strangest hobby:

_____

_____

_____

Redecorating Your Room

Your parents give you $200 to redecorate your room and you must not make any holes in your walls!

Draw a plan to show how your room will look:

Floor plan of my room	Side view of my room

My color scheme will be the following:

Walls: _____   Curtains: _____

Ceiling: _____   Bedspread: _____

Other items: _____

I have chosen this color scheme because of the following reasons:

_____

_____

Budget for the cost of redecorating my room:

Item	Cost	Item	Cost
		Total Cost =	

If you go over budget with your project, how would you convince your parents to allow you to go ahead with your planned room?

_____

_____

Future Fame

Imagine that you are given the opportunity to become famous. What would you choose to be?

_____

Why would you choose this?

_____

_____

_____

Draw yourself at work.

```
+-------------------------------------------------------------+
|                                                             |
|                                                             |
|                                                             |
|                                                             |
|                                                             |
|                                                             |
+-------------------------------------------------------------+
```

What would you do in your new life? Where would you go? What results would you hope to achieve?

Write a diary about your first three days of being famous.

Day One: _____

_____

_____

Day Two: _____

_____

_____

Day Three: _____

_____

Moon Colony

You have to lead a moon colonization mission. You can take five people with you to live on the moon. You need to take enough food and supplies to last until you can produce more food. As the leader, you need to establish some rules and consequences.

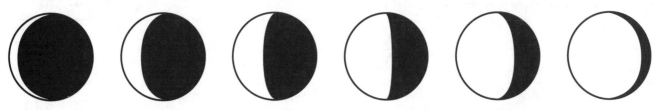

People I would include: (List their profession, e.g. doctor, craftsperson)

Who?   Why?

1. _____   _____

2. _____   _____

3. _____   _____

4. _____   _____

5. _____   _____

Draw and label the essential supplies you would need to take.

Write five rules for your colony and the consequences if the rules are broken.

Rule   Consequence

1. _____   _____

2. _____   _____

3. _____   _____

4. _____   _____

5. _____   _____

Stars and Planets

Circle whether the following statements are true or false.

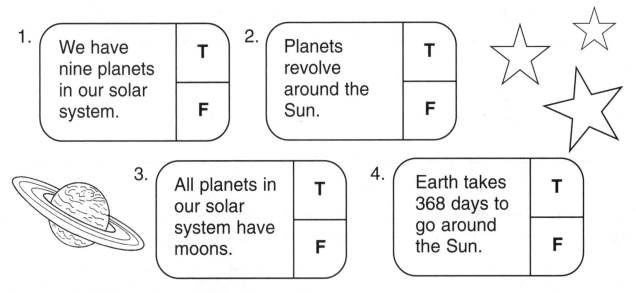

1. We have nine planets in our solar system.   T   F

2. Planets revolve around the Sun.   T   F

3. All planets in our solar system have moons.   T   F

4. Earth takes 368 days to go around the Sun.   T   F

Illustrate all the true statements.

Write three other TRUE statements about our solar system.

_____

_____

_____

Write three other FALSE statements about our solar system.

_____

_____

_____

Food and Exercise Diary

1. Keep a daily record of what you eat for one week. Complete this table about foods you like to eat.

Foods I should eat and drink often:	Foods I shouldn't eat and drink often:

2. Compare how much time you spend sitting down and how much time you spend doing physical activities. The table below will help you.

Sitting Activities	Mon.	Tues.	Wed.	Thurs.	Fri.	Sat.	Sun.
Reading							
Watching TV							
Studying							
Homework							
At School							
Physical Activities	Mon.	Tues.	Wed.	Thurs.	Fri.	Sat.	Sun.
Games							
Sport							
Walking							
Shopping							

Dream Homes

Choose one of the following home descriptions and design a home.

- The ideal home for a family with six children.

- A home suitable for an elderly person.

Show the floor plan for the house. Accompany your plan with some details that explain why you think special features are important.

Use Your Head!

- Imagine you have been transported to the year 3000. Draw a model "television set" of that era.

- Do you agree that young people watch too much television? Give reasons for your answer.

- Television was created to improve communication, but has also been blamed for reducing communication within families. What do you think?

_____

_____

_____

_____

_____

Sand

We find sand at the beach and in rivers. Sand can be coarse or fine. It can be made from particles of shells, rocks, and coral, so it is often different colors.

We have many uses for sand.

- We use it for modeling things like sandcastles at the beach.
- We use it as a filling for soft toys and beanbags.
- Mined sand is used to make glass.

1. Can you think of three other uses for sand?

A. _____

B. _____

C. _____

2. Draw a diagram to help you explain how shells, rocks, and coral are made into grains of sand that are found on the beach or in rivers.

3. In the past, sand was often used to measure time. Design a new device that uses sand to measure time. Illustrate your invention below and describe how it works.

Landmark Match-Up

How's your LIQ (Landmark Intelligence Quotient)? Try matching these famous landmarks to their country of origin.

Who's the Oldest?

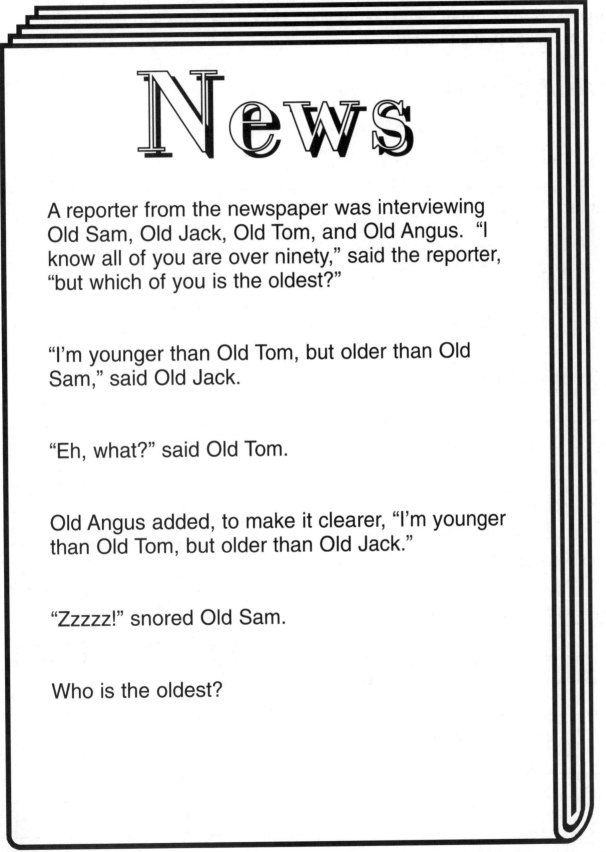

News

A reporter from the newspaper was interviewing Old Sam, Old Jack, Old Tom, and Old Angus. "I know all of you are over ninety," said the reporter, "but which of you is the oldest?"

"I'm younger than Old Tom, but older than Old Sam," said Old Jack.

"Eh, what?" said Old Tom.

Old Angus added, to make it clearer, "I'm younger than Old Tom, but older than Old Jack."

"Zzzzz!" snored Old Sam.

Who is the oldest?

Abbreviations

OK is an abbreviation of "okay" that most people recognize. Here are some abbreviations from e-mails and computing. How many can you figure out? Each has a clue to the meaning.

1. WYSIWYG: this will print out how you see it

_____

2. B4: previously

_____

3. 2nite: this evening

_____

4. EZ: not difficult

_____

5. cuz: for that reason

_____

6. <g>: smile

_____

7. <s>: breathe out deeply

_____

8. THX: expression of gratitude

_____

9. ROTFL: expressing great amusement

_____

10. OTOH: alternatively

_____

11. LTNS: haven't seen you in a while

_____

12. BTW: introducing a new topic

_____

13. CU: goodbye

_____

Top 10 Math

Here's this week's top 10 Rock n' Roll chart. Next to each song is its movement since last week. For example, "Rock Around the Clock" has moved up seven places so it must have been number 8 last week. Use the information to work out all of last week's chart. Who was at the top of the charts?

This Week	Last Week
1. Rock Around the Clock (up 7)	1.
2. Shake, Rattle 'n' Roll (up 8)	2.
3. That'll Be the Day (down 2)	3.
4. Peggy Sue (steady)	4.
5. Love Potion No. 9 (down 2)	5.
6. Wild One (up 3)	6.
7. Run Around Sue (down 2)	7.
8. Heartbreak Hotel (down 2)	8.
9. Shakin' All Over (down 2)	9.
10. Da Doo Ron Ron (down 8)	10.

Which Maze?

To make more money, Tom plans to build a small maze. He draws four designs but can't decide between them. Which design should he choose if he wants his customers to enter and leave from one side? They must go through every door only once.

A

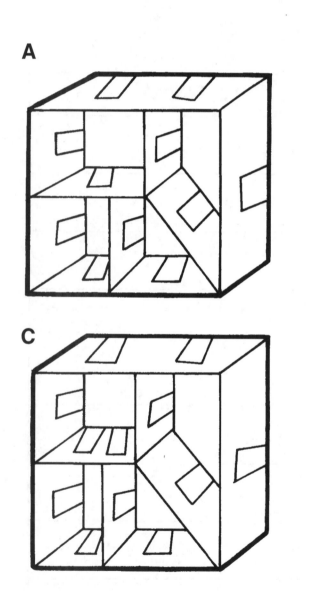

B

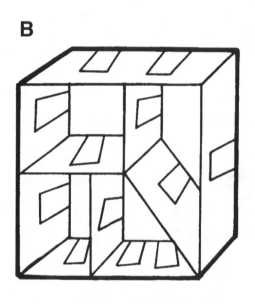

C

D

Rhyming Word Pairs

Find an adjective that rhymes with a noun so that together the two words have about the same meaning as the phrase given. An example has been done for you.

Example: a soaked dog = soggy doggy

1. a friend who does not arrive on time _____

2. an overweight rodent_____

3. a naughty boy _____

4. a crude guy _____

5. a beetle's cup _____

6. a lengthy tune _____

7. a plump feline _____

8. twice as much bother _____

9. a large hog _____

10. a girl from Switzerland _____

11. a skinny horse_____

12. a blinding bulb_____

13. a comical rabbit_____

14. a happy boy_____

15. a loafing flower _____

16. an unhappy father _____

17. a home for a rodent_____

18. without money _____

19. an irritated employer _____

20. fake coins _____

IQ Test

Here are 10 questions that are similar to those found in IQ tests. Complete the pattern with the next letter, number, or shape in the pattern.

1. 1, 2, 4, 7, 11, . . . _____

2. 23, 21, 19, 17, . . . _____

3. 1, 4, 9, 16, . . . _____

4. A, C, D, F, G, I, . . . _____

5. Z, A, Y, B, X, C, . . . _____

6. A, E, I, O, . . . _____

7.

8.

9. I, III, V, VII, . . . _____

10. Which word is least like the other four? cow, bull, sheep, calf, heifer?

_____

Train of Thought

Arrrgh! Disaster is imminent! Locomotive driver Arnie Watson is walking slowly back to the railroad depot along the Spring Gully railroad track. Because he is hearing impared Arnie can't hear the *Spring Gully Express* roaring up directly behind him. He's wearing dark clothing and isn't carrying a lantern. The express had turned off its lights, and there's no moon or stars. There are no lights in this darkly wooded area, yet the Express driver still manages to screech to a halt only meters away from Arnie's back. How?

Picture the Scene

Why is the airplane's arrival delayed? Think of at least five reasons.

_____

_____

_____

_____

_____

How is a cloud like a pillow? List at least eight attributes or characteristics that are similar.

_____

_____

_____

_____

_____

Imagine that all the clocks have stopped. How could this affect you?

_____

_____

_____

_____

More Hidden Meanings

Explain the meaning of each box.

1. _____

2. _____

3. _____

4. _____

5. _____

6. _____

7. _____

8. _____

9. _____

10. _____

11. _____

12. _____

Whodunit?

Ah, a case worthy of the great Sherlock Holmes himself! Read the mystery story and see if you can figure out "whodunit."

When Harry left his house it was early on a fine warm day. He fished at his favorite hole for most of the morning, then drove into town to pick up some supplies. It was almost dark when he returned home to discover his home had gone. Vanished. Stolen? Perhaps, but most certainly missing.

At the police station the duty officer was a little bewildered.

"It was there this morning, sir?"

"Yes! Of course it was! Would I not see my own house?"

"Er, were there any tracks—footprints or tire tracks?"

"Only from my vehicle."

"Any other clues that might help us, sir?"

"Well, I had left the fire going, and . . . "

"And what, sir?"

"The ground where it had been was very wet when I got back."

"Ah," said the officer. "That explains it all!"

It does? Can you figure out where Harry's house went?

_____

_____

_____

_____

Crazy Cartoon

Create a cartoon strip which tells about the story of all these unusual characters meeting and having an adventure:

- ✦ Prince Charming with bad breath,

- ✦ Jack and Jill as visitors from outer space,

- ✦ Rapunzel who loves to break dance, and

- ✦ Snow White who is in love with the Gingerbread Man.

Design an ending with a twist.

Brain Challenges

The French Revolutionary Calendar

See if you can calculate what the date of your birthday would be under the calendar adopted by France after the revolution. It had 12 months of 30 days each, and there were 5 days of national holidays from September 17–21.

Summer Months

(starting September 22)

Messidor: the harvesting month

Thermidor: the heat month

Fructidor: the fruit month

Autumn Months

(starting December 21)

Vendémiaire: the vintage month

Brumaire: the fog month

Frimaire: the frost month

Winter Months

(starting March 21)

Nivôse: the snow month

Pluviôse: the rain month

Ventôse: the wind month

Spring Months

(starting June 19)

Germinal: the seeds month

Floréal: the blossoms month

Prairial: the meadows month

According to the French Revolutionary calendar my birthday would be _____.

Follow the Yellow Brick Road

Information

Each brick in the yellow brick road is 30 cm long by 15 cm wide by 10 cm deep.

Each brick weighs 3.5 kg.

Each brick is worth $585.00.

Solve the following problems.

1. How many bricks would be needed to create a path approximately 9 m long by 3 m wide? _____

2. The road to Emerald City is about 40 km long and 3 m wide. How many bricks would be needed for this path? _____

3. What would its area be? _____

4. How much would it cost? _____

5. If the bricks were all piled one on top of the other, how high would the pile be? _____

6. How much would they weigh altogether? _____

The Race

Ali's sponsor, Cheap Stuff for Bikes, has donated a new helmet for the big endurance race. It is not a very good one though. Fifteen kilometers into the race the sponsor's sticker falls off.

For the next 1/4 of the distance it rains, and Ali discovers the helmet isn't waterproof.

The next 1/7 of the distance seems better, although Ali can't see— the helmet's paint has run down her face. Then, the strap breaks and Ali spends the next 1/5 of the distance holding it on with one hand. Ali's helmet falls off, and she spends the last 3/10 of the race hoping the police don't see her. They don't, but she only comes in third. She throws the helmet away.

How long is the race? _____

(Hint: What number has the divisors 4, 7, 5, and 10?)

Orbital Math

Two spacecraft (A and B) are orbiting the earth. They are both traveling at the same speed, but A's orbit takes 90 minutes to complete while B's orbit takes 180 minutes.

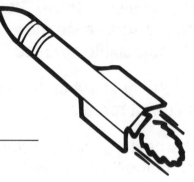

1. How many orbits does A complete each
   day? _____

2. How many orbits does B complete? _____

3. Which satellite is in the higher orbit? _____

4. Both pass over Melbourne, Australia together at 9 A.M. When will they pass
   over Australia next? _____

5. Spacecraft A is over South America 45 minutes later. Is it day or night?

   _____

6. How often during the day are the two spacecraft over the same spot?

   _____

7. Name the satellite that orbits the sun once every 365 days.

   _____

Leaping Leap Years!

A leap year is a year that is exactly divisible by four. However, if the year is exactly divisible by 100, it is not a leap year. Except, years that are exactly divisible by 400 are leap years.

Which of these years would have been, were, are, or will be leap years? Circle your answers.

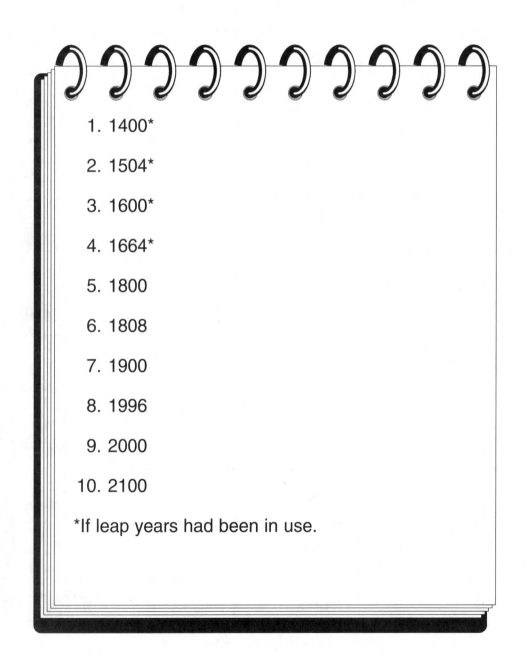

1. 1400*

2. 1504*

3. 1600*

4. 1664*

5. 1800

6. 1808

7. 1900

8. 1996

9. 2000

10. 2100

*If leap years had been in use.

Launch Time

It is launch time at the rocket pad. Since there are so many people who speak other languages, the interpreters are translating the countdown into French and Spanish. Unfortunately, somebody's put the countdown into alphabetical rather than reverse numerical order. Can you use your linguistic skills to translate the numbers and then write them in the correct order again?

French	English	Spanish	English
cinq		cero	
deux		cinco	
dix		cuatro	
huit		diez	
neuf		dos	
quatre		nueve	
sept		ocho	
six		seis	
trois		siete	
un		tres	
zero		uno	

Number Trivia

How many number questions can you answer?

1. Who is code-named Agent 007? _____

2. How many dog years are there for every human year? _____

3. How many years in:

   one decade? _____

   one score? _____

   one century? _____

   one millennium? _____

4. How many cards in a full deck, excluding Jokers? _____

5. What is a 747? _____

6. Who wrote:

   20,000 Leagues Under the Sea? _____

   Around the World in 80 days? _____

   1984? _____

7. Think of three number trivia questions of your own.

   _____

   _____

   _____

   _____

20 Questions

The answer is 100. What are 20 questions?

100

1. _____

2. _____

3. _____

4. _____

5. _____

6. _____

7. _____

8. _____

9. _____

10. _____

11. _____

12. _____

13. _____

14. _____

15. _____

16. _____

17. _____

18. _____

19. _____

20. _____

20 More Questions

The answer is _____ (you choose). What are 20 questions?

1. _____

2. _____

3. _____

4. _____

5. _____

6. _____

7. _____

8. _____

9. _____

10. _____

11. _____

12. _____

13. _____

14. _____

15. _____

16. _____

17. _____

18. _____

19. _____

20. _____

Everyday Math

Every day we use many different types of mathematical operations. Look at the following activities and write down all the things you would do involving mathematics. An example has been done for you. Write your answers on the next page.

Example

Activity: You go to the store to buy three flavors of ice cream.

Things that involve math:

    a. Find the cost of one ice cream.

    b. Multiply that cost by three.

    c. Check that you have enough money to pay for the ice cream.

    d. Check if you were given the correct change.

---

1. Winning a fishing competition with the biggest fish

2. Deciding which CD to buy—the new release or two at a 20 percent discount

3. Going to the movies by bus

4. Buying two fast food meals

5. Having new carpet installed in your house

6. Buying jeans and a shirt

With a friend, write down all the things you do during the day. Sort them into things that involve math and things that don't.

Things I do that involve math:	Things I do that don't involve math:

Everyday Math (cont.)

1. _____

_____

_____

2. _____

_____

_____

3. _____

_____

4. _____

_____

_____

5. _____

_____

_____

6. _____

_____

_____

How Many?

How many different ways can you get the correct answer?

You throw a die ten times.

The total number you have to throw is 47.

What numbers could you have thrown to arrive at the right answer?

Lilies

Water lilies double in area every 24 hours. At the beginning of summer there is one water lily on the lake. It takes 60 days for the lake to be completely covered. On what day is it half covered?

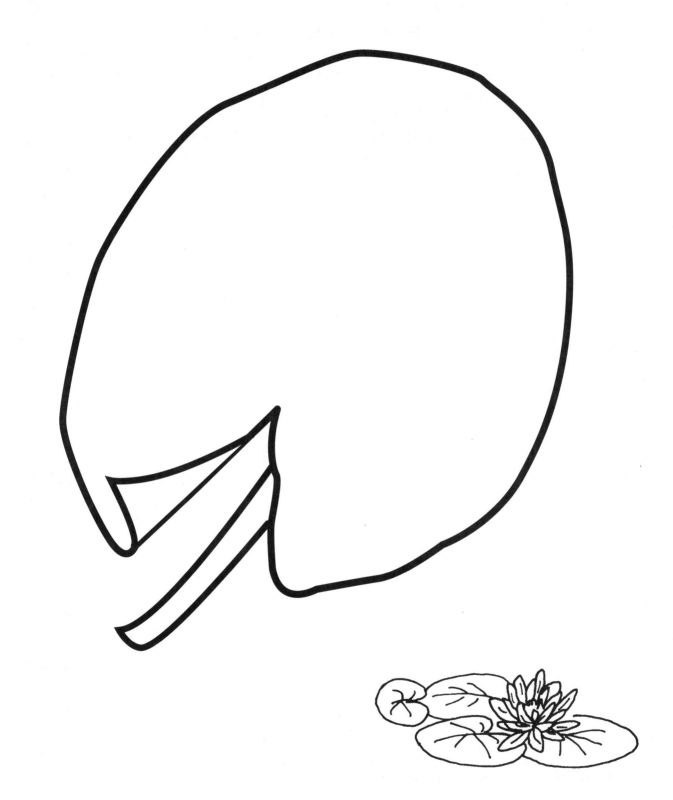

Sam's Solution

Sam worked out that eight nines equal 1125.

He proved to his teacher he was right.

How did he do it?

More How Many?

How many days, hours, and minutes from today until:

New Year's Day?   _____ days

_____ hours

_____ minutes

The Fourth of July   _____ days

_____ hours

_____ minutes

Your 14th birthday   _____ days

_____ hours

_____ minutes

Summer vacation begins   _____ days

_____ hours

_____ minutes

Mother's Day   _____ days

_____ hours

_____ minutes

Fibonacci Numbers

Look at these numbers. They are all in a family called *Fibonacci numbers*. They have a rule that allows them to belong to this family.

Can you figure out the rule to fill in all the blanks?

_____ ,_____ ,_____ ,_____ , 3, 5, 8, 13, 21,_____ ,_____ ,_____ ,_____ ,_____

What is the rule?_____

Fibonacci numbers occur in nature: in pine cones, pineapples, and the petals of many flowers. How many examples can you find that follow this sequence?

What's in a Number?

The name of each of the following objects includes a reference to a number associated with the object. Draw or make a model of each and provide labels.

Write a short description to go with each one.

Tripod	**Quintuplets**
Unicorn	**Binoculars**
Octopus	**Centipede**
Hexapod	**Dodecahedron**

Let's Go Shopping

Four friends spent the day shopping at a clothing store. From the clues given below, determine how much each spent and which item she purchased. Use an "O" for the correct answers and an "X" for the incorrect answers.

1. The skirt cost more than the shirt but less than the dress and shorts.

2. Shari spent more than Jenna or Margaret but less than the person who bought the dress.

3. Jenna spent more than Margaret.

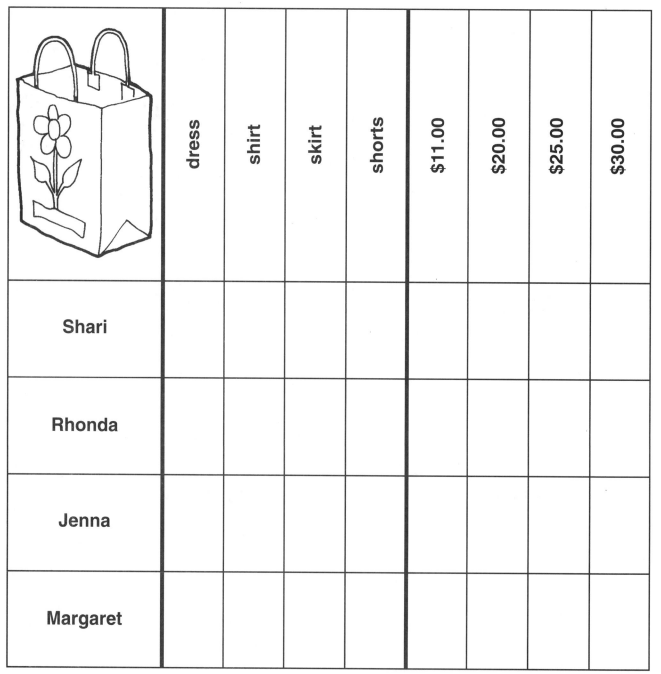

	dress	shirt	skirt	shorts	$11.00	$20.00	$25.00	$30.00
Shari								
Rhonda								
Jenna								
Margaret								

An Ancient Problem

There once was a king who had a great kingdom and great riches. The king discovered a young scholar who showed great promise. He offered the young scholar half of his kingdom or one grain of wheat on a chessboard doubled for every square. What do you suppose the young scholar chose?

Make this ancient problem more meaningful to you by solving the following problem: Someone has offered you a million dollars or one penny doubled for every square of a checkerboard. The board is drawn below. Use the checkerboard and some paper to calculate which is the better choice.

Write your decision here: _____

_____

_____

_____

Numerical Palindromes

A palindrome is a word, phrase, or number that is the same when it is read frontwards or backwards. Words like toot and dad are simple palindromes. "A Toyota" and "Madam, I'm Adam" are examples of phrases that are palindromes. Numbers like 1221 and 576675 are numerical palindromes.

NOON

MOM

12321

401104

DID

The following is a method to generate a numerical palindrome.

1. Start with any four-digit number.	1563
2. Reverse the digits.	3651
3. Add the original number.	1563 + 3651 = 5214
4. Reverse the digits.	4125
5. Add the numbers.	5214 + 4125 = 9339

This is a palindrome!

Do this for six different numbers to test the process. The number of times that you will have to repeat the process of reversing and adding will vary. Can you find another way to produce palindromes?

Supermarket Competition

These are the four finalists' shopping carts in the local supermarket's "Dash for Cash" competition. They had just one minute to fill their carts with cash. How much did each finalist get, and who won? Use the chart to determine how much each cart collected. For example, cart 1 collected 33 five dollar bills, which equals $165.00.

Bills	Cart 1	Cart 2	Cart 3	Cart 4
$5	33	5	26	11
$10	10	15	8	12
$20	5	8	8	12
$50	4	5	4	5
$100	4	5	4	5
Totals				

Show your work here.

Who Won? _____

Missing Numbers

The missing numbers in this puzzle are the digits 1 to 9. Each digit is used only once. Complete the puzzle using the clues below.

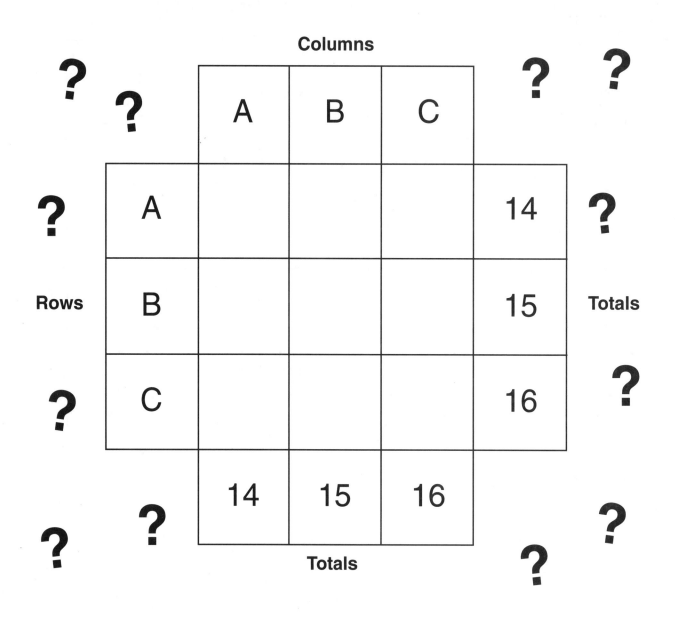

Clues

✎ Row A has all even digits.   ✎ Row B has all odd digits.

✎ 4 and 6 are in the same column.   ✎ 6 is not in the same row as 4.

✎ 1 and 9 are in the same row.

Handshakes

There are eight people at a party. If every person shakes hands with everyone else at the party, how many handshakes will there be? _____

Show your work and explain your answer.

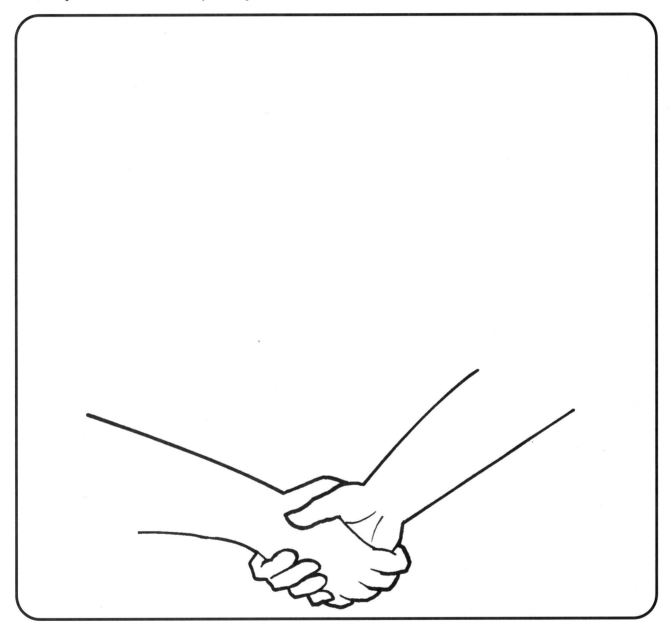

Extension: How many handshakes would there be in your family? _____

What's in the Bag? #5

Read the words on the next page. Then match the letters with the correct synonyms in the clues. (You will not use all the letters.) Put the five clues together and discover what's in the bag!

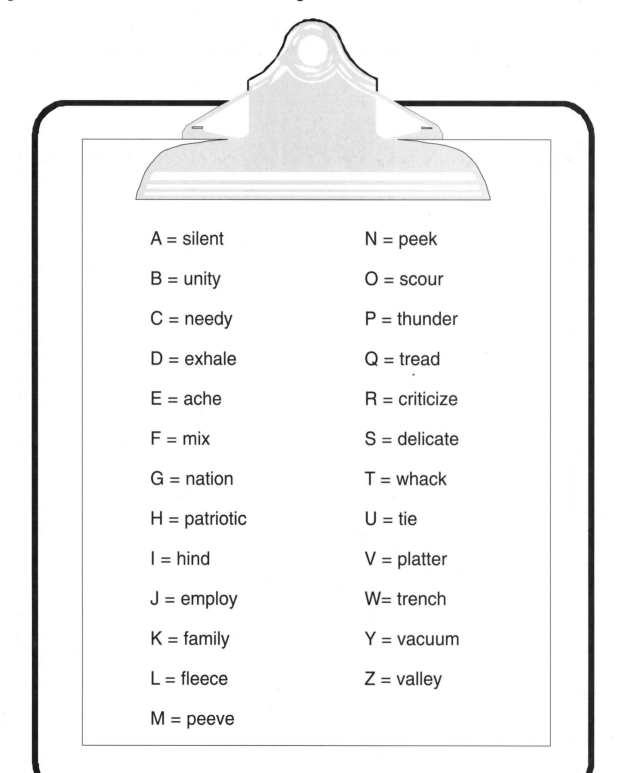

A = silent	N = peek
B = unity	O = scour
C = needy	P = thunder
D = exhale	Q = tread
E = ache	R = criticize
F = mix	S = delicate
G = nation	T = whack
H = patriotic	U = tie
I = hind	V = platter
J = employ	W = trench
K = family	Y = vacuum
L = fleece	Z = valley
M = peeve	

What's in the Bag? #5 *(cont.)*

Clue 1:

____ ____ ____ ____ ____ ____

rumble   mute   breathe   breathe   hurt   breathe

Clue 2:

____ ____ ____ ____ ____

loyal   hurt   mute   wool   tender

Clue 3:

____ ____ ____ ____ ____ ____

rear   glance   hire   knot   scold   sweep

Clue 4:

____ ____ ____ ____ ____ ____

tender   club   rear   poor   kin   sweep

Clue 5:

____ ____ ____ ____ ____

tender   club   scold   rear   rumble

What's in the bag? _____

What's in the Bag? #6

Read the words on the next page. Then match the letters with the correct synonyms in the clues. (You will not use all of the letters.) Put the five clues together and discover what's in the bag!

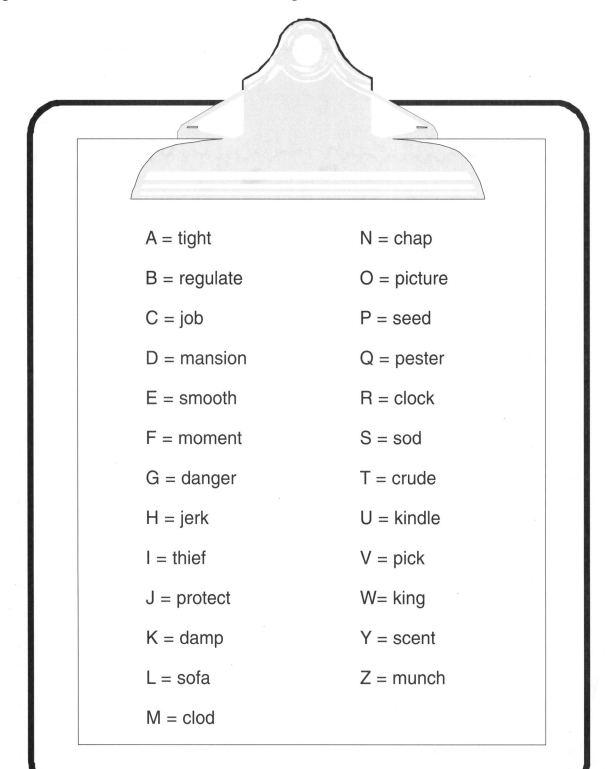

A = tight

B = regulate

C = job

D = mansion

E = smooth

F = moment

G = danger

H = jerk

I = thief

J = protect

K = damp

L = sofa

M = clod

N = chap

O = picture

P = seed

Q = pester

R = clock

S = sod

T = crude

U = kindle

V = pick

W= king

Y = scent

Z = munch

What's in the Bag? #6 (cont.)

Clue 1:

_____   _____   _____   _____   _____   _____

hazard   taut   palace   peril   silky   coarse

Clue 2:

_____   _____   _____   _____   _____   _____

choose   crook   silky   ruler   silky   timer

Clue 3:

_____   _____   _____   _____   _____   _____   _____   _____

career   twitch   taut   fellow   fellow   silky   couch   grass

Clue 4:

_____   _____   _____   _____   _____   _____   _____   _____

portrait   grain   silky   timer   taut   coarse   silky   grass

Clue 5:

_____   _____

coarse   choose

What's in the bag? _____

What's in the Bag? #7

Read the words on the next page. Then match the letters with the correct synonyms in the clues. (You will not use all of the letters.) Put the five clues together and discover what's in the bag!

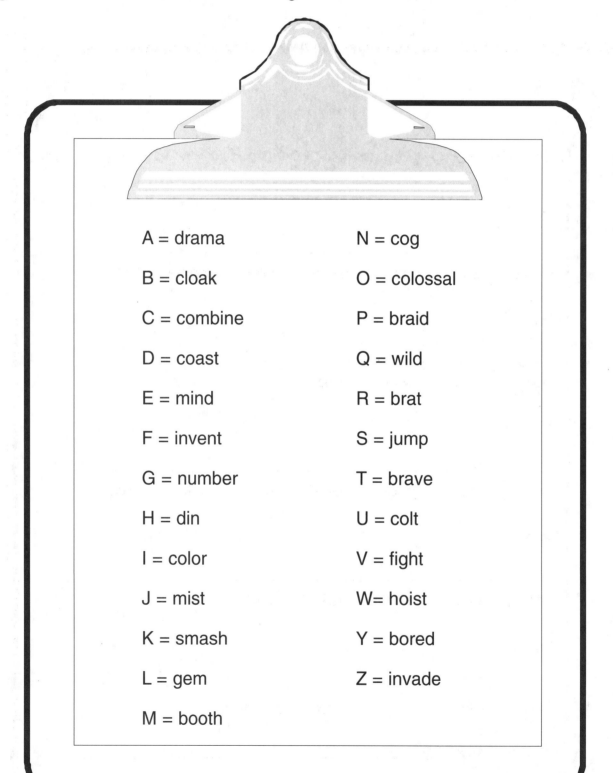

A = drama

B = cloak

C = combine

D = coast

E = mind

F = invent

G = number

H = din

I = color

J = mist

K = smash

L = gem

M = booth

N = cog

O = colossal

P = braid

Q = wild

R = brat

S = jump

T = brave

U = colt

V = fight

W = hoist

Y = bored

Z = invade

What's in the Bag? #7 *(cont.)*

Clue 1:

_____ _____ _____ _____ _____ _____ _____

weave   rascal   hue   battle   play   bold   brain

Clue 2:

_____ _____ _____ _____

brain   play   rascal   skip

Clue 3:

_____ _____ _____ _____ _____ _____ _____

mix   play   rascal   rascal   hue   brain   skip

Clue 4:

_____ _____ _____ _____ _____

stall   horse   skip   hue   mix

Clue 5:

_____ _____ _____ _____ _____

mix   jewel   play   stall   weave

What's in the bag? _____

What's in the Bag? #8

Read the words on the next page. Then match the letters with the correct synonyms in the clues. (You will not use all of the letters.) Put the five clues together and discover what's in the bag!

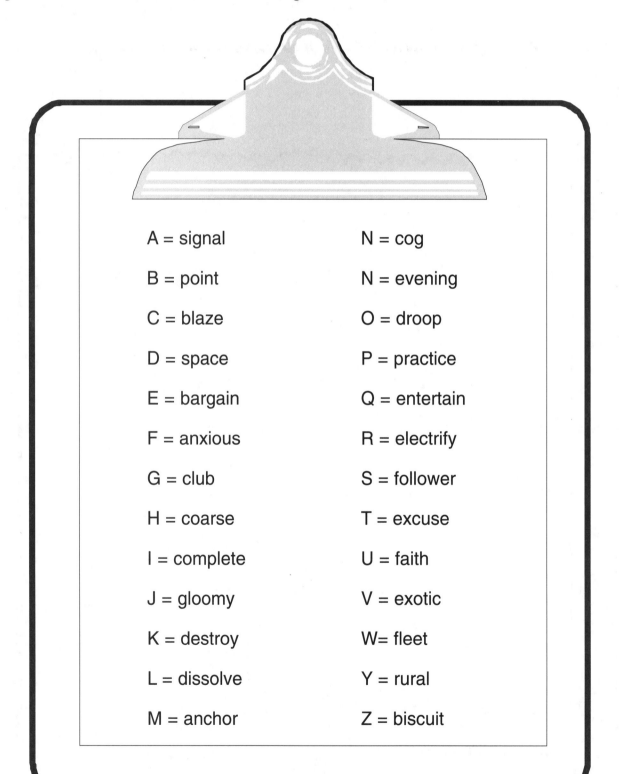

A = signal	N = cog
B = point	N = evening
C = blaze	O = droop
D = space	P = practice
E = bargain	Q = entertain
F = anxious	R = electrify
G = club	S = follower
H = coarse	T = excuse
I = complete	U = faith
J = gloomy	V = exotic
K = destroy	W = fleet
L = dissolve	Y = rural
M = anchor	Z = biscuit

What's in the Bag? #8 *(cont.)*

Clue 1:

_____   _____   _____   _____   _____   _____

rough   alarm   dusk   area   melt   sale

Clue 2:

_____   _____   _____   _____   _____

fan   dock   alarm   fire   ruin

Clue 3:

_____   _____   _____   _____   _____   _____

ships   finish   dusk   group   sale   area

Clue 4:

_____   _____   _____   _____   _____   _____

finish   dusk   fan   sale   fire   forgive

Clue 5:

_____   _____   _____

rough   finish   forgive

What's in the bag? _____

Procrastination Rules!

Here's a bunch of scrambled words that all mean to procrastinate, delay, hold back, or ignore. How many of them can you find? Or should you just put it all off until later?

FFO-TUP	RINLGE	EMIPED	ROITEL
DEEFR	NETIDA	DRIHEN	OOOVERKL
PONESTOP	TRESRA	DELWAD	SSUPDEN
TINDISCONUE	TLALS	YATS	

How Sharp Are You Today?

You can change "blunt" into "sharp" in 13 steps! Read each clue then change just one letter of the previous answer to make the new word.

B	L	U	N	T	
					The main force of a blow
					A low, pig-like noise
					Let have
					$1000
					A heated iron
					Has no taste or flavor
					Empty, not written in
					A straight length of wood
					To put seeds in the ground
					Not level
					Abbreviation of "shall not"
					Boy's name
					To give out a fair portion
S	H	A	R	P	

Constellation Word Search

Find and circle the words in the word search that are in the box. All of the words are the names of constellations.

Aquarius	Capricorn
Libra	Scorpio
Aries	Gemini
Pisces	Taurus
Cancer	Leo
Sagittarius	Virgo

```
S   U   R   U   A   T   A   U   S   T   R

V   I   R   G   O   A   L   I   A   S   S

C   A   P   R   I   C   O   R   N   O   P

U   A   R   B   I   L   T   H   E   R   I

S   A   G   I   T   T   A   R   I   U   S

N   S   U   I   R   A   U   Q   A   O   C

S   C   O   R   P   I   O   C   R   E   E

O   S   R   E   C   N   A   C   S   L   S

G   E   M   I   N   I   S   E   I   R   A
```

Your Name

Write all of the letters of your first and last name. How many words of three or more letters can you make from your name?

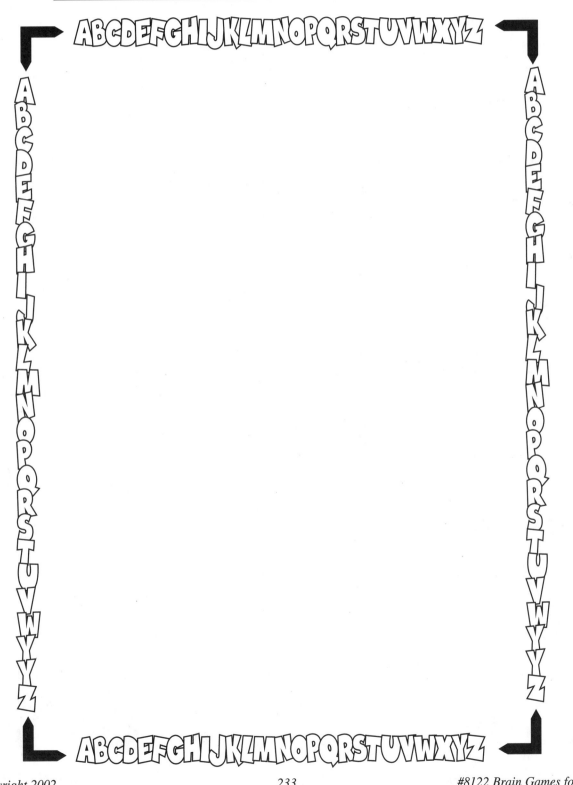

Jumbled Music Styles

Remove the indicated letters and then unscramble the remaining letters to spell out a musical style. (example: AWNINGS – AN = WINGS = swing)

1. BUGLES – G = _____

2. CHIP SHOP – CS = _____

3. CODFISH – FH = _____

4. CROAK – A = _____

5. CRYING OUT – GI = _____

6. FLOCK – C = _____

7. HIPPO – HI = _____

8. LOCK, STOCK, AND BARREL – ABCEKST = (three words) _____

   _____

9. MISCALCULATES – EMTU = _____

10. NOTCHED – D = _____

11. THAMES VALLEY – LS = (two words) _____

12. UNPACK – AC = _____

Style Search

Rock, jazz, classical, country, gospel . . . the list of musical styles can seem never-ending. Here's a list of 22 styles. Find them all, and the leftover letters will spell out the names of four other styles that are thought to have come together to create rock and roll.

be bop, bluegrass, blues, country, dance, disco, Dixieland, gospel, grunge, heavy metal, heavy rock, hip hop, rap, rave, rock, rock and roll, speed, metal, surf, swing, synth pop

```
B D N A L E I X I D O S P H O G
R O C K A N D R O L L P O E L E
C O U N T R Y I E W O E P A E G
E G E K E P O H P I H E H V P N
C N V C M O G I E S J D T Y S U
N I A O Y U M P B E L M N R O R
A W R R V U E F R U S E Y O G G
D S S S A R G E U L B T S C S R
D P O B E B O O W B O A P K A H
O N K Y H D I S C O T L O P N K
```

The four other styles: _____ _____

_____ _____

Across-Word

Though this puzzle is less than witty, low on fun and jollity,
a plus is in its brevity, and that each word must end in "ity."

Energy from electrons

							i	t	y

An object's ability

						i	t	y

Steadiness

					i	t	y

The smaller of two groups

					i	t	y

The attractive force of the earth

				i	t	y

A game or pursuit

				i	t	y

Being long-lived

					i	t	y

Quality of being admired

						i	t	y

Being sensitive

							i	t	y

The Clipper Ship Crossword

1. A ship's living quarters

2. Where food is cooked

3. Left (direction)

4. The back of a ship

5. A ship's body

6. The front of a ship

7. They leave a sinking ship

8. Dropped to keep a ship from moving

9. Replaces sails on modern ships

10. Right (direction)

What is the special name for a mariner who sailed around the tip of South America?

Bulb Additions

Add "bulb" to the letter *r*. Rearrange into a promotional statement on a book jacket and you have a "blurb." Can you complete these nine other "bulb additions"?

bulb + ae = an ornament

```
┌─────────────────────────────────────────┐
│                                         │
│                                         │
└─────────────────────────────────────────┘
```

bulb + be = a hollow globule of gas

```
┌─────────────────────────────────────────┐
│                                         │
│                                         │
└─────────────────────────────────────────┘
```

bulb + eh = an orbiting space telescope

```
┌─────────────────────────────────────────┐
│                                         │
│                                         │
└─────────────────────────────────────────┘
```

bulb + er = the remains of a broken building

```
┌─────────────────────────────────────────┐
│                                         │
│                                         │
└─────────────────────────────────────────┘
```

bulb + cde = to have been hit with a heavy stick

```
┌─────────────────────────────────────────┐
│                                         │
│                                         │
└─────────────────────────────────────────┘
```

bulb + eiq = to argue over a small item

```
┌─────────────────────────────────────────┐
│                                         │
│                                         │
└─────────────────────────────────────────┘
```

bulb + adeer = a famous pirate

```
┌─────────────────────────────────────────┐
│                                         │
│                                         │
└─────────────────────────────────────────┘
```

bulb + begmu = a kind of chewing gum

```
┌─────────────────────────────────────────┐
│                                         │
│                                         │
└─────────────────────────────────────────┘
```

Con Job

Every answer to these clues begins with "con"—and all the letters can be found in Constantinople. What a convenient word!

solid shape with a circular base rising to a point

〇〇〇〇

agree to

〇〇〇〇〇〇

to comfort a sad person

〇〇〇〇〇〇〇

keep within a boundary

〇〇〇〇〇〇〇

happy

〇〇〇〇〇〇〇

competition between rivals

〇〇〇〇〇〇〇

uninterrupted

〇〇〇〇〇〇〇〇〇

a speech sound that is not a vowel

〇〇〇〇〇〇〇〇〇〇

a large land mass

〇〇〇〇〇〇〇〇〇

Buttery Words

Butter certainly crops up in all manner of places, recipes, and words—so read the clues and work out these buttery words!

B U T T E R +		=	
	I		1. a special TV show honoring a person
	EN		2. a person with brown hair
	SS		3. a stone support for a building
	NO		4. to button again
	JO		5. a type of engine
	EIQ		6. a charcoal fuel block
	CPU		7. a flower
	GIL		8. someone who litters
	GIJ		9. a dance from the '50s
	CGSY		10. a famous battle of the Civil War

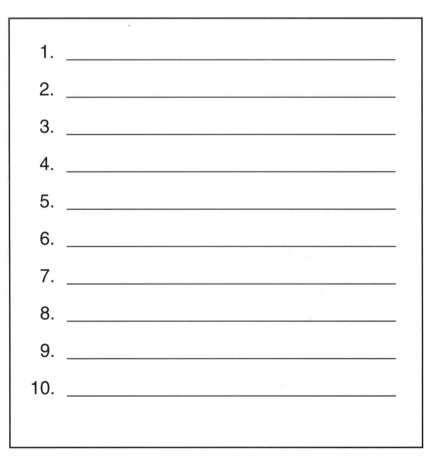

1. _____

2. _____

3. _____

4. _____

5. _____

6. _____

7. _____

8. _____

9. _____

10. _____

All Roads Lead to Rome

Here are eight roads leading to Rome. The names are scrambled but you know that each one contains the letters "R-O-M-E." Use the clues to identify each road.

1. Old-fashioned women's underpants
2. A tropical plant often found in a swamp.
3. Someone who pays for goods or services.
4. A person who employs people.
5. A person who creates original music.
6. Very large
7. Examined and noted similarities and differences
8. The mathematics of points, lines, curves, and surfaces.

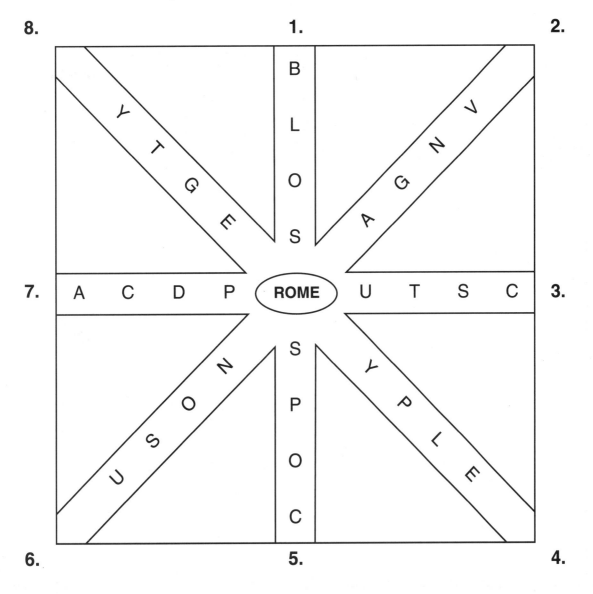

My Turn to be a Hero

The letters A–Z are written on this page and the next page. For each letter, think of a situation in which you could become a hero. For example: Avalanche—I could help to rescue someone from beneath the snow.

A_____

B_____

C_____

D_____

E_____

F_____

G_____

H_____

I_____

J_____

K_____

L_____

M_____

My Turn to be a Hero (cont.)

N _____

O _____

P _____

Q _____

R _____

S _____

T _____

U _____

V _____

W _____

X _____

Y _____

Z _____

Leo's Likes and Dislikes

The following are some questions using made-up facts about Leonardo Da Vinci. Leonardo Da Vinci liked the shape of an OVAL but not a SQUARE; he invented the ROAD but not the PATH; he liked to LEND money but not BORROW it. Using his name as a clue, try to answer the questions.

1. Paint a DANDELION or a ROSE? _____

2. Predict GLOBAL WARMING or ACID RAIN? _____

3. Invent the AIRLINE or the TRAIN? _____

4. Invent the THEATER or the DRIVE-IN? _____

5. Design the RADIO or the TV? _____

6. Make RADIAL or CROSS-PLY tires?_____

7. Make a CRADLE or a CRIB? _____

8. Invent COMPUTER games or ARCADE games? _____

9. Draw a portrait of an ALIEN or a BIGFOOT? _____

10. Invent the CASSETTE or the VIDEO? _____

Complete a Word

Use the 26 letters of the alphabet to complete the words below. Use each letter only one time. (*Hint:* Cross off the letters as you use them.) Write what the word means on the line below.

| a b c d e f g h i j k l m |
| n o p q r s t u v w x y z |

1. ◯ u i d e

   _____

2. ◯ c c o ◯ d ◯ o n

   _____

3. s c r a ◯ ◯ ◯ e

   _____

4. a ◯ u e ◯ u c t

   _____

5. ◯ u f ◯ i ◯

   _____

6. ◯ ◯ e s s

   _____

7. ◯ a ◯ n

   _____

8. s ◯ r ◯ e ◯

   _____

9. e x c ◯ r p t

   _____

10. s c o r p i ◯ ◯

   _____

11. ◯ i ◯ h e r

   _____

12. ◯ u n ◯

   _____

                                                       #8122 Brain Games for Kids

Palindrome Word Find

Palindromes are words, phrases, sentences, or numbers that read the same forward and backward. Two examples are *121* and *Anna*. See how many palindromes you can find in this puzzle. (There are 34 words in all.)

```
S  J  B  L  A  D  B  B  U  O  F  M  B  E  W  E  Z  C
L  O  P  E  A  C  O  I  D  L  N  U  N  T  R  H  N  H
E  C  O  E  C  B  Q  O  B  J  T  M  M  O  E  A  B  T
V  T  M  Y  E  P  D  K  P  K  N  L  T  A  O  N  P  B
E  O  O  L  Z  P  M  H  E  V  E  I  Q  D  D  N  E  A
L  X  W  T  U  X  N  A  T  S  Q  M  T  H  I  A  E  T
A  T  J  P  S  R  N  U  Y  Z  K  A  R  S  T  H  M  X
N  A  D  D  B  D  R  R  Z  P  L  J  O  O  U  Q  O  J
J  Z  S  O  Z  I  A  T  K  W  O  H  A  L  T  R  X  O
D  E  E  D  M  G  D  A  B  S  S  P  W  O  C  O  L  T
B  Y  A  O  A  M  A  G  K  V  A  L  P  S  I  K  R  T
T  E  R  A  N  X  R  G  W  D  G  Z  F  R  V  G  V  O
E  A  R  K  N  L  S  L  O  I  A  L  U  P  I  K  M  O
R  E  P  A  P  E  R  U  W  D  S  N  I  O  C  M  O  T
R  X  H  Y  S  X  P  S  N  J  E  O  N  T  E  R  M  G
E  O  K  A  F  O  I  U  D  U  D  M  B  A  C  E  B  I
T  H  A  K  D  J  M  N  X  R  G  H  E  W  C  A  B  T
S  E  E  S  U  N  X  W  O  A  L  S  K  A  G  Z  P  O
```

More Letter Answers

Use one, two, or three letters of the alphabet to "spell" a word corresponding to each of the following clues. The first one has been done for you.

1. Used in a pool game   _____Q_____

2. Happiness   _____

3. A foe   _____

4. Jealousy   _____

5. A woman's name   _____

6. In debt   _____

7. A written composition   _____

8. What makes a movie exciting   _____

9. A boy's name   _____

10. To say good-bye   _____

11. The number after 79   _____

12. A drink, hot or iced   _____

13. An exclamation   _____

14. To be good at something   _____

15. To rot   _____

Tutu Entanglement

What would we do without tutus? We would not have any of the following words or phrases, that's for sure! Add TUTU to the letters below and then unscramble them using the clue.

TUTU + ERBENPTA AND JELLY = PEANUT BUTTER
(Clue)

		clue	word or phrase
T U T U +	OP	things produced	
	RON	attendance for an event	
	HNR	a lie	
	PREB	to flatter	
	ROBS	sudden violent happening	
	BIMK	a city in Africa	
	FLHR	honest	
	ABNOR	rotate through a half circle	
	PRECB	flower	
	EFOON	unmusical	

Alphabet Elevator

At the alphabet convention, letters using the elevator have to arrange themselves into words. Use the clues and figure out what words the letters made on each floor.

						7	A story
						6	To take a trip
						5	A lift
						4	Eat too much
						3	To vote again
						2	A person who votes
						1	Above
R	E	V				G	Speed up an engine

V, E, and R get in the elevator on the ground floor.

On the first floor, O joins them.

T gets in on the second floor.

E's twin (E) joins them on floor 3.

A hurries in on the 4th floor.

L gets in on the 5th floor—the elevator is full!

O and E get out on the 6th floor.

V and R get out on the 7th floor.

Symphony Orchestra Word Search

Find all these instruments in the word search below. The leftover letters will tell you what the musician standing out in front of the orchestra has to do.

alto clarinet, bass clarinet, bassoon, cello, cor anglais, double bass, flute, French horn, gong, piano, piccolo, snare, timpani, triangle, trombone, trumpet, tuba, viola, violin

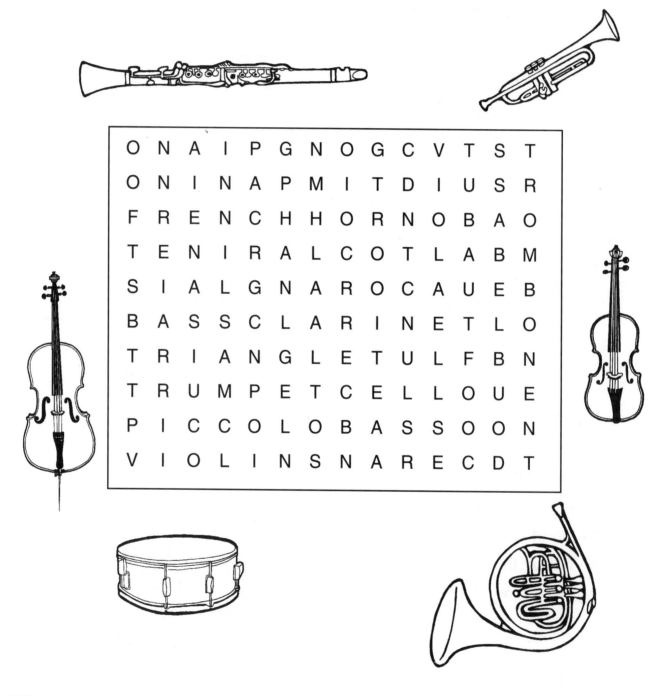

```
O N A I P G N O G C V T S T
O N I N A P M I T D I U S R
F R E N C H H O R N O B A O
T E N I R A L C O T L A B M
S I A L G N A R O C A U E B
B A S S C L A R I N E T L O
T R I A N G L E T U L F B N
T R U M P E T C E L L O U E
P I C C O L O B A S S O O N
V I O L I N S N A R E C D T
```

What does the musician standing out in front of the orchestra do? _____

Jelly Legs

Imagine that your body is made of jelly. List everyday things you would not be able to do, and how your jelly body would affect your daily activities. What would you be able to do that you can't do with your current body?

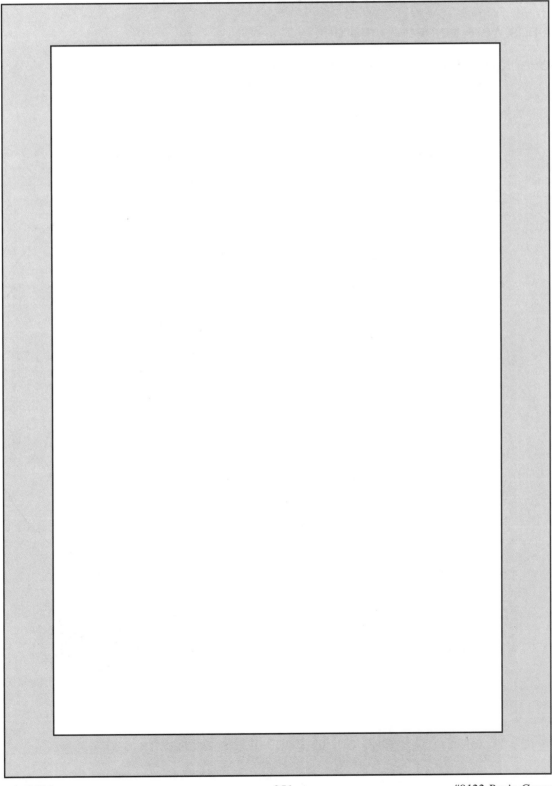

Hammurabi's Codes

Hammurabi, King of Mesopotamia in about 1792 B.C., brought great changes to the laws of his country. Two of his laws were the following:

1. Wrongdoers were judged and punished by the decision of the society, rather than by the victim and/or the victim's family.

2. All killings were treated as murder.

List the advantages and the disadvantages of these two laws.

Advantages   **Disadvantages**

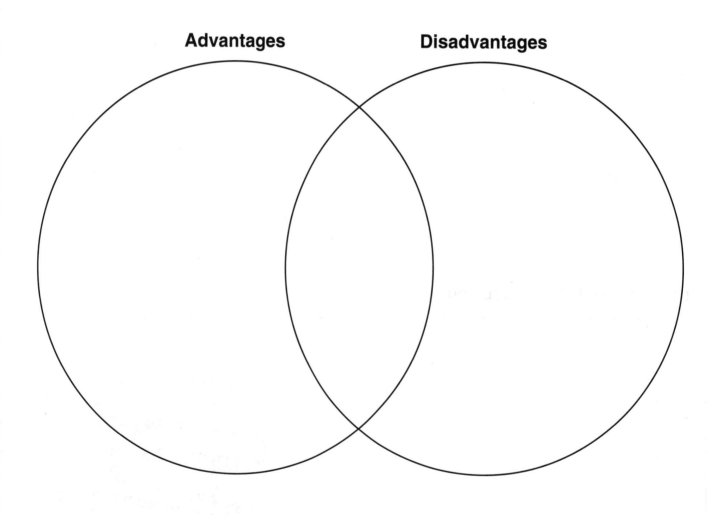

Funny Books

Identify what makes a book or character funny.

Name some of the humorous books you have read.

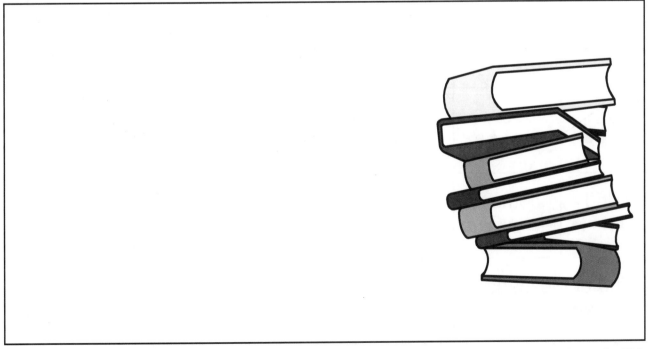

Morse Code

Here is what Morse code looks like. It sounds like this: dot = quick sound or tap, dash = longer sound. Using Morse code, write a note to a friend using only the dots and dashes of the code. Be sure to allow enough space between each letter so that the letters don't run into each other. Write your letter on the next page.

Morse Code

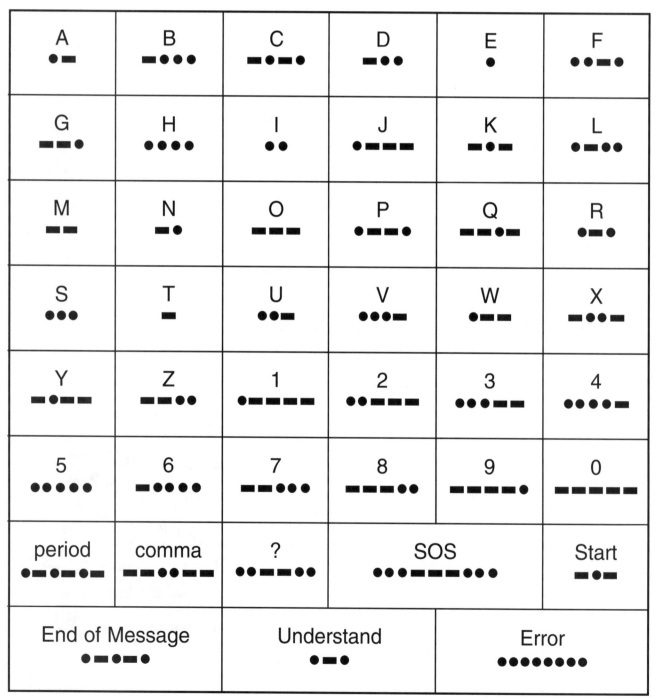

Morse Code *(cont.)*

Write your letter here.

_____

_____

_____

_____

_____

_____

_____

_____

_____

_____

_____

My Hero

From all of the people you have ever known, read about, or heard about choose one person who impresses you most.

Write a haiku or limerick about this person.

_____

_____

_____

_____

_____

_____

_____

_____

_____

_____

_____

City Link

Each of these cities begins with the last letter of the previous answer. Join them up in one long city link.

1. Previous U.S. capital

2. Capital of Kuwait

3. Capital of Japan

4. Capital of Norway

5. Capital of Canada

6. Capital of Greece

7. Capital of South Korea

8. Capital of England

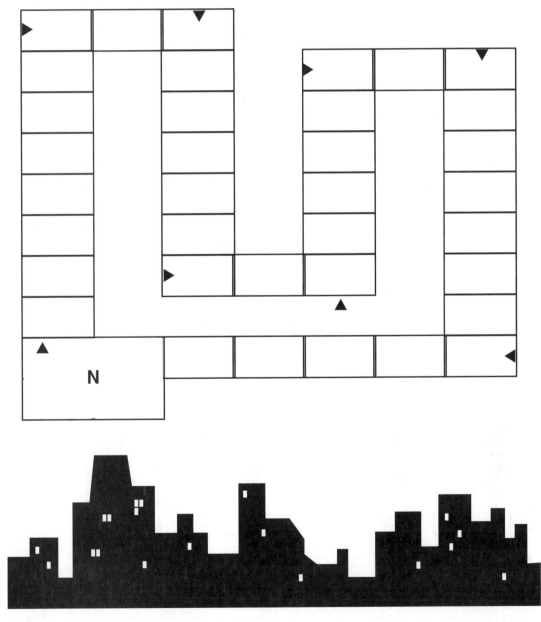

Stunt Puzzle

Jim Band is a hero in movies. In his latest movie, the hero is forced to escape from a maze. While escaping, Jim Band (or at least his stunt double) must do the following:

- Wrestle a lion
- Escape from ropes
- Jump from a building (it's a big maze)
- Carry a bomb
- Swim in shark-infested water
- Swing beneath a bridge
- Jump a double-decker bus (okay, it's a really BIG maze!)

He must enter via the North entrance, and in completing all of these stunts, he must cover every path but not travel the same path twice.

1. Where does the stunt double exit? _____

2. In what order are the stunts done? _____

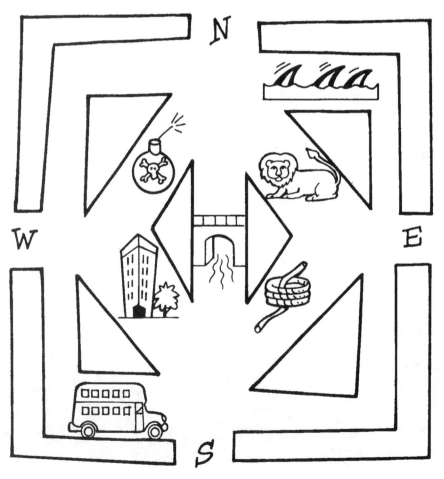

Muddled (and Endangered) Creatures

Look at this list of animals. Do the names seem unfamiliar? If they're not saved from extinction, then children 100 years from now may find the real names unfamiliar, too. So, unscramble them and find the names of 11 endangered mammals, reptiles, and birds.

raptor_____

hateech _____

conrod_____

roodiccle _____

pheelnat _____

leglaze_____

orchesrion _____

lutter _____

halwe_____

poorweekcd_____

Be Creative

Design a device in the box that will save time by doing something that is normally done manually (by hand). Explain how it will work.

Detailed explanation of how the device will work:

_____

_____

_____

_____

Using Technology

Name all of the machines that you could possibly use during an average day.

_____

_____

_____

_____

Imagine you were living in the 19th century and were suddenly transported to the present day. What do you imagine you would find most surprising?

_____

_____

_____

_____

What do you think would be most frightening?

_____

_____

What would be most amusing?

_____

_____

What would be most useful out of all the inventions in the 20th century?

_____

_____

Listing Change

Write a list of things that change rapidly and a second list of things that change slowly.

Rapid change	Slow change
_____	_____
_____	_____
_____	_____
_____	_____
_____	_____
_____	_____
_____	_____
_____	_____
_____	_____

Write a list of things that change daily, for example, world population.	List things that never change.
_____	_____
_____	_____
_____	_____
_____	_____
_____	_____
_____	_____
_____	_____

Buckets

List as many uses as you can for a bucket.

Stamp Out Poverty

World governments should abandon space travel and all money should be directed to help eliminate poverty throughout the world because one-quarter of the world's population is badly malnourished.

Examine the statement above. List all the positive and negative arguments and any questions that arise.

Positives	Negatives	Questions
_____	_____	_____
_____	_____	_____
_____	_____	_____
_____	_____	_____
_____	_____	_____
_____	_____	_____
_____	_____	_____
_____	_____	_____
_____	_____	_____

What decision(s) did you reach? Do you support the statement? _____

_____

New and Improved

Design a new shower, and explain the reasons for any changes. You may like to use the BAR strategy to help decide on features that could be improved and ways of doing it. Illustrate your new shower design below.

B = make **bigger** or **smaller**

A = **add** something

R = **remove** something and **replace** it with something else

Change: _____

Reasons:_____

_____

Change: _____

Reasons:_____

_____

Change: _____

Reasons:_____

Before   **After**

What a Legend!

Describe a hero or heroine who is living at the present time. This can be a fictional person. Start with a physical description and then move beyond this to explain the other qualities he or she has. Think of 12 heroic tasks that he or she must complete.

Description of hero or heroine   **Explain the twelve heroic tasks.**

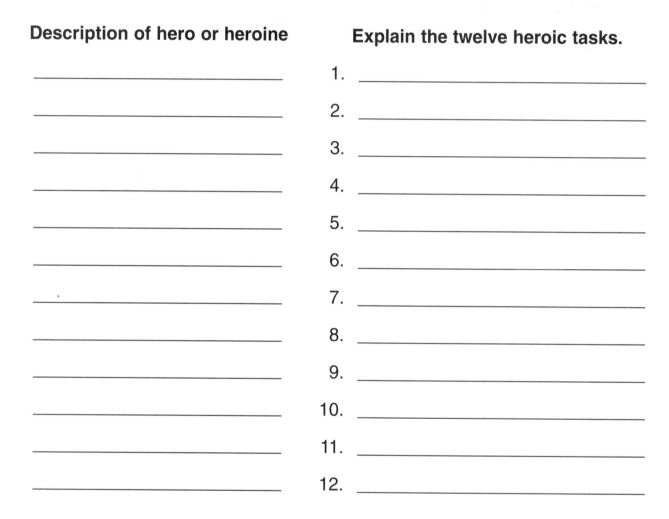

You, as the hero, have to select three of the following objects to help with the tasks. Which would you choose and why would they be selected?

matches, jellybeans, a deck of cards, a rope, a skateboard, a magnifying glass, newspaper, a hat, a blanket, a boat, bicycle, a hammer, nails, money, shoes, soap, spoon, mirror, pocket knife, screwdriver, a spade

Choice   **Reasons**

_____   _____

_____   _____

_____   _____

Space Invention

Invent something unusual that can be used in space.

Suggestions: A feeding machine which can be used in a weightless environment, an alien-greeting robot, a space probe that can be sent out to analyze each new planet you approach.

Describe your invention in the squares below.

What it is	Description of components
How it works	What it can be used for
Special features	Illustration

Snow for Sale

Think of some innovative uses for snow.

Design an advertising campaign to sell snow.

Public Transportation

Brainstorm solutions for this problem:

People don't like using public transportation.

Improving Transportation

Choose one form of transportation. Improve this form so that it could move more people than at present and would be more comfortable for a long trip. Draw your new form of transportation and describe the improvements you have made.

Pyramids of Egypt

Below is a drawing of an Egyptian pyramid.

The purpose of the Egyptian pyramid was _____

Substitute something: _____

Combine it with something else: _____

Adapt it to make it suitable for another purpose: _____

Modify the size: _____

Divide it into portions: _____

Eliminate part of it: _____

Reverse it: _____

After you have written your ideas for the changes to the Egyptian pyramid, draw your own version. Label all of the changes you have made.

My new design is called _____

Its purpose is _____

Clothing

1. List six things that affect the type of clothing people wear and make a note of how each thing makes a difference to their choices.

Influence	How does it make a difference?
1.	
2.	
3.	
4.	
5.	
6.	

2. Quickly select five letters from the alphabet (do not include Q). Find an article of clothing beginning with each of these letters. In the table below, note what type of clothing it is, where it comes from, and who wears it.

Name of Item	What is it?	Where from?	Who wears it?
1.			
2.			
3.			
4.			
5.			

3. Now illustrate and label one of these articles of clothing.

Clothing *(cont.)*

1. Speaking of items of clothing, what do these expressions mean?

   Keep your shirt on:_____

   Treat her with kid gloves:_____

   If the shoe fits, wear it:_____

   He'd give you the shirt off his back:_____

2. How does climate affect the clothing you wear? Draw yourself sensibly dressed for the following conditions. Include any accessories you may also need.

Extremely hot	Extremely cold	Extremely wet	Extremely windy

Hats

1. List, draw, and label as many types of hats as you can. Show who wears the hat and where you'll find him or her (in which country).

2. Why are there so many different types of head coverings? Give as many reasons as you can.

_____

_____

_____

_____

_____

_____

_____

_____

Hats *(cont.)*

3. Make a hat for all occasions. Put your mind to work to create a useful hat that is also formal, sporty, protective, etc.

4. What do these hat expressions mean?

   Keep it under your hat: _____

   Throw your hat in the ring:_____

   Pass the hat around: _____

   Take your hat off to someone: _____

Lunch Special

Organize a lunch special for your school cafeteria. Make sure that it tastes good and is healthful.

Describe and illustrate your meal in the box below.

Name of lunch special:	Illustration
Description: _____ _____ _____ _____ _____	

Design and produce an advertising poster for your lunch special.

Scratch and Smell

List all of the ways you could be protected by your sense of smell. Now list all of the ways you could be protected by your sense of touch. Write about the importance of these two senses to the survival of human beings.

Mouth Watering!

Ponder this question and come up with as many answers as you can think of.

How can your sense of taste help you other than telling you that you like or dislike your food? Create a poster telling about the sense of taste and what it does.

Seeing is Believing!

What are some things that you have learned using:

- your sense of sight?
- your sense of hearing?

Draw a picture showing what you have learned.

Design with Numbers

Design a house floor plan. It must consist of four bedrooms, a kitchen, a living room, bathroom, laundry room, dining room, family room, and garage. Decide on the area of each room and the total area of the house.

Hidden Meanings

Explain the meaning of each box.

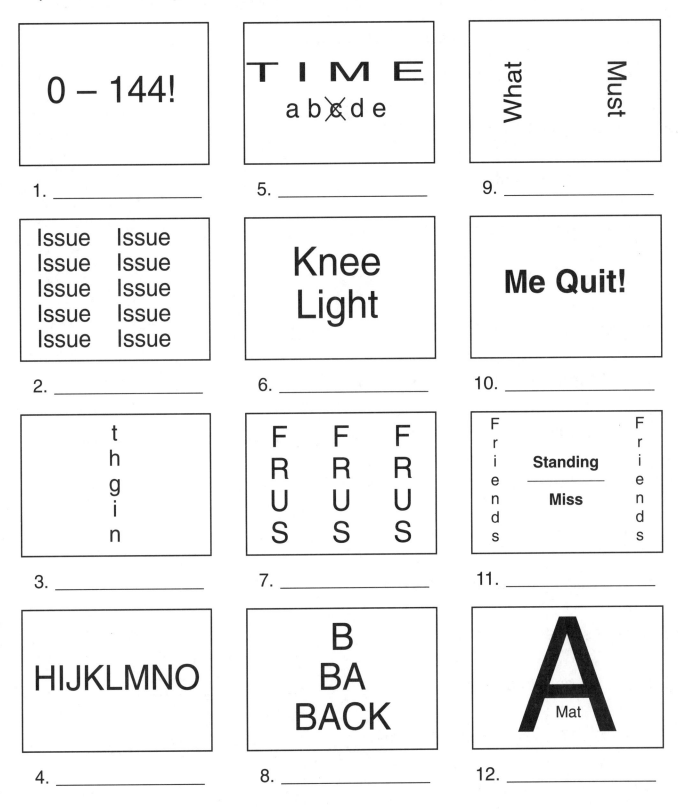

0 – 144!

1. _____

Issue   Issue
Issue   Issue
Issue   Issue
Issue   Issue
Issue   Issue

2. _____

t
h
g
i
n

3. _____

HIJKLMNO

4. _____

TIME
ab⊠de

5. _____

Knee
Light

6. _____

FRUS FRUS FRUS

7. _____

B
BA
BACK

8. _____

What   Must

9. _____

Me Quit!

10. _____

Friends Standing Miss Friends

11. _____

A Mat

12. _____

Reverse Words

Reverse words are words that become different words when read backwards. Write the words and their reverses from the clues below. An example has been done for you.

physician/fish = doc/cod

1. sticky substance/rodent = _____

2. doodle/large hospital room = _____

3. cooking container/the best = _____

4. cat and dog/part of staircase _____

5. not die/cruel = _____

6. not later/opposite of lost = _____

7. half of twenty/tennis court separation = _____

8. a belt/pieces = _____

9. flying mammals/knife injury = _____

10. pullout from a dresser/prize = _____

11. take a quick look/not give away = _____

12. baby rests/section of a bridge = _____

13. heavenly body/rodents = _____

14. takes skin off vegetables/nightly rest = _____

15. part of body/hair slicker = _____

Initializations and Acronyms

Acronyms are words formed from the initial letters of the words for which they stand. An example is VIP, which means "very important person." What do the

1. SWAK _____

2. HQ _____

3. RR _____

4. ERA _____

5. CPA _____

6. AWOL _____

7. TLC _____

8. GI _____

9. SOS _____

10. HEW _____

11. ASAP _____

12. PA _____

13. UFO _____

14. DJ _____

15. COD _____

Palindromes

Palindromes are words, phrases, sentences, or numbers that read the same forward and backward. Write a palindrome that relates to each word or phrase below. An example has been done for you.

Example: trick or joke = gag

1. midday _____

2. past tense of the verb *do* _____

3. a female sheep _____

4. robert's nickname _____

5. a small child _____

6. a little chick's noise _____

7. an organ of the body used for sight _____

8. a father's nickname _____

9. something that fails to work _____

10. the sound of a horn _____

11. something a baby wears _____

12. songs sung alone _____

13. a mother's nickname _____

14. an Eskimo canoe _____

15. even, flat _____

16. soda _____

17. a woman's name _____

18. a small dog _____

19. a brave or skillful act _____

20. relating to government or citizenship _____

Shipwrecked!

List three people you would like to be shipwrecked with and give reasons for your choices.

_____

_____

_____

_____

_____

List things you would need to retrieve from the ship to help in your survival.

_____

_____

_____

_____

_____

_____

_____

The Amazing Hat

Design a hat that has at least four uses. Draw it here, and label the parts.

Describe how the hat works and for whom it would be useful.

_____

_____

_____

_____

_____

_____

Progress Chart

Page	Title	Date	Completed

#8122 Brain Games for Kids

Progress Chart (cont.)

Page	Title	Date	Completed

Progress Chart *(cont.)*

Page	Title	Date	Completed

Progress Chart *(cont.)*

Page	Title	Date	Completed

Answer Key

Brain Warmups

Page 16

Answers will vary.

Page 17

1. 27 animals
2. 300 students
3. Answers will vary. Samples:
   200+85
   2 hundreds, eight tens, and five ones
   15 x 19
   300–15

Page 18

Answers will vary.

Page 19

Answers will vary.

Page 20

7, 21, 49, 70, 77, 28
35, 70, 84, 21, 14
35, 42, 49, 70, 77
28, 14, 7, 14, 28
35, 77, 56, 35, 42
56, 63, 14, 49

Page 21

Across	Down
1. 28	1. 38
2. 18	2. 88
3. 85	3. 89
	4. 48

Page 22

M-A-B-C-D-F-G-J-L-N-O-M

Page 23

12, 3, 15, 20, 14, 22, 2, 19, 8, 2, 12

Page 24

5 + 7 + 4 + 18 = 34

Page 25

C = 80 miles

Page 26

1. □
2. △
3. ○
4. ♡
5. ○
6. □
7. ⊃
8. △
9. ♡
10. ▭

Page 27

Δ's
sun
slide
swings
table
hills
O's
tree
fruit on tree
sun
slide
cup

Page 28

8 triangles

Page 29

Answers will vary.

Page 30

1. a. 50 students
   b. 4th grade
2. a. 98 kilometers
   b. no

Page 31

3. a. $284.95
   b. yes, $228.60
4. a. 7 team members
   b. 0

Page 32

5. a. $3.07
   b. $29.19
6. a. $37.36
   b. $34.64

Page 33

Bob Johnson, age 7
Bobby Wilson, age 8
Robert Anderson, age 9

Page 34

There are many answers. Some possible answers include the following:

1. h d
2. 2 q
3. 1 q, 2 d, 1 n
4. 1 q, 1 d, 3 n
5. 5 d
6. 10 n
7. 4 d, 2 n
8. 3 d, 4 n
9. 2 d, 6 n
10. 1 d, 8 n
11. 8 n, 10 p

Answer Key *(cont.)*

12. 6 n, 20 p
13. 4 n, 30 p
14. 2 n, 40 p
15. 1 n, 45 p
16. 10 p, 4 d
17. 20 p, 3 d
18. 30 p, 2 d
19. 40 p, 1 d
20. 50 p

Page 35

Ted Agee, age 9
Theodore Chin, age 8
Teddy Dalton, age 10

Page 36

Circle, triangle, square, rectangle
Shapes are fun.

Page 37

The safe way across is 60 ÷ 15, 16 kg x 4, 112 m +
36 m, 17 − 9 − 4, $4.20 − $3.80, 32 ÷ 8, 1 + 2 + 3 + 4
− 6, 10 + 3 − 9

Page 38

1. Fill the 5 L jug. Pour 3 L into the 3 L jug from
   the 5 L jug. Empty the 3 L jug. Pour 2 L from
   the 5 L jug into the now empty 3 L jug. Fill the
   5 L jug. That makes 7 L.
2. 7 new walls
3. 1 + 2 = 3
   3 x 2 = 1
   1 x 3 = 3
   4 − 3 = 1
   3 + 3 = 1
   2 − 3 = 4

Page 39 and 40

Answers will vary.

Page 41

Straight letters: A, E, F, H, I, K, L, M, N, T, V, W, X, Y,
Z
Curved letters: C, J, O, S, U
Both: B, D, G, P, Q, R

Page 42

Some examples: (there are many)
adult, alien, arise, atlas, drain, drier, easel, enter,
erase, learn, lined, lunar, radar, rider, rinse, risen,
ruled, ruler, rural, sinus, slate, slide, snail, stand, stare,
steal, tease

Page 43

Do you promise to tell the tooth, the whole tooth, and
nothing but the tooth?

Page 44

stars

spars
spare
space

Page 45

23 words: alone, Anne, lane, lean, leap, Leon, loan,
lone, neon, Nepal, Noel, none, nope, opal, open, pale,
pane, panel, peal, plan, plane, plea, pole

Page 46

1. DAD
2. BAGGAGE
3. DEAF
4. ACE

Page 47

32 words: ash, can, cap, has, hip, his, nap, nip, pan,
pin, sap, sin, spa, cash, chap, chin, chip, hasp, Inca,
inch, pain, scan, shin, ship, snip, span, spic, spin,
chain, china, panic, Spain

Page 48

Names can be in any order:
Peter Pan
Roger Rabbit
Doctor Doolittle
Donald Duck
Mickey Mouse
Black Beauty
Miss Muffett
Goosey Gander
Mister McGregor
Tommy Tucker
Maid Marion

Page 49

rain, hail, cloud, fog

Page 50

Reading is lots of fun!

Page 51

1. hen pen
2. far star
3. hot pot
4. hare chair
5. ship trip
6. loose goose
7. best rest
8. mad dad
9. big wig
10. book nook
11. slow crow
12. lunch bunch
13. wet jet
14. nice mice
15. cat hat

Answer Key (cont.)

Page 52
1. job
2. mad
3. new
4. old
5. ill
6. all
7. car
8. fix
9. use
10. fat
11. end
12. boy
13. cat
14. say
15. try

Page 53
1. deep sleep
2. other brother
3. can Dan
4. large barge
5. bare hare
6. tall mall
7. wild child
8. peg leg
9. dome home
10. fish dish
11. eat meat
12. silly Billy
13. fat cat
14. rude dude
15. spare fare
16. brief grief
17. more score
18. old mold
19. sad dad
20. lazy daisy

Page 54
Here are 41 words:
3 letters: cod, cud, cue, die, doe, due, duo, ice, led, lid, lie, oil, old
4 letters: cell, clue, code, coil, cold, deli, dice, dole, duel, dull, iced, idle, idol, lied, loud, lull
5 letters: cello, cloud, could, lucid, oiled, oldie
6 letters: coiled, collie, docile, lolled, lulled
7 letters: collide

Page 55
Answers will vary.
Samples: came, ram, camera, rice, are, care, mice, race, ice, ear, ace, mace

Pages 56–73
Answers will vary.

Page 74
1. nose
2. ears
3. cannister
4. ball
5. ring
6. boat
7. wheel
8. lemon

Pages 75–85
Answers will vary.

Page 86
4 colors

Page 87
1. five (counting you and the driver)
2. plane

Page 88
1. stamp value
2. tree is reversed
3. seagull missing
4. coconuts have fallen
5. footprints
6. extra shark
7. one less perforation on the right side
8. sun has moved
9. a bottle
10. torn corner

Page 89
1. Turkey
2. New Zealand
3. Britain
4. Iran
5. France
6. Wales
7. Canada
8. Israel
9. Peru

Page 90
1. clocktower—different times
2. sun's position
3. clear sky/rain
4. birds/no birds
5. leaves on tree/no leaves
6. ducks on pond/no ducks
7. clean chair/newspaper and leaves on chair
8. different flowers
9. different paths to tower
10. empty trash can, trash on ground/full trash can

Answer Key *(cont.)*

Page 91

1. He couldn't sleep with the light on.
2. to become a light housekeeper
3. It's always waving.
4. Both crews were marooned.
5. and cargoes go in ships?
6. The spiral staircase drove him around the bend.
7. They beam all the time.
8. a nervous wreck

Pages 92–93
Answers will vary.

Page 94
B

Page 96

1. 26 letters in the alphabet
2. 52 cards in a deck
3. 88 piano keys
4. 3 blind mice (see how they run)
5. 4 quarts in a gallon
6. 11 players on a football team
7. 7 continents on the Earth
8. 50 states in the United States
9. 6 points for a touchdown
10. 20,000 leagues under the sea
11. 1,001 Arabian Nights
12. 5 digits in a zip code
13. 5 fingers on the right or left hand
14. 4 seasons in the year
15. 8 sides on a stop sign

Page 97
Answers will vary.

Page 98
No correct answer—if the joke is funny it must be right!

Pages 99–103
Answers will vary.

Brain Workouts

Page 105

1. 43 small holes
2. 576 onions
3. $10.76 each

Page 106

4. 855 holes
5. 14 bundles
6. 5 potatoes in each pot

Page 107

7. $7.11
8. 9 rows
9. $19.83
10. 264 apples

Pages 108–110
Answers will vary.

Page 111

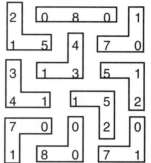

Page 112
Answers will vary.

Page 113

a. 6¢ change
b. 2 sackets of potatoes with 12¢ left

Page 114 and 115
Answers will vary.

Page 116

1. 490 km/hour
2. 5 cm/minute
3. 19 km/hour
4. 160 km/hour
5. 50 m/minute
6. 0.5 km/hour (It was being towed to the launch pad.)

Page 117
Phonograph—1877
Gramophone—1887
Tape recorder—1898
LP—1948
Cassette—1960
DAT—1970
CD—1980
DVD—1997

Page 118
1492 x 1
746 x 2
373 x 4

Page 119

1. (35 ÷ 5) x (27 ÷ 3) = 63
2. (32 ÷ 4) x (49 ÷ 7) = 56
3. (72 ÷ 9) x (24 ÷ 8) = 24
4. (56 ÷ 7) x (64 ÷ 8) = 64
5. (36 ÷ 6) x (35 ÷ 7) = 30

Page 120
Melanie—wolves, potato chips
Sarah—gorillas, hot dogs
Rachael—jaguars, lollipops
Jessica—ponies, chocolate bars

Answer Key (cont.)

Page 121
Answers will vary.

Page 122
Fat Chance, 8.9

Page 123
All have the lucky number three in them but 37 x 9 = 333 has three threes.

Page 124
Andre—letter, aunt, no stamp
Cindy—postcard, mom, pet stamp
Daphne—parcel, dad, flower stamp
Ben—bill, baker, building stamp

Page 125

Page 126
Abigail won, then Bernard, Cathryn, Denise, Edward, Francis, Gabby

Page 127
1. duck
2. penguin
3. pelican
4. swan
5. gull
6. goose
7. loon
8. crane
9. egret
10. sandpiper

Pages 128 and 129
Clue 1: steel
Clue 2: sharp
Clue 3: joins
Clue 4: wood
Clue 5: hammer
What's in the bag? a nail

Pages 130 and 131
Clue 1: scales
Clue 2: slither
Clue 3: coils
Clue 4: long
Clue 5: molt
What's in the bag? a snake

Pages 132 and 133
Clue 1: strange
Clue 2: aircraft
Clue 3: hovers
Clue 4: mystery
Clue 5: light

What's in the bag? a U.F.O.

Pages 134 and 135
Clue 1: chewy
Clue 2: dough
Clue 3: baked
Clue 4: sugary
Clue 5: dozens
What's in the bag? cookies

Page 136
1. Alan
2. Anne
3. Arab
4. band
5. bank
6. bran
7. barn
8. nana
   Extra Points: bandana

Page 137

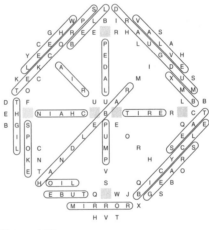

Page 138
Ideograph

Page 139
1. duo
2. duet
3. dual
4. couple
5. couplet
6. pair
7. two
8. twosome
9. deuce

Page 140

1. farms		6. roams
2. grams		7. warms
3. harms		8. ramps
4. crams		9. reams
5. marsh		10. smart

Answer Key (cont.)

Page 141

The Complete Angler

Page 142

1. beats
2. teary
3. swear
4. artsy
5. strew
6. beast
7. waste
8. retry
9. water
10. yeast

Page 143

1. tomato
2. olive
3. elderberry
4. yam
5. mango
6. onion
7. nectarine
8. eggplant

Page 144

cars

oars

ours

furs

firs

fire

file

film

Page 145

Order of answers may vary: buzzard, cardinal, chicken, cormorant, eagle, ostrich, parrot, pigeon, sparrow, vulture, woodpecker

Page 146

Persephone

Page 147

Catherine of Aragon

Anne Boleyn

Jane Seymour

Anne of Cleves

Catherine Howard

Catherine Parr

Page 148

1. ice skating
2. pewter
3. spoon
4. stocks
5. dugout
6. bayberry
7. samplers
8. peddlers
9. linen
10. trencher
11. dame school
12. indigo
13. linseed
14. lye
15. quoits
16. hornbook
17. doublet
18. johnnycake
19. saltbox
20. sabbath

Page 149

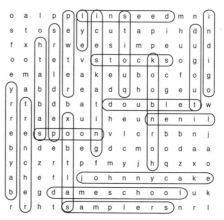

Page 150

sand

sank

dank

dane

done

dune

dune

june

jane

sane

sand

Page 151

Answers will vary.

Page 152

1. pinch
2. pink
3. pint
4. pinball
5. Ping-Pong
6. pinnacle
7. pineapple
8. pinpoint
9. pin cushion

Page 153

mint

candy

toffee

popcorn

licorice

chocolate

chewing gum

marshmallow

butterscotch

Answer Key *(cont.)*

Pages 154–180
Answers will vary.

Page 181
T
T
F
F

Pages 182–185
Answers will vary.

Page 186
1. England
2. France
3. Italy
4. Egypt
5. U.S.A.
6. England
7. France
8. Australia
9. India
10. Japan

Page 187
Old Tom

Page 188
1. What you see is what you get.
2. before
3. tonight
4. easy
5. because
6. grin
7. sigh
8. thanks
9. rolling on the floor laughing
10. on the other hand
11. long time no see
12. by the way
13. see you

Page 189
Last weeks charts:
1. That'll Be the Day
2. Da Doo Ron Ron
3. Love Potion No. 9
4. Peggy Sue
5. Run Around Sue
6. Heartbreak Hotel
7. Shakin' All Over
8. Rock Around the Clock
9. Wild One
10. Shake, Rattle 'n Roll

Page 190
Answers will vary.

Page 191
1. late date
2. fat rat
3. bad lad
4. rude dude
5. bug's mug
6. long song
7. fat cat
8. double trouble
9. big pig
10. Swiss miss
11. bony pony
12. bright light
13. funny bunny
14. glad lad
15. lazy daisy
16. sad dad
17. mouse house
18. no dough
19. cross boss
20. funny money

Page 192
1. 16
2. 15
3. 25
4. J
5. W
6. U
7. 8.
9. IX
10. sheep

Page 193
It was daylight and the Express driver could see him.

Page 194
Answers will vary.

Page 195
1. scatterbrained
2. six feet below the ground
3. a square meal
4. neon light
5. little league
6. big man on campus
7. pain in the neck
8. check up
9. Tiny Tim
10. once over lightly
11. keep it under your hat
12. high school

Answer Key (cont.)

Page 196
The house burned down, and the firefighters tried to save it.

Page 197
Answers will vary.

Brain Challenges

Page 199
Answers will vary.

Page 200
1. 9 m x 3 m = 30 bricks x 20 bricks = 600 bricks
2. 40 km x 3 m = 133,333 bricks x 20 bricks = 2,666,660
3. 40,000 m x 3 m = 120,000 m²
4. 2,666,660 bricks x $585 = $1,559,996,100
5. 2,666,660 x 10 cm = 266,666 m
6. 2,666,660 x 3.5 kg = 9,333,310 kg

Page 201
140 km long

Page 202
1. 16
2. 8
3. B: the orbit takes longer, must be higher
4. A: 10:30 A.M.
   B: 12 noon
5. night—it's on the opposite side of the world
6. 8 times a day
7. the earth

Page 203
1. no
2. yes
3. yes
4. yes
5. no
6. yes
7. no
8. yes
9. yes
10. no

Page 204
French: dix, neuf, huit, sept, six, cinq, quatre, trois, deux, un, zero
Spanish: diez, nueve, ocho, siete, seis, cinco, cuatro, tres, dos, uno, cero

Page 205
1. James Bond
2. 7
3. 10
   20
   100
   1,000

4. 52
5. a plane
6. a. Jules Verne
   b. Jules Verne
   c. George Orwell
7. Answers will vary.

Pages 206–209
Answers will vary.

Page 211
Day 59

Page 212
One possible answer is: 99 + 999 + 9 + 9 + 9 = 1,125

Page 213
Answers will vary.

Page 214
0, 1, 1 ,2, 3, 5, 8, 13, 21, 34, 55, 89, 144, 233
rule: add the last two numbers to get the next number.

Page 215
Answers will vary.

Page 216
Shari bought the shorts for $25.
Rhonda bought the dress for $30.
Jenna bought the skirt for $20.
Margaret bought the shirt for $11.

Page 217
Answers will vary.

Page 218
Answers will vary.

Page 219
Cart 1: 165 + 100 + 100 + 200 + 400 = $965
Cart 2: 25 + 150 + 160 + 250 + 500 = $1,085
Cart 3: 130 + 80 + 160 + 200 + 400 = $970
Cart 4: 55 + 120 + 240 + 250 + 500 = $1,165
Cart 4 won

Page 220

	A	B	C	
A	2	4	8	14
B	3	5	7	15
C	9	6	1	16
	14	15	16	

Page 221
28 handshakes
Extension: Answers will vary.

Pages 222 and 223
Clue 1: padded
Clue 2: heals
Clue 3: injury
Clue 4: sticky
Clue 5: strip
What's in the bag: a bandaid

Answer Key *(cont.)*

Pages 224 and 225
Clue 1: gadget
Clue 2: viewer
Clue 3: channels
Clue 4: operates
Clue 5: T.V.
What's in the bag: a remote control

Pages 226 and 227
Clue 1: private
Clue 2: ears
Clue 3: carries
Clue 4: music
Clue 5: clamp
What's in the bag: headphones

Pages 228 and 229
Clue 1: handle
Clue 2: smack
Clue 3: winged
Clue 4: insect
Clue 5: hit
What's in the bag: a flyswatter

Page 230
put-off
defer
postpone
discontinue
linger
detain
arrest
stall
impede
hinder
dawdle
stay
loiter
overlook
suspend

Page 231
blunt
brunt
grunt
grant
grand
brand
bland
blank
plank
plant
slant
shan't
Shane
share
sharp

Page 232

S U R U A T A U S T R
V I R G O A L I A S S
C A P R I C O R N O P
U A R B I L T H E R I
S A G I T T A R I U S
N S U I R A U Q A O C
S C O R P I O C R E E
O S R E C N A C S L S
G E M I N I S E I R A

Page 233
Answers will vary.

Page 234
1. blues
2. hip hop
3. disco
4. rock
5. country
6. folk
7. pop
8. rock and roll
9. classical
10. techno
11. heavy metal
12. punk

Page 235
Boogie Woogie, Jump Blues, Doo Wop, Honky Tonk

Page 236
electricity
capability
stability
minority
gravity
activity
longevity
likability
sensitivity

Page 237
1. cabin
2. galley
3. port
4. stern
5. hull
6. bow
7. rats
8. anchor
9. engine

Answer Key (cont.)

10. starboard

Capehorner

Page 238

bauble

bubble

hubble

rubble

clubbed

quibble

bluebeard

bubblegum

Page 239

cone

consent

console

contain

content

contest

constant

consonant

continent

Page 240

tribute

brunette

buttress

rebutton

turbo-jet

briquette

buttercup

litterbug

jitterbug

gettysburg

Page 241

1. Bloomers Rd.
2. Mangrove Rd.
3. Customer Rd.
4. Employer Rd.
5. Composer Rd.
6. Enormous Rd.
7. Compared Rd.
8. Geometry Rd.

Pages 242–243

Answers will vary.

Page 244

1. dandelion
2. acid rain
3. airline
4. drive-in
5. radio
6. radial

7. cradle
8. arcade
9. alien
10. video

(word whose letters are found in Leonardo Da Vinci)

Page 245

1. guide—lead
2. accordian—wind instrument
3. scramble—mix up
4. aqueduct—water channel
5. suffix—word ending
6. chess—game
7. pawn—chess piece
8. survey—look over
9. excerpt—passage from a book
10. scorpion—poisonous animal
11. zither—string instrument
12. junk—trash

Page 246

Page 247

1. Q
2. XTC
3. NME
4. NV
5. B, D, K, or L
6. O
7. SA
8. FX
9. J
10. CU
11. AT
12. T
13. G or O
14. XL
15. DK

Answer Key (cont.)

Page 248

output

turnout

untruth

butter up

outburst

Timbuktu

truthful

about-turn

buttercup

out of tune

Page 249

tale

travel

elevator

overeat

revote

voter

over

rev

Page 250

conduct

Pages 251–256

Answers will vary.

Page 257

1. New York
2. Kuwait
3. Tokyo
4. Oslo
5. Ottawa
6. Athens
7. Seoul
8. London

Page 258

1. South Entrance
2. bridge, ropes, lion, bomb, building, bus, water

Page 259

parrot

cheetah

condor

crocodile

elephant

gazelle

rhinoceros

turtle

whale

woodpecker

Pages 260–280

Answers will vary.

Page 281

1. O Gross!
2. Tennis Shoes or 10 issues
3. Night falls
4. H_2O
5. Long Time No See
6. Neon Light
7. Surfs Up
8. Quarterback, Halfback, Fullback
9. What goes up must come down
10. Quit following me
11. Misunderstanding between friends
12. Matinee

Page 282

1. tar/rat
2. draw/ward
3. pot/top
4. pets/step
5. live/evil
6. now/won
7. ten/net
8. strap/parts
9. bats/stab
10. drawer/reward
11. peek/keep
12. naps/span
13. star/rats
14. peels/sleep
15. leg/gel

Page 283

1. Sealed With a Kiss
2. Headquarters
3. Railroad
4. Equal Rights Amendment
5. Certified Public Accountant
6. Absent Without Leave
7. Tender Loving Care
8. Government Issue
9. Save Our Ship
10. Health, Education, and Welfare
11. As Soon as Possible
12. Public Address
13. Unidentified Flying Object
14. Disc Jockey
15. Cash on Delivery

Page 284

1. noon
2. did
3. ewe
4. Bob
5. tot
6. peep
7. eye
8. pop or dad
9. dud
10. toot
11. bib
12. solos
13. mom or mum
14. kayak
15. level
16. pop
17. Answers will vary. They include Anna, Eve, Hannah, and Nan.
18. pup
19. deed
20. civic

Pages 285 and 286

Answers will vary.

Super Solver Award

To: _____

From: _____

Date: _____

Super Solver Award

To: _____

From: _____

Date: _____

Brain Games
for Kids

Part 2

Part 2 Table of Contents

Part 2 Table of Contents *(cont.)*

Part 2 Table of Contents *(cont.)*

Part 2 Table of Contents *(cont.)*

Part 2 Table of Contents *(cont.)*

Part 2 Table of Contents *(cont.)*

Part 2 Table of Contents *(cont.)*

Part 2 Table of Contents *(cont.)*

Brain Warm-ups

What Makes 12?

6 x 2 = 12. Think of 10 different ways to arrive at the number 12.

Patterns

Look at the patterns that have been started. Complete the patterns. The first row has been started for you. Trace over the dotted shapes and complete the rest of the page.

Standard Measurements

1. List the standard units of measurement that you know.

_____

_____

2. Write down some reasons why we need standard measurements.

_____

_____

3. What do you think people used before there were standard weights?

_____

_____

4. Write down some difficulties of using these different types of measurement.

_____

_____

_____

5. You have a two-pound and a three-pound weight. How will you measure the following amounts of bananas? (There may be more than one way.)

7 pounds	10 pounds
1 pound	**20 pounds**

Scaling Scales

Draw as many different types of scales as you can.

Invent your own weighing machine. It needs to be able to show objects that are heavier, lighter, or equal in weight. Draw and label your scales.

John, Jack, and the Nuggets

"This is tricky," said Jack to his friend John. "We've got 10 large nuggets of gold, and 11 smaller ones. How are we going to divide them up?"

"Well," said John. "What if I count clockwise around the circle and take each fifth nugget? When I've got 10, you can have the 11 that are left."

"That sounds pretty fair," replied Jack.

But it wasn't. John ended up with all 10 big nuggets. From where did he start counting?

Tortoise Trails

These four tortoises are trotting off to a juicy patch of grass. They're all waddling at the same speed, so which one will get there first? (Hint: You need to measure!)

Answer: _____

House Math

What a house! It has thousands of windows, doors, floors, ceilings—very strange. It is almost as strange as the house that—that what? Read the written numbers. Then write the matching letter in the answer space. Read the answer vertically.

	Written Numbers	Answer
1	seven hundred fourteen	
2	two thousand four	
3	nine thousand, three hundred seven	
4	three hundred fifty-seven, doubled	
5	seventy-four	
6	ten thousand minus six hundred ninety-three	
7	six hundred twelve	
8	two thousand, four hundred eighty-one	
9	one hundred eleven	
10	nine hundred eight	
11	six thousand sixty-five	
12	two hundred forty-two	
13	one hundred two, times seven	

A	B	C	F	H	I	J	K	L	M	O	T	U
9307	111	612	8759	2004	6065	74	2481	242	3512	90	714	908

Invasion: Earth!

The Martians are invading! They're fed up with seeing themselves portrayed on Earth TV as horrible two-headed monsters (when actually they are horrible three-headed monsters), and they are out for revenge. They have filled up their spaceship tanks with gas and headed here as fast as they can. But will they make it? Their tanks only hold 50 million gallons of gas and Earth is . . . how far away is Earth? Follow the maze by adding the numbers to find the shortest distance to Earth.

Will they make it? _____

How far away is Earth? _____

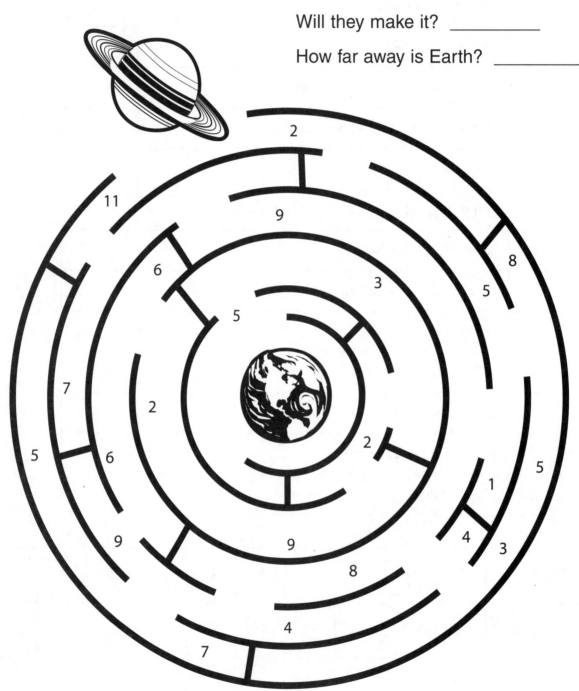

Door-to-Door

It's a hard life, selling door-to-door, especially when you are selling doors.
Anyhow, here are nine doors. Start with the equation that has an answer of one,
and end at the number nine, drawing a line from one to the next. Don't go to the
wrong door at the wrong time—it could easily unhinge you . . . .

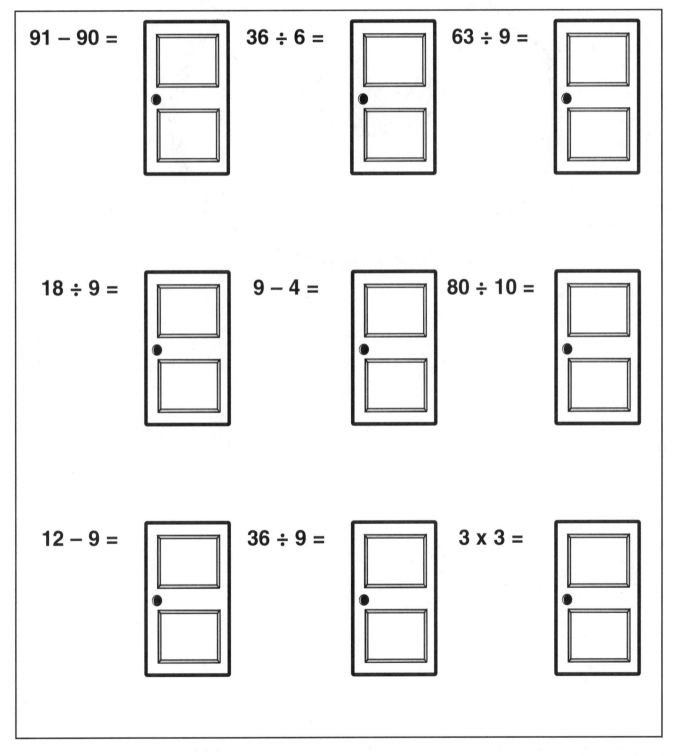

Doughnut Decision

There is only one doughnut, but there are eight people. Can you cut the doughnut into equal pieces, using only three cuts? Show your work.

Exam Time

As Mr. Teran prepared to pass back the last spelling exam, five anxious students awaited their grades. Using the clues below, determine each child's grade. Mark an **X** in each correct box.

1. Lucy, who did not get an A on her test, scored higher than Martin and Gwen.

2. Cara and Gwen both scored higher than Donald.

3. Martin received a C on his test.

4. No two students received the same grade.

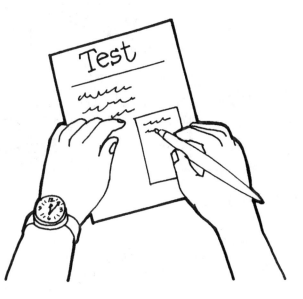

	A	B	C	C-	D
Lucy					
Gwen					
Cara					
Martin					
Donald					

Proverbial Codes

Use this code to decode and finish the sentences.

Number	6	7	8	9	0	1	2	3	4	5	16	17	18
Code	A	B	C	D	E	F	G	H	I	J	K	L	M

Number	19	20	21	22	23	24	25	26	27	28	29	30	31
Code	N	O	P	Q	R	S	T	U	V	W	X	Y	Z

1. (17 20 20 16) _____ before you (17 0 6 21)
   _____ .

2. Never put off until (25 20 18 20 23 23 20 28)
   _____ what can be done (25 20 9 6 30)
   _____ .

3. A (1 23 4 0 19 9) _____ in (19 0 0 9)
   _____ is a (1 23 4 0 19 9) _____
   (4 19 9 0 0 9) _____ .

4. The early (7 4 23 9) _____ catches the (28 20 23 18)
   _____ .

5. All that (2 17 4 25 25 0 23 24) _____ is not (2 20 17 9)
   _____ .

6. Don't (8 23 30) _____ over (24 21 4 17 17 0 9)
   _____ milk.

7. You never (16 19 20 28) _____ what you can do
   (26 19 25 4 17) _____ you (25 23 30) _____ .

8. Make (30 20 26 23 24 0 17 1) _____ necessary to
   (24 20 18 0 20 19 0) _____ .

Word Problems

Read each word problem and then answer the questions.

1. Daniel bought two candy bars at 47 cents each. How much did he spend?

2. Laura had 92 cents. She wanted to buy a 35 cent juice and a 49 cent hot dog. How much did she spend? How much change does she receive?

3. Jim put his pennies into two small boxes. He put 1,396 pennies into each box. How many pennies did he have?

Word Problems *(cont.)*

Read each word problem and then answer the questions.

4. The Wilson's drove their car 10,483 miles one year and 19,768 miles the next year. How far did they drive during the two years?

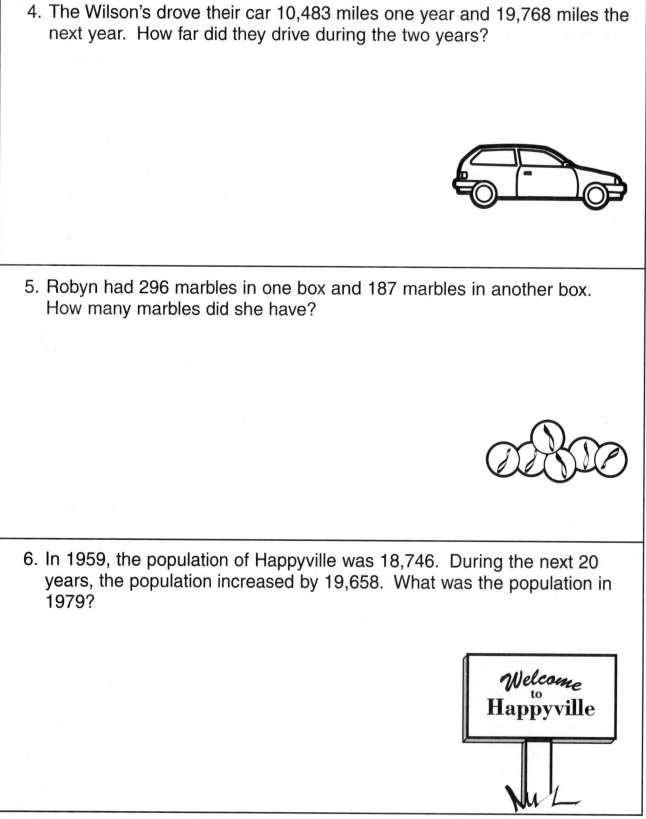

5. Robyn had 296 marbles in one box and 187 marbles in another box. How many marbles did she have?

6. In 1959, the population of Happyville was 18,746. During the next 20 years, the population increased by 19,658. What was the population in 1979?

Welcome to **Happyville**

Word Problems *(cont.)*

Read each word problem and then answer the questions.

7. Russell bought four bags of chips at 60 cents each, two sodas at 35 cents each, and two cookies at 25 cents each. How much did he spend?

8. Tamara wanted to go bowling. She rented shoes for $10.00, paid for two games at $2.00 a game, and bought one soda for $.35. How much did she spend?

9. Kristen had 12 red socks, 27 green socks, 13 blue socks, and 32 pink socks. How many socks did she have?

10. Paul has 75 rocks in his collection. His Uncle Joe has 139 and wants to give them to Paul. How many will he then have?

Time

Imagine that all the clocks have stopped. How many different ways can you invent to measure time?

Which one do you think would work best? Why?

Frog Hop!

Here are the results for the Calaveras County Frog Jumping Competition. The only question is, who won? Remember: the frog's score is the aggregate (total) of their jumps.

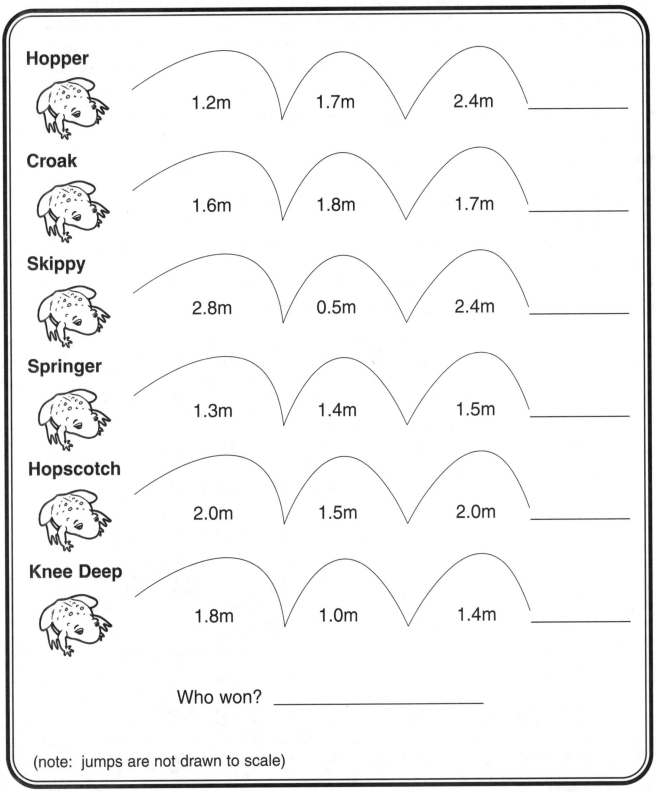

Hopper

1.2m   1.7m   2.4m   _____

Croak

1.6m   1.8m   1.7m   _____

Skippy

2.8m   0.5m   2.4m   _____

Springer

1.3m   1.4m   1.5m   _____

Hopscotch

2.0m   1.5m   2.0m   _____

Knee Deep

1.8m   1.0m   1.4m   _____

Who won? _____

(note: jumps are not drawn to scale)

Prime Time

Mathematicians put numbers into two categories—*prime* or *composite*. A *prime number* is a number with only two factors: one and itself. A *composite number* has more than two factors.

A Greek mathematician named Eratosthenes invented a method to see if a number is prime or composite; that method is called the *Sieve of Eratosthenes*. He arranged the numbers from 1 to 100 and used divisibility rules to find the prime numbers. Use the numbers in the box below and follow the steps to find the prime numbers.

- The number 1 is a special case. It is neither prime nor composite. Put a box around number 1.
- Number 2 is a prime number, so circle 2. Cross out all the numbers divisible by 2.
- Number 3 is a prime number, so circle 3. Then cross out all numbers divisible by 3.
- The next uncrossed number is 5. Circle 5 and then cross off all the multiples of 5.
- Circle 7. Seven is a prime number. Cross off all the multiples of 7.
- Any numbers that are left are prime, so circle them.

1	2	3	4	5	6	7	8	9	10
11	12	13	14	15	16	17	18	19	20
21	22	23	24	25	26	27	28	29	30
31	32	33	34	35	36	37	38	39	40
41	42	43	44	45	46	47	48	49	50
51	52	53	54	55	56	57	58	59	60
61	62	63	64	65	66	67	68	69	70
71	72	73	74	75	76	77	78	79	80
81	82	83	84	85	86	87	88	89	90
91	92	93	94	95	96	97	98	99	100

Word Stair Puzzle

Use the clues to fill in the grid.

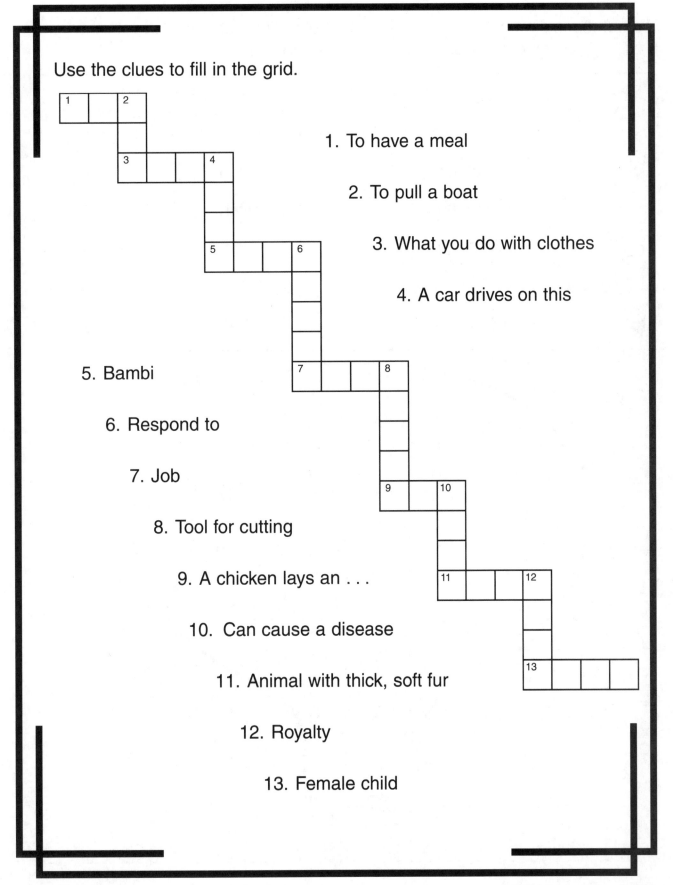

1. To have a meal

2. To pull a boat

3. What you do with clothes

4. A car drives on this

5. Bambi

6. Respond to

7. Job

8. Tool for cutting

9. A chicken lays an . . .

10. Can cause a disease

11. Animal with thick, soft fur

12. Royalty

13. Female child

Light Bulb Word Search

Find all of these light bulb words in the light bulb. The letters left over in the light bulb will tell you how many light bulbs you can buy.

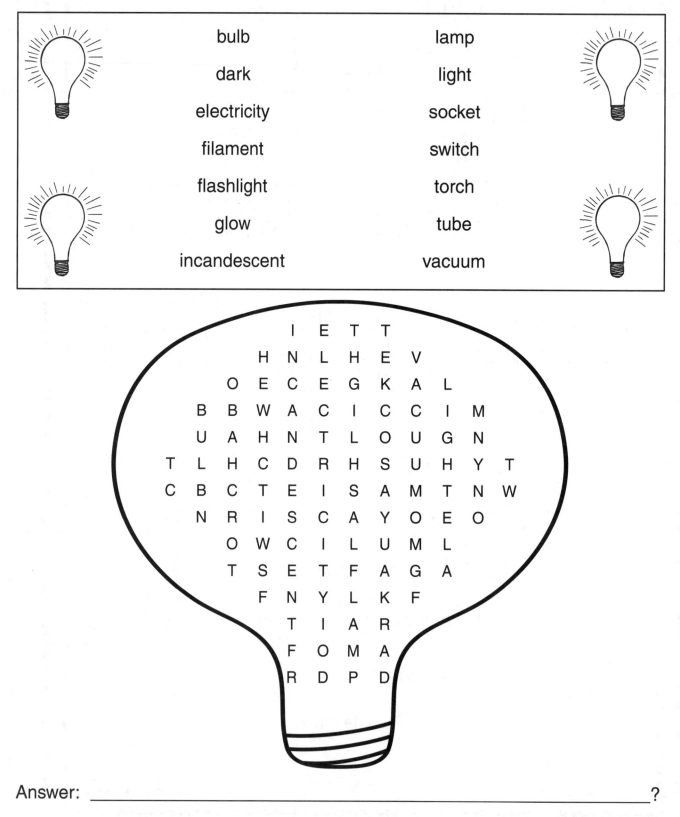

bulb	lamp
dark	light
electricity	socket
filament	switch
flashlight	torch
glow	tube
incandescent	vacuum

```
        I  E  T     T
     H  N  L  H  E  V
  O  E  C  E  G  K  A  L
B B W  A  C  I  C  C  I  M
U A H  N  T  L  O  U  G  N
T L H  C  D  R  H  S  U  H  Y  T
C B C  T  E  I  S  A  M  T  N  W
N R I  S  C  A  Y  O  E  O
O W C  I  L  U  M  L
T S E  T  F  A  G  A
   F  N  Y  L  K  F
      T  I  A  R
      F  O  M  A
      R  D  P  D
```

Answer: _____?

Keyboarding

How many five-letter words can you make using the middle row of the keyboard? You can only use each letter once.

(Hint: There aren't very many!)

The Dvorak keyboard (a special keyboard claimed to be much faster to type on) looks like this:

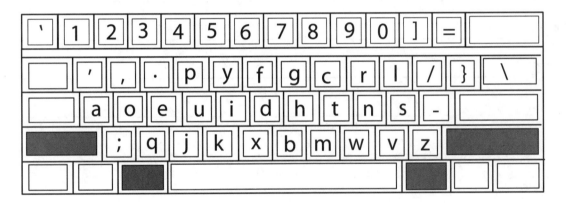

How many five-letter words can you make using the middle row of letters on this keyboard?

Abbreviations

Write the meaning of each abbreviation.

1. Pres. _____

2. ASAP _____

3. Adj. _____

4. Lbs. _____

5. Max. _____

6. Etc. _____

7. Sept. _____

8. M.A. _____

9. I.O.U. _____

10. P.M. _____

11. C.O.D. _____

12. R.S.V.P. _____

13. S.A.S.E. _____

14. S.A. _____

15. Bldg. _____

16. RR _____

17. Prep. _____

18. Hdqrs. _____

19. D.A. _____

20. D.S.T. _____

Summertime

List words related to summertime that begin with each letter of the alphabet.

A _____

B _____

C _____

D _____

E _____

F _____

G _____

H _____

I _____

J _____

K _____

L _____

M _____

N _____

O _____

P _____

Q _____

R _____

S _____

T _____

U _____

V _____

W _____

X _____

Y _____

Z _____

Pinocchio

Pinocchio was made from a magic piece of wood. How many words of three letters or more can you make out of the word "Pinocchio"?

P	I	N
O	C	C
H	I	O

_____

_____

_____

_____

_____

_____

_____

_____

Oyster Antics

Here is a bunch of oysters all sleeping in a shallow pool. Eight of them have pearls inside; the rest do not have pearls. To help you find the pearls, the oysters have labeled themselves. They have also arranged themselves into a helpful pattern. Find the pearls and circle the oysters with pearls. One has been circled for you. (Hint: What are pearls often made into? a _____)

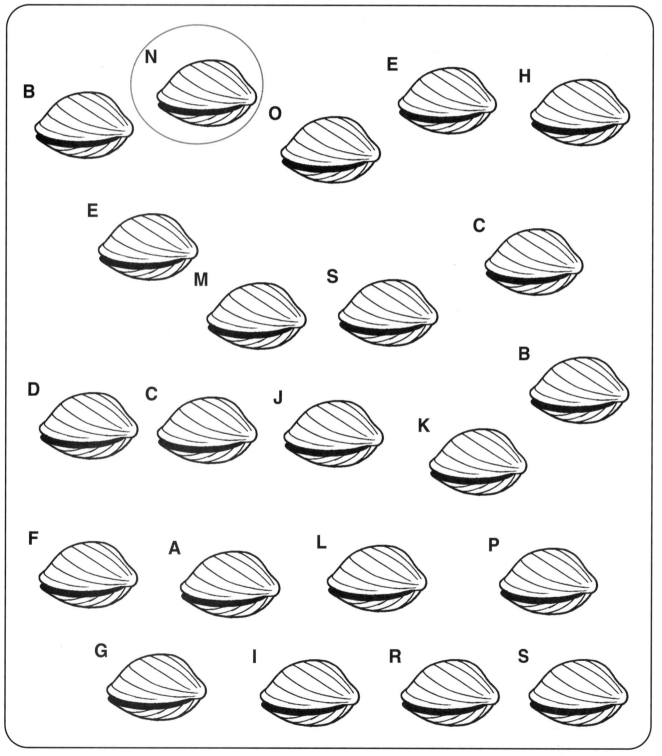

Word Twins

Some words just seem to fit together, like "day and night" or "bread and butter."
They are almost like twins! Below are two lists of 17 separated word twins.
Read the two lists of words and put the "twins" back together.

List 1		List 2	
aches	fish	again	paste
again	night	bolts	pepper
alive	nuts	cheese	pieces
bacon	odds	chips	roll
bells	rock	day	square
bits	salt	eggs	stripes
crackers	stars	ends	thin
cut	thick	kicking	whistles
fair		pains	

_____   _____

_____   _____

_____   _____

_____   _____

_____   _____

_____   _____

_____   _____

_____

Winnie-the-Pooh Word Puzzle

Solve the clues by using the letters of Winnie-the-Pooh's name as a guide.

1. Owl's spelling of his name

2. A bouncy tiger

3. A bouncy kangaroo

4. Winnie-the-Pooh sometimes went under this name

5. The entrance to this character's house seems smaller after eating honey.

6. A grumpy friend

7. Pooh Bear's best friend

8. Pooh Bear's favorite food

9. The characters live in the 100 _____ wood.

10. A small pig

11. A wise bird

12. Christopher's last name

13. How Rabbit spells house

Cornflake Word Chase

You might find snap, crackle, and pop in some cereals—but what can you find in a cornflake? How about more than 20 three-letter (or longer) words, all beginning with C!

O	R	N
F	C	L
A	K	E

Reading Scramble

Unscramble the letters to find words about books and reading.

1. ookb   _____

2. brayrli   _____

3. eard   _____

4. sodrw   _____

5. ictreup   _____

6. tnpri   _____

7. epga   _____

8. rutaho   _____

9. trtsai   _____

10. etpy   _____

11. ytrso   _____

12. ptol   _____

13. rcveo   _____

14. cahatrcre   _____

15. lusitariotnl   _____

Alphabetical Order

Put the words in ABC order.

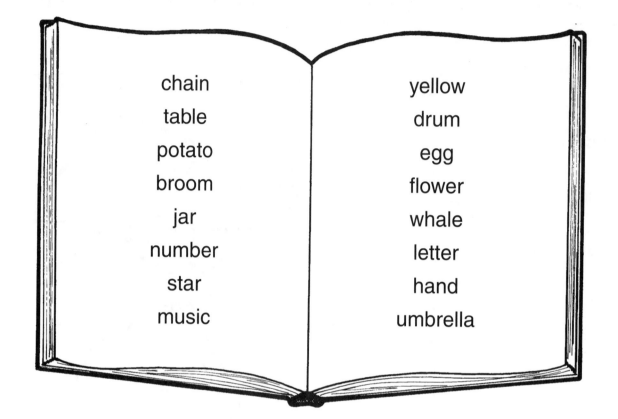

chain	yellow
table	drum
potato	egg
broom	flower
jar	whale
number	letter
star	hand
music	umbrella

1. _____

2. _____

3. _____

4. _____

5. _____

6. _____

7. _____

8. _____

9. _____

10. _____

11. _____

12. _____

13. _____

14. _____

15. _____

16. _____

Five-Letter Words

Each of the following words has a synonym that contains five letters. Write them on the lines.

1. big   __ __ r __ __

2. understand   __ __ __ __ n

3. tale   __ t __ __ __

4. correct   __ __ __ __ t

5. begin   s __ __ __ __

6. robber   __ __ i __ f

7. world   __ __ r __ __

8. cost   p __ __ __ __

9. record   __ r __ __ __

10. rush   __ __ r __ y

11. below   u __ __ __ __

12. permit   __ __ __ __ w

13. fetch   __ r __ __ __

14. glad   h __ __ __ __

15. yell   __ h __ __ __

The Great Outdoors

List words related to what you see outdoors. Write as many words as you can for each letter.

A _____

B _____

C _____

D _____

E _____

F _____

G _____

H _____

I _____

J _____

K _____

L _____

M _____

N _____

O _____

P _____

Q _____

R _____

S _____

T _____

U _____

V _____

W _____

X _____

Y _____

Z _____

Word Pairs

Write the missing half of each pair.

1. _____ and puff

2. _____ and feather

3. _____ and dogs

4. _____ and cranny

5. _____ and thin

6. _____ and match

7. _____ and nail

8. _____ and sugar

9. _____ and dandy

10. _____ and forth

11. _____ and holler

12. _____ and stones

13. _____ and down

14. _____ and cents

15. _____ and cream

16. _____ and order

17. _____ and fall

18. _____ and peace

19. _____ and out

20. _____ and white

21. _____ and proper

22. _____ and soul

23. _____ and satin

24. _____ and ladder

25. _____ and paper

Geography Pairs

The first definition in each pair is for a geography word. Fill in the blanks to spell the word. Change one letter in the geography word to spell the word that fits the second definition.

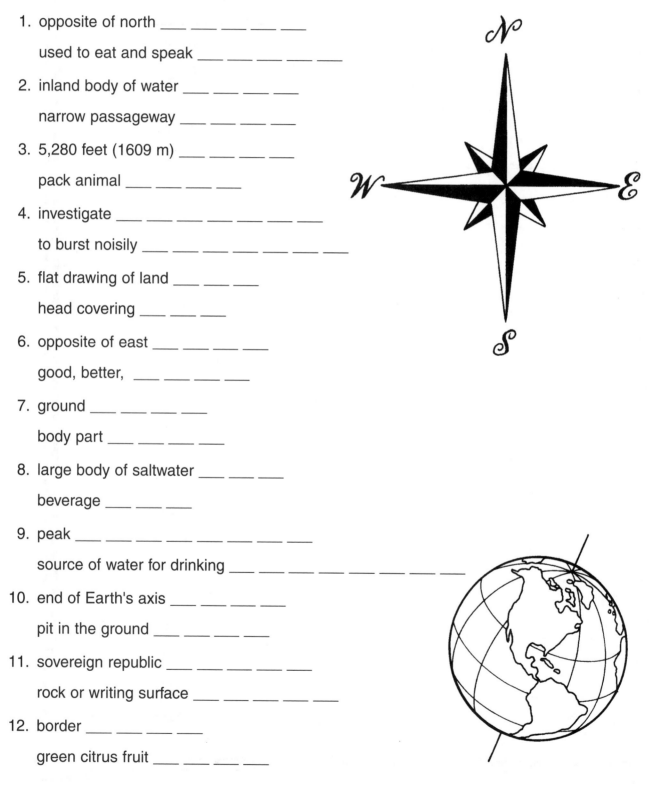

1. opposite of north ___ ___ ___ ___ ___

   used to eat and speak ___ ___ ___ ___ ___

2. inland body of water ___ ___ ___ ___

   narrow passageway ___ ___ ___ ___

3. 5,280 feet (1609 m) ___ ___ ___ ___

   pack animal ___ ___ ___ ___

4. investigate ___ ___ ___ ___ ___ ___ ___

   to burst noisily ___ ___ ___ ___ ___ ___ ___

5. flat drawing of land ___ ___ ___

   head covering ___ ___ ___

6. opposite of east ___ ___ ___ ___

   good, better, ___ ___ ___ ___

7. ground ___ ___ ___ ___

   body part ___ ___ ___ ___

8. large body of saltwater ___ ___ ___

   beverage ___ ___ ___

9. peak ___ ___ ___ ___ ___ ___ ___ ___

   source of water for drinking ___ ___ ___ ___ ___ ___ ___ ___

10. end of Earth's axis ___ ___ ___ ___

    pit in the ground ___ ___ ___ ___

11. sovereign republic ___ ___ ___ ___ ___

    rock or writing surface ___ ___ ___ ___ ___

12. border ___ ___ ___ ___

    green citrus fruit ___ ___ ___ ___

History Homophones

Read each word. Write a word that sounds the same but is spelled differently on the line next to each word. The words you write will relate to the settling of America.

1. piece _____

2. seas _____

3. plane _____

4. sale _____

5. whirled _____

6. heard _____

7. sight _____

8. hoarse _____

9. straight _____

10. billed _____

11. fur _____

12. pour _____

13. rain _____

14. tacks _____

15. capital _____

16. seed _____

17. core _____

18. root _____

19. thrown _____

20. wore _____

What Did You See Today?

What did you see when you first woke up today? What did you see when you walked through the house? What did you see on your way to school? List everything you have seen today.

Playing Games

Imagine an old tire. What does it look like? How heavy is it? How does it feel? How does it smell?

_____

_____

_____

_____

How many games can you make up using an old car tire?

_____

_____

_____

_____

_____

If the tire was chopped into pieces, what could you use the different bits for? Remember that some bits of the tire are rough and some are smooth, and some have letters on them.

_____

_____

_____

_____

_____

_____

The Pink Shirt

Your aunt has given you a pink shirt for your birthday, but you don't like the color pink. You don't want to hurt her feelings, but you don't want to wear it.

Write five good excuses why you can't wear the shirt.

1. _____

   _____

2. _____

   _____

3. _____

   _____

4. _____

   _____

5. _____

   _____

Write five ways that you could use the shirt instead of wearing it.

1. _____

   _____

2. _____

   _____

3. _____

   _____

4. _____

   _____

5. _____

   _____

Tennis, Anyone?

Write at least 10 uses for a tennis ball. They can be as silly as you like.

1. _____

2. _____

3. _____

4. _____

5. _____

6. _____

7. _____

8. _____

9. _____

10. _____

bonus _____

bonus _____

Is It a Ghost?

Write down all the things that this cloud looks like.

_____

_____

_____

_____

_____

_____

_____

All About Me

Make a little cartoon about yourself. The title is:

My Favorite Things to Do Every Day

1.	2.	3.
4.	5.	6.
7.	8.	9.

What a Hero!

Invent a story which tells about a heroic act by a tightrope-walker.

Road Rules

What changes would you recommend to the current road rules to prevent traffic accidents?

Future Travel

Predict how students will travel to school in the future.

_____

_____

_____

_____

_____

_____

_____

_____

_____

_____

_____

_____

_____

No Cars?

What would happen if there were no more cars in the world?

_____

_____

_____

_____

_____

_____

_____

_____

_____

_____

_____

_____

_____

The Handy Dandy Fairy Tale Writer

Use our Handy Dandy Fairy Tale Writer to construct your next fairy tale! Just take a main character from column one and a second one from column two, add in a location from column three, add a problem from column four, and a solution from five. Bingo! A brand new fairy tale!

1. _____ +
2. _____ +
3. _____ +
4. _____ =
5. _____

There are also five real fairy tales. Can you name them?

1. _____
2. _____
3. _____
4. _____
5. _____

Main Character One	Main Character Two	Location	Problem	Solution
A wolf	Large, smelly goat	Bridge	Collecting straw-into-gold-weaving debt	Blow down house
Another wolf	Selfish girl	Castle in the air	Collecting trolls	Dress up as grandmother
Elf with unusual name	Spoiled girl	Dark wood	Fending off starvation	Grind bones to make bread
Giant	Uncooperative pig	Dungeon	Finding pork	Take first born child
Troll	Young lout	House of bricks	Keeping Englishman out	Wait for bigger brother to come along

A Talking Shark

If you met a shark that could talk, what questions would you ask it?

_____

_____

_____

_____

_____

_____

_____

_____

_____

_____

_____

You Ask the Questions

The answer is "a rose." Write at least three questions.

_____

_____

_____

_____

_____

_____

The answer is "in the middle of the night." Write at least three questions.

_____

_____

_____

_____

_____

_____

Recycle

What could you do with . . .

felt-tip pens that don't write anymore?

_____

_____

_____

a trampoline that has lost its bounce?

_____

_____

_____

cereal that has gone stale?

_____

_____

_____

It doesn't matter how silly the ideas are. Think of as many as you can.

Predicting the Future

What do you think children will wear to school 100 years in the future?

_____

_____

_____

_____

What do you think you will be doing, and where will you be, in twenty years?

_____

_____

_____

_____

How will you travel to school in the future?

_____

_____

_____

_____

_____

It Won't Happen!

Name 10 things you can't hear.

Name five people you will never meet.

Name seven things that can't be photographed.

Brainstorm!

There are no right or wrong answers, so be creative.

Name all the things that you can think of that move.

_____

_____

_____

_____

What are things that are found underground? List as many as you can.

_____

_____

_____

_____

List everything that you can think of that is pink.

_____

_____

_____

_____

Redesign Your Object

Choose an object that you could redesign. It could be a spade, or a kitchen utensil, such as tongs, a colander, a whisk, a spoon or fork, or anything else that you choose.

Describe what the object is used for.

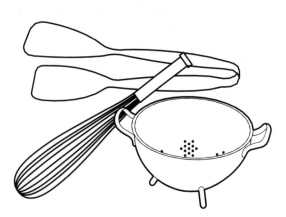

_____

_____

_____

Brainstorm other uses.

_____

_____

_____

Imagine that the object was re-made a hundred times larger. What uses would it have now?

_____

_____

_____

Choose one part of the object to change. List its new uses.

_____

_____

_____

Reverse or rearrange part of the object. Draw what it looks like now.

The Evolving Classroom

Brainstorm ways that the classroom could be made a more comfortable, exciting, and interesting place.

Choose one of the possible changes and think of what would need to be done to make the change.

BAR

> **B** stands for bigger
>
> **A** stands for add on
>
> **R** stands for replace/rearrange/change

Example: Draw a shoe

Ask what could be made **bigger**. For example, the sole of the shoe could be a platform three feet high, so that the wearer can see over people's heads in a crowd.

Add wings or a motor, to go places fast.

Replace the laces with snaps to make it easier to get the shoes off.

Use the BAR process using your pencil as the object, giving reasons for each change. Silly and innovative ideas are encouraged.

What Is That?

Make up a new and strange animal and draw it here.

What is it called?

_____

Where does it live?

_____

What does it eat?

_____

Do You Want a Ride?

How many different things can you ride?

_____

_____

_____

_____

_____

_____

List all the things that you can push.

_____

_____

_____

_____

_____

_____

The Old Fire Engine

This fire engine is too old to be used as a fire engine anymore. It is going to be broken down into pieces. What could all the pieces be used for?

wheels _____

_____

ladder _____

_____

headlights _____

_____

seats _____

_____

steering wheel _____

_____

windshield _____

_____

hose _____

_____

other pieces _____

_____

What a Face!

Divide these faces into groups.

A   B   C   D   E   F

Explain your reasons for each group.

_____

_____

_____

_____

_____

_____

_____

Join the Pictures

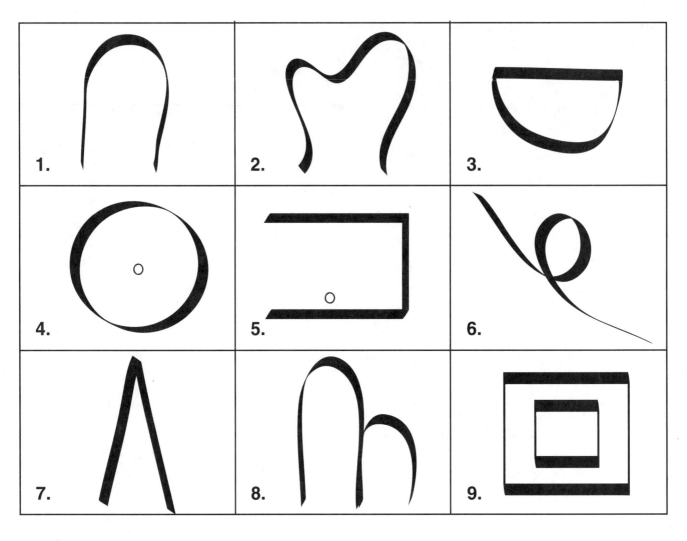

1. If picture one is a finger, what is picture four?_____

2. If picture seven is a mountain, what is picture six? _____

3. If picture two is a tooth, what is picture three? _____

4. If picture eight is a kennel, what is picture nine?_____

5. If picture four is a hat (you are looking down on it), what is picture five?

   _____

6. If picture eight is an igloo, what is picture four? _____

7. If picture eight shows two rocks, what is picture one? _____

8. If picture five is a door (turn the page sideways), what do you see when you open the door at picture nine?_____

Travel

How many ways can you travel from one place to another?

List all the ways you know and draw pictures for each.

Talking About Birds

Ducks, geese, turkeys, and chickens are all domestic birds called fowls. They can all fly a bit, and some fly better than others.

1. In the table, rank these birds from worst to best flyers:

Worst Flyer	Okay Flyer	Better Flyer	Best Flyer

2. Why are ducks and geese able to swim, but turkeys and chickens are not? Illustrate your answer.

Movement

1. Write down four reasons why animals need to move.

a. _____   c. _____

b. _____   d. _____

2. Choose three animals and fill in the table to show some of the ways each one moves.

Animal	Method 1	Method 2	Method 3

3. Of your three animals, draw the fast movers on the left and the slow movers on the right.

Fast Movers	Slow Movers

4. Invent a creature that would be the best mover ever. Draw and label your "pet" to show the special purposes for the special parts.

Sundials

1. Draw some instruments that have been used to measure time.

2. Draw a sundial below and describe what it will be made from.

My sundial will look like this:

My sundial is made from:

_____

_____

_____

_____

_____

_____

3. Explain how sundials work.

_____

_____

4. Where would be the best place to put your sundial on the playground? Explain why you chose that location.

_____

_____

_____

Bicycles and Things

1. The first bicycle was built in England over 350 years ago. It had no pedals, and riders had to push it along with their feet! Draw this invention.

Bicycle from the year 1642

---

2. Now think about a 21st century "personal transport machine."

   How would it move? _____

   What would it be made of? _____

   What would it look like? _____

   Draw your invention here.

Personal Transport Machine for the year 2042

A Different Dog Kennel

Draw a dog kennel.

Can you make it different by:

making one part bigger?

adding something extra?

replacing one part with something else?

Not a Good Pet!

List animals which would not make good pets.

_____

_____

_____

_____

Why did you choose these animals?

_____

_____

_____

Draw pictures of three of the animals from your list.

Extinct Animals

Name five animals that are extinct.

1. _____

2. _____

3. _____

4. _____

5. _____

What are five questions you would liked to have asked one of the extinct animals?

1. _____

2. _____

3. _____

4. _____

5. _____

Draw pictures of all five animals.

The Circus

How many circus words can you think of in two minutes?

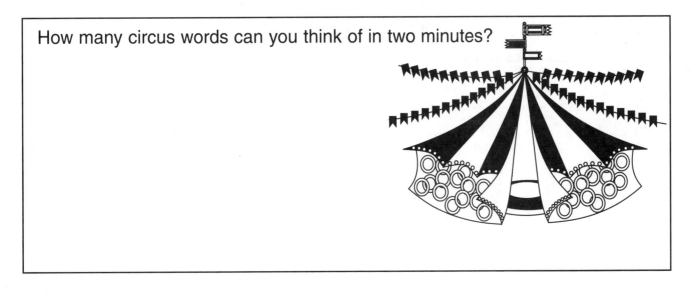

List all the people associated with the circus. Remember that there are many behind-the-scenes people, such as those who look after the animals, those who make the costumes, and those who sell food and tickets.

Separate the list of circus people into different categories such as funny acts, dangerous acts, etc.

A Different Kind of House

What would our houses look like if they had no corners?

Spot the Forgery

Look at the two pictures—the one on the left is the original, the one on the right is a forgery. How many differences can you find between the two?

List the differences here:

Railway Words

Look carefully at these four word puzzles. Can you work out what each says?

Pipeline Puzzle

All those pipes, and so many in need of repair! So, the water goes in at the arrow—and where does it come out?_____

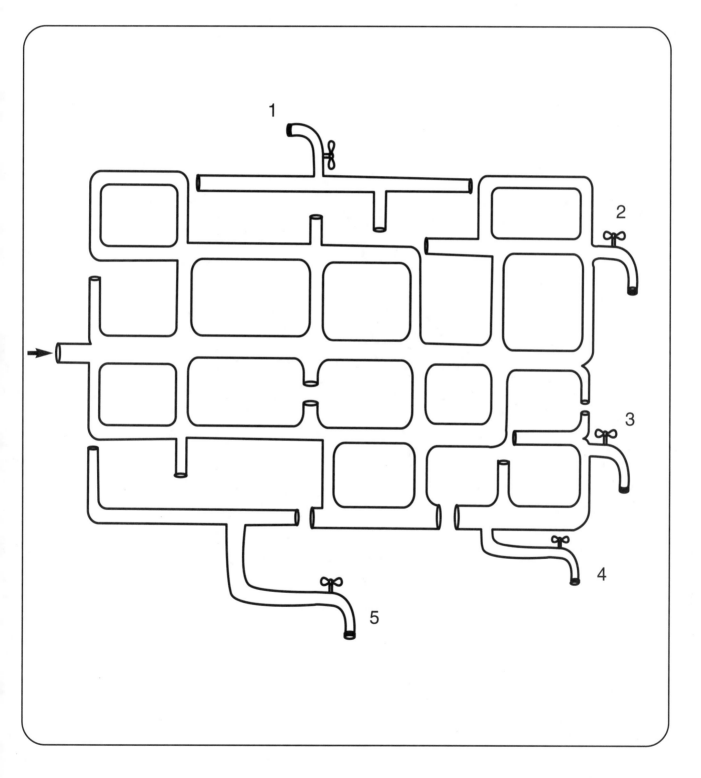

To Bee or Not to Bee . . .

This bee is confused. Its mate has just done a stunning dance to communicate exactly where the pollen is, but it got confused. Follow the trail and see where the bee ends up.

Lightning Rod

Benjamin Franklin was one of the first scientists to conclusively prove that lightning is a form of electricity. He achieved this by flying a kite in a thunderstorm. Later he tried it again, but with four kites. Unfortunately, he's only holding onto one of them. Two of the other kites are attached to each other, and the fourth is flying free. So, which kites are doing what?

A: _____

B: _____

C: _____

D: _____

Amazing!

Here's an April Fool's maze. Can you find your way from "in" to "out"?

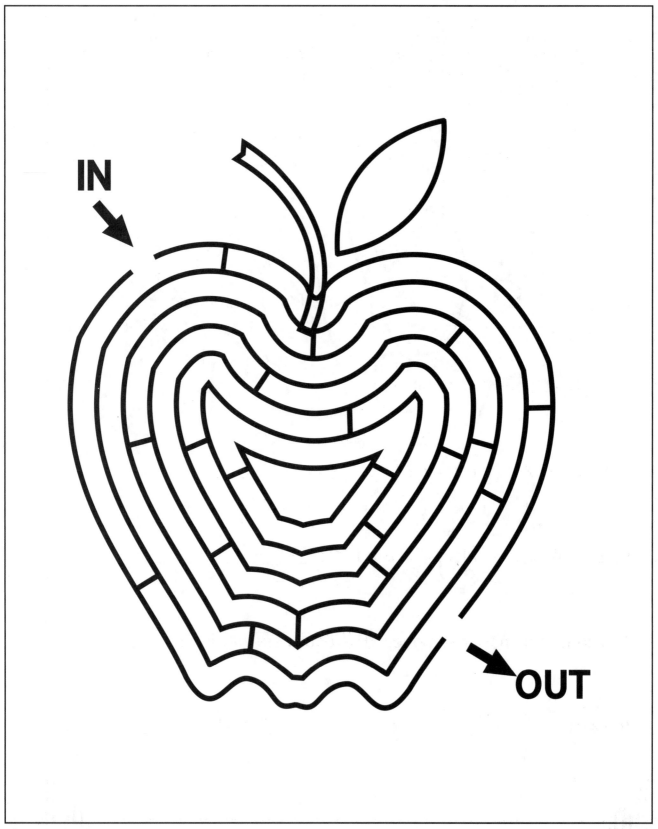

Colorful Language

Don't get the blues—get colorful! Complete each of these sentences with a color.

1. Don't run so fast—you're going _____in the face!

2. You coward! You're just _____!

3. Wait until Josh sees my new bike, he'll be _____with envy.

4. Oh dear, you've gone as _____as a ghost!

5. Watch out! The captain's face is_____as thunder!

6. Everything's wonderful! We're in the _____!

7. The whole show lost money. The books are way in the _____.

8. Fetch an _____from the fruit bowl please.

Assembly Line Blues

Unlike the car in the circle, the other five cars below have defects. The assembly line quality control supervisor spotted them. Can you?

A. _____

B. _____

C. _____

D. _____

E. _____

How Amazing!

Follow the maze to get the car in the garage.

Homes

Three children live on the same street. Each of their houses is a different color. Can you use the clues to match each child to his or her house? Draw a line between each child and home. Color the houses when you are through.

> 1. Marla's house is the color of cotton candy.
>
> 2. Pepper's house is the color of some apples.
>
> 3. Rosa's house is the color of corn on the cob.

Marla

Red House

Pepper

Yellow House

Rosa

Pink House

In the Library

Draw a picture of a library with the following in it:

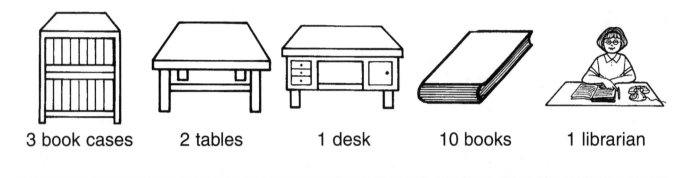

| 3 book cases | 2 tables | 1 desk | 10 books | 1 librarian |

Which One Does Not Belong?

In each line below, one of the four words does not belong with the other three. Circle the one that does not fit. Explain what the others have in common. An example has been done for you.

relish, (hot dogs,) mustard, ketchup = condiments

1. October, November, December, June _____

2. boot, shoe, glove, slipper _____

3. notebook, pencil, pen, crayon _____

4. king, queen, prince, page _____

5. Bob, Robert, Rich, Robby _____

6. ebony, mahogany, carnation, cherry _____

7. chocolate chip, ginger snap, layer cake, animal cookie _____

8. girl, lass, nephew, woman _____

9. tape recorder, television, telephone, microphone _____

10. table, chair, sofa, flower _____

11. cantaloupe, casaba, grapefruit, watermelon _____

12. strange, thud, cry, hiss _____

13. cougar, jaguar, lion, elephant _____

14. hammer, screwdriver, drill, lightbulb _____

15. exclamation mark, question mark, colon, period _____

All Alike

Read the words on each line. Explain how they are alike. An example has been done for you.

north, south, east = cardinal directions

1. jazz, tap, ballet _____

2. tennis, soccer, basketball _____

3. lily, daffodil, gardenia _____

4. tiger, lion, jaguar _____

5. cookies, candy, ice cream _____

6. wrench, drill, hammer _____

7. mad, silly, grumpy _____

8. diamond, ruby, amethyst _____

9. milk, butter, cheese _____

10. single, alone, individual _____

11. orange, tennis ball, marble _____

12. plane, blimp, helicopter _____

13. pencil, pen, marker _____

14. Helena, Hillary, Heather _____

15. pumpkin, zucchini, acorn _____

Categorizing

In the word box below are 42 words, each of which belongs in one of the six categories—wood, metals, water, space, colors, and furniture. Place each of the words under the correct category. For example, **bay** would belong in the water category. Seven words belong under each category.

• bay	• oak	• chest	• river	• chartreuse
• Mars	• lake	• pond	• beige	• aluminum
• rocket	• ocean	• orbit	• copper	• weightless
• creek	• dresser	• board	• iron	• countdown
• sea	• tan	• cabinet	• forest	• pencil
• lamp	• scarlet	• couch	• titanium	• maple
• lumber	• platinum	• steel	• rocker	
• tin	• red	• blue	• walnut	
• mirror	• moon	• green	• astronaut	

Wood

_____
_____
_____
_____
_____
_____
_____

Metals

_____
_____
_____
_____
_____
_____
_____

Water

_____
_____
_____
_____
_____
_____
_____

Space

_____
_____
_____
_____
_____
_____
_____

Colors

_____
_____
_____
_____
_____
_____
_____

Furniture

_____
_____
_____
_____
_____
_____
_____

How Is Your Memory?

Study the picture for three minutes. Then, turn the page and write down as many items from the picture as you can remember.

How is Your Memory? *(cont.)*

New Products

Brainstorm ideas for each list.

Different types of clothing	Different modes of transportation

With your eyes closed, select one object from each list. Combine them to form a new object. Sketch and name the combined idea.

How would this new product affect your life? Describe what it could do.

My New Invention!

Use this shape as the basis for a new invention.

Draw the invention. Write its name on the line below your drawing.

_____

What is it used for?

_____

_____

_____

Family Categories

Draw a chart to show all the ways in which your family members can be categorized, for example, by size, weight, gender, interests. Can you think of 10 different categories?

Brain Workouts

School Days

Complete this pie graph to show how you spend your day at school. Show all
your subjects, lunch and recess breaks, and the amount of time each one takes.

Your Ideal Day

Draw a pie graph showing how your ideal day would be spent.

Number Trivia

Imagine you are a contestant on the television quiz show called Number Trivia.
How will you score?

1. What numbers are inferred by these words?

    Gross   _____   Binoculars   _____

    Octopus   _____   Unicorn   _____

    Centipede   _____

2. Which country has these currencies?

    Baht   _____   Pound   _____

    Lira   _____   Rupee   _____

    Yen   _____

3. In a garden there are 20 flowers. Seven are roses, eight are carnations,
   and five are daisies. If the garden had 28 roses, there would be _____
   carnations, _____ daisies, and _____ flowers altogether.

4. Five athletes competed in the 100 meter sprint. The athlete from Canada
   won. The athlete from Mexico came last. The athlete from Australia was
   ahead of the athlete from South Africa and just behind the athlete from the
   United States.

    Who came in second? _____

5. Here is an example of one way to plant five trees in two rows so that each
   row contains three trees. Can you think of another way?

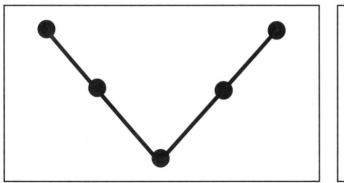 

Rearrange the Numbers

Rearrange the numbers below so that six sets of three numbers each add up to 18.

12   11   1

10   4

8   17   3

9   2

6   7   5

New Order:

Make Up Your Own

How many number sentences can you make using combinations of these numbers? You may use the same number more than once.

Try to use all operations (addition, subtraction, multiplication, division).

6 + 9 = 15

9 − 2 = 7

Vegetable Matters

A vegetable garden was found to have an area of 75 square feet. Draw different shapes that the garden could be and still have the same area.

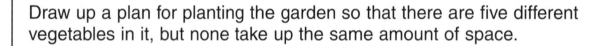

Draw up a plan for planting the garden so that there are five different vegetables in it, but none take up the same amount of space.

Ten-Pin Puzzle

Each pin below has a point value, shown at the right.

If a black circle shows a knocked down pin,
how many points does each pattern show?

What's the highest score possible? _____

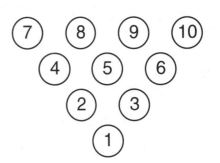

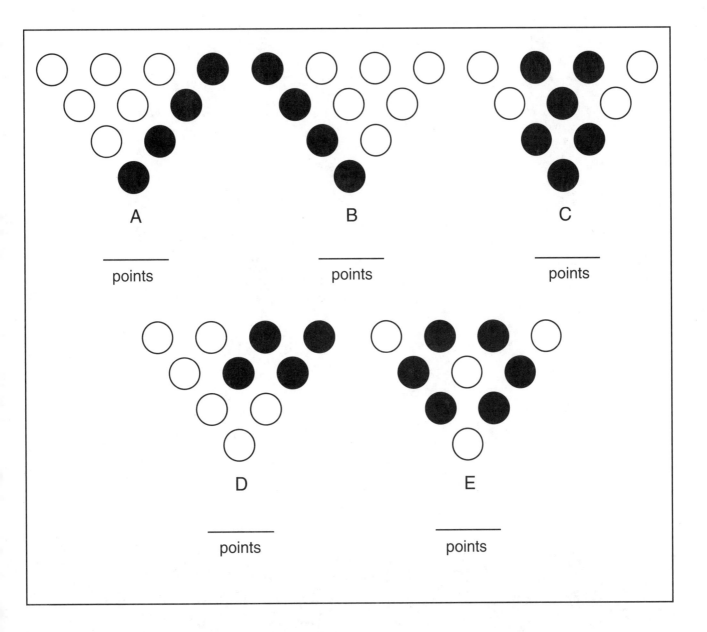

A

_____
points

B

_____
points

C

_____
points

D

_____
points

E

_____
points

Sports Teams

You are to organize the sports teams for your grade. There are 130 students in your grade level, and there are five sports to play. You need to have at least 10 teams.

Solve:

How many students should be on each team? _____

How many reserves do you need for each team? _____

What will you do with the students left over? _____

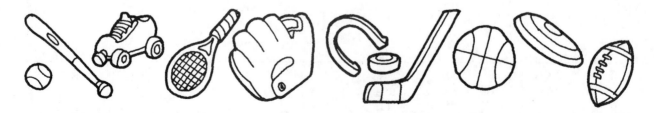

Triangular Tabulations

How many triangles are there? (Hint: don't forget the upside-down ones or the ones made from other triangles.)

There are _____ triangles.

What Is the Question?

Answer: There were only 14 students left on the bus. Write 10 questions that could fit with this answer.

1. _____

   _____

2. _____

   _____

3. _____

   _____

4. _____

   _____

5. _____

   _____

6. _____

   _____

7. _____

   _____

8. _____

   _____

9. _____

   _____

10. _____

   _____

Looking at Solids

1. How many sports or board games can you name that use some of these solids as part of the playing equipment? Some of the boxes are filled in as an example.

Game	Cube	Rectangle	Triangular Prism	Pyramid	Sphere	Cone	Cylinder
Volleyball		net			ball		
Monopoly	Dice	Money					

Looking at Solids *(cont.)*

2. Devise a team game or a board game in which at least three solid shapes from the previous page are used.

Number System

Devise a number system to compete with the Roman numeral system. What would the symbols look like and what are they called?

Show what these numbers would look like in your new number system.

7	19	58
257	830	2645

Rewrite these questions using your new number system (and answer them)!

7 + 5 =	20 − 11 =
5 x 10 =	84 ÷ 7 =

Estimation

Estimate how many glasses of water would fill a 10-gallon container.

How would you check your answer without pouring the water into the container?

Would this be an accurate way of checking your prediction?

Find the Patterns

The number sentences in each exercise follow a pattern. Find the pattern, continue it for two more lines, and then check your answer on a calculator.

$91 \times 1 = 91$ $37 \times 3 = 121$ $9 \times 9 + 7 = 88$

$91 \times 2 = 182$ $37 \times 33 = 1221$ $98 \times 9 + 6 = 888$

$91 \times 3 = 273$ $37 \times 333 = 12321$ $987 \times 9 + 5 = 8888$

_____   _____   _____

_____   _____   _____

Now make up some number sentences of your own that follow a pattern.

_____   _____   _____

_____   _____   _____

_____   _____   _____

_____   _____   _____

_____   _____   _____

_____   _____   _____

Change the Triangles

Move four toothpicks so that exactly three equilateral triangles are formed.

Strike It Rich!

Whose picture is on the $100,000 bill?

To discover the answer, find the difference in each problem below. Decode the name by matching the answer to its letter. Write the letter in the box below the difference.

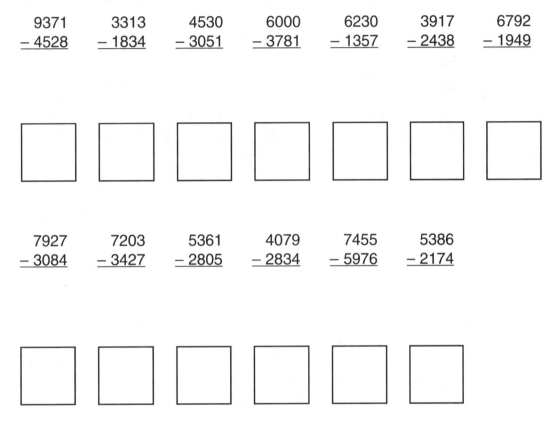

9371	3313	4530	6000	6230	3917	6792
− 4528	− 1834	− 3051	− 3781	− 1357	− 2438	− 1949

7927	7203	5361	4079	7455	5386
− 3084	− 3427	− 2805	− 2834	− 5976	− 2174

1479	3776	4843	2219
O	I	W	D
4873	2556	3212	1245
R	L	N	S

Did you know?

The $100,000 bill is the highest-value bill ever printed by the United States. It was used only by government banks. The bill is no longer issued.

          #8122 Brain Games for Kids

Birthday Parties

Eight children in one neighborhood will turn 10 this year. From the clues below, determine the month of each child's birthday. Mark the correct boxes with an **X**.

	January 1	February 21	March 25	April 7	May 7	July 15	August 3	October 30
Victor								
Mary								
Marco								
Christina								
Vicky								
Mike								
Danielle								
Peter								

1. Everyone celebrates on Mary's birthday.

2. Danielle's birthday is before Mike's but after Marco's and Victor's.

3. Victor's birthday is exactly one month after Marco's.

4. Christina's birthday is during a winter month.

5. Vicky's birthday comes after Danielle's but before Mike's.

Money Maze

Find your way through the money maze. Mark the path of correct money amounts. You may go ↕ ↔ ↗ or ↘ .

	7 pennies + 7 dimes = 70 cents	Start $	4 nickels + 3 dimes = 60 cents
$ End			
3 pennies + 2 dimes + 2 quarters = 73 cents	4 nickels + 2 dimes + 3 quarters = $1.25	5 nickels + 1 dime + 1 quarter = 55 cents	6 pennies + 6 dimes + 1 quarter = 91 cents
8 pennies + 5 dimes = 58 cents	2 pennies + 3 quarters = 76 cents	8 nickels + 3 quarters = $1.15	11 pennies + 7 dimes = 78 cents
4 quarters + 2 dimes = $1.25	2 pennies + 6 nickels + 7 dimes = $1.02	1 penny + 1 dime + 2 quarters = 61 cents	2 nickels + 3 dimes = 45 cents
8 dimes = 40 cents	17 nickels = 85 cents	7 pennies + 5 nickels = 33 cents	10 quarters = $2.50
2 pennies + 5 nickels + 3 quarters = 87 cents	11 pennies + 4 nickels = 41 cents	7 nickels + 7 dimes = $1.05	3 nickels + 1 dime + 1 quarter = 45 cents
3 pennies + 3 dimes = 35 cents	4 pennies + 7 nickels = 39 cents	3 nickels + 3 dimes + 3 quarters = $1.20	4 pennies + 3 nickels = 19 cents

Solve These If You Can!

Can you find the answers to these word problems?

1. Paul went horseback riding. He paid two five-dollar bills and three quarters. He received one dollar bill and a dime in change. How much did it cost Paul to go riding?

   _____

   _____

2. Amy gave the fast food clerk three one-dollar bills, a quarter, two dimes, and three pennies. The clerk told her she still owes a nickel. How much was Amy's lunch?

   _____

   _____

3. When Lan went bowling, he gave the clerk two one-dollar bills, a half dollar and a quarter. The clerk gave him two dimes in change. How much did it cost Lan to bowl?

   _____

   _____

4. Kimi wanted to buy a cake mix. She looked in her wallet and counted two one-dollar bills and three nickels. She would need a half-dollar more. How much was the cake mix?

   _____

   _____

5. Alvaro bought a ticket to a concert.   He paid with a ten-dollar bill and a five-dollar bill. He received two one-dollar bills in change. How much was the concert ticket?

   _____

   _____

6. Sheila wanted to buy a new swimsuit. She had two ten-dollar bills, but would need a five-dollar bill and two one-dollar bills. How much would the new swimsuit cost?

   _____

   _____

What Is on the Road?

Next to each letter of the alphabet, write at least one thing that starts with that letter that you might find beside or on the road. For example: A – ant, ambulance, artwork, arch.

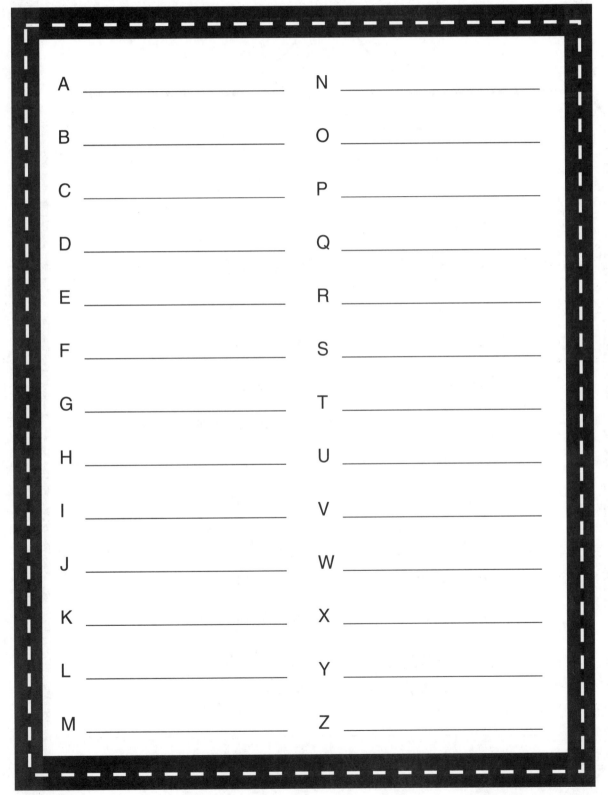

A _____   N _____

B _____   O _____

C _____   P _____

D _____   Q _____

E _____   R _____

F _____   S _____

G _____   T _____

H _____   U _____

I _____   V _____

J _____   W _____

K _____   X _____

L _____   Y _____

M _____   Z _____

What's in the Bag? #1

Read the words on the next page. Then match the letters with the correct synonyms in the clues. (You will not use all of the letters.) Put the five clues together and discover what's in the bag!

A = nap	N = shift
B = chuckle	O = mute
C = confront	P = chubby
D = garment	Q = daze
E = tiff	R = brief
F = necessity	S = endeavor
G = dense	T = repent
H = baffle	U = raise
I = shaggy	V = road
J = placid	W = embrace
K = mood	X = drink
L = depart	Y = sport
M = settler	Z = zone

What's in the Bag? #1 (cont.)

Clue 1:

_____   _____   _____   _____
hug   doze   short   pioneer

Clue 2:

_____   _____   _____   _____   _____   _____
region   hairy   plump   plump   dispute   short

Clue 3:

_____   _____   _____   _____   _____   _____
plump   doze   clothing   clothing   dispute   clothing

Clue 4:

_____   _____   _____   _____
face   doze   pioneer   plump

Clue 5:

_____   _____   _____
giggle   dispute   clothing

What's in the bag? _____

What's in the Bag? #2

Read the words on the next page. Then match the letters with the correct synonyms in the clues. (You will not use all of the letters.) Put the five clues together and discover what's in the bag!

A = shelter

B = harvest

C = light

D = dive

E = shabby

F = turf

G = solar

H = spongy

I = little

J = live

K = hatchet

L = corn

M = divine

N = honor

O = powder

P = antelope

Q = revise

R = lockup

S = myth

T = cease

U = canteen

V = cent

W = poke

X = cluster

Y = dryness

Z = rhyme

What's in the Bag? #2 *(cont.)*

Clue 1:

_____

jail   worn   beam   stop   haven   tribute   sun   maize   worn

Clue 2:

_____

sod   haven   crop   jail   mini   beam

Clue 3:

_____

jab   haven   penny   worn

Clue 4:

_____

fable   drought   godly   crop   dust   maize

Clue 5:

_____

tribute   haven   stop   mini   dust   tribute

What's in the bag? _____

What's in the Bag? #3

Read the words on the next page. Then match the letters with the correct synonyms in the clues. (You will not use all of the letters.) Put the five clues together and discover what's in the bag!

A = abandon	N = needy
B = barbarous	O = option
C = captivity	P = prickly
D = debris	Q = quake
E = exhale	R = recycle
F = flicker	S = ship
G = germinate	T = thread
H = hectic	U = unity
I = immoral	V = violin
J = juvenile	W = wharf
K = kinsman	X = swoop
L = lease	Y = yonder
M = shack	Z = zest

What's in the Bag? #3 *(cont.)*

Clue 1:

_____   _____

choice   poor

Clue 2:

_____   _____   _____

choice   sparkle   sparkle

Clue 3:

_____   _____   _____   _____   _____   _____   _____   _____

thorny   choice   reuse   string   vacate   savage   rent   breathe

Clue 4:

_____   _____   _____   _____   _____   _____   _____   _____   _____

savage   vacate   string   string   breathe   reuse   evil   breathe   yacht

Clue 5:

_____   _____   _____   _____

savage   breathe   vacate   shelter

What's in the bag? _____

What's in the Bag? #4

Read the words on the next page. Then match the letters with the correct synonyms in the clues. (You will not use all of the letters.) Put the five clues together and discover what's in the bag!

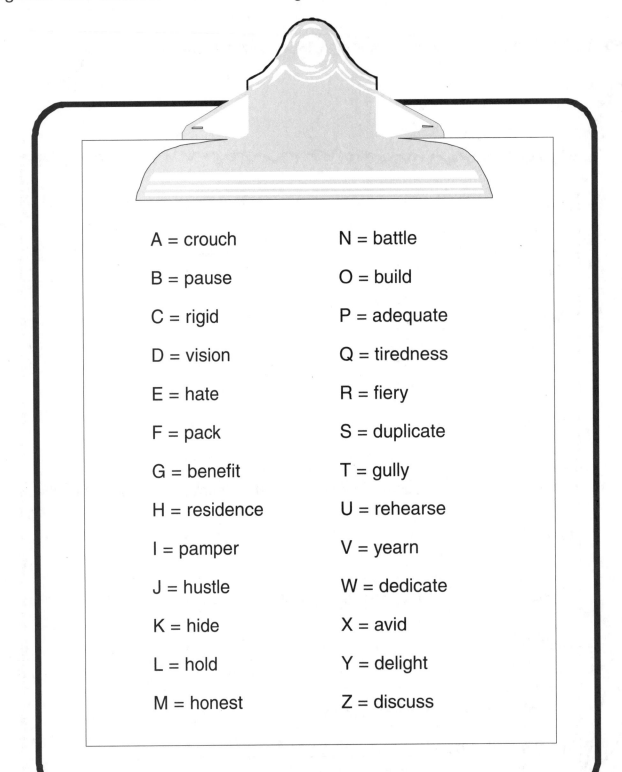

A = crouch

B = pause

C = rigid

D = vision

E = hate

F = pack

G = benefit

H = residence

I = pamper

J = hustle

K = hide

L = hold

M = honest

N = battle

O = build

P = adequate

Q = tiredness

R = fiery

S = duplicate

T = gully

U = rehearse

V = yearn

W = dedicate

X = avid

Y = delight

Z = discuss

What's in the Bag? #4 (cont.)

Clue 1:

_____   _____   _____   _____   _____   _____

frank   stoop   frank   frank   stoop   retain

Clue 2:

_____   _____   _____   _____   _____   _____

stoop   hot   stiff   ditch   spoil   stiff

Clue 3:

_____   _____   _____   _____   _____   _____   _____

copy   devote   spoil   frank   frank   abhor   hot

Clue 4:

_____   _____   _____   _____   _____   _____   _____

stop   retain   practice   stop   stop   abhor   hot

Clue 5:

_____   _____   _____   _____   _____

ditch   practice   copy   conceal   copy

What's in the bag? _____

Encyclopedias

Encyclopedias have a language all of their own. How many of these encyclopedia-related words can you identify?

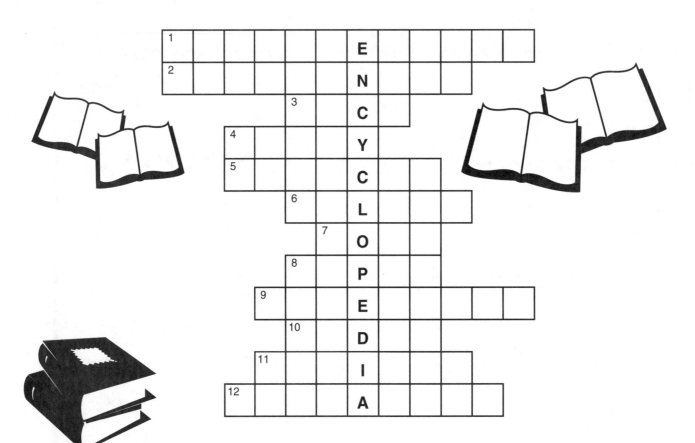

1. arranged in order according to the alphabet

2. a reference book of words and their meanings

3. a piece of true information

4. an item in a reference work

5. a dictionary

6. a book in a set

7. a written or printed work

8. an entry in an encyclopedia

9. a book to which you can refer for facts

10. a list of all main words in a book and their context

11. a section of a reference work

12. a book of synonyms

Kite Safety Rules

Use these clues to solve the puzzle about the important rules of flying kites!

Across

2. Never fly a kite in the rain or a _____.
6. A _____ is a good target for lightning!
7. Keep away from cars and _____.
9. A kite's _____ keeps it balanced.
10. You should follow _____ the safe flying rules.
11. Keep away from buildings and tall _____.

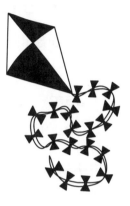

Down

1. _____ _____ will give you a shock if your kite hits them.
3. The kite's string is attached to this: _____.
4. Always fly kites in a wide _____ _____.
5. A _____ is a good place for kite flying.
8. Remember the kite _____ rules and keep safe!

Cheese Words

So many cheeses, so little time to try them all! Can you find them in the puzzle below?

Blue Stilton	Cottage	Munster
Brie	Cream	Parmesan
Camembert	Edam	Ricotta
Cheddar	Mozzarella	Swiss

```
        N  G  I  N  I  C
        O  A  G  A  E  A
  P  A  B  T  L  N  S  G  M  M  P  N
  R  T  R  L  L  A  E  A  E  U  M  I
  A  T  I  I  E  R  M  M  M  N  A  T
  D  O  E  T  R  O  R  O  B  S  E  T
  D  C  M  S  A  K  A  R  E  T  R  O
  E  I  A  E  Z  I  P  F  R  E  C  R
  H  R  D  U  Z  K  S  L  T  R  A  C
  C  N  E  L  O  E  G  A  T  T  O  C
        B  M  D  B  L  U
        S  S  I  W  S  E
```

Hidden Words

How many words of four or more letters beginning with **S** can you make from the word saxophone?

S	A	X
O	P	H
O	N	E

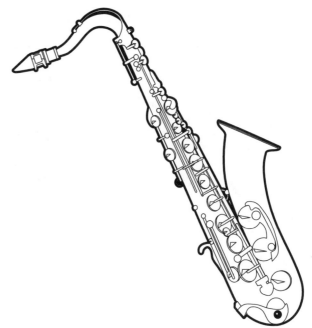

_____   _____

_____   _____

_____   _____

_____   _____

_____   _____

_____   _____

                                       #8122 Brain Games for Kids

The Mercedes Wheel

Here's a Mercedes wheel. How many words can you make by traveling from one letter to the next along the lines? You can't use a letter twice unless it's on the wheel twice.

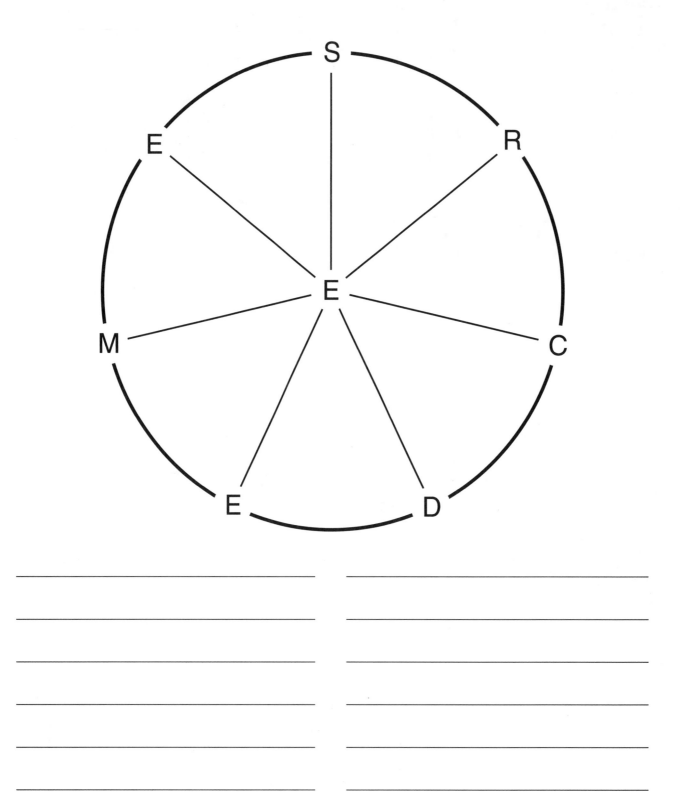

_____ _____

_____ _____

_____ _____

_____ _____

_____ _____

Solar System Mystery

Here are the nine planets of the solar system. Look very carefully at their spelling. Can you give three reasons why Mars's name is the odd one out?

Mars's name is the odd one out because:

1. _____

_____

2. _____

_____

3. _____

_____

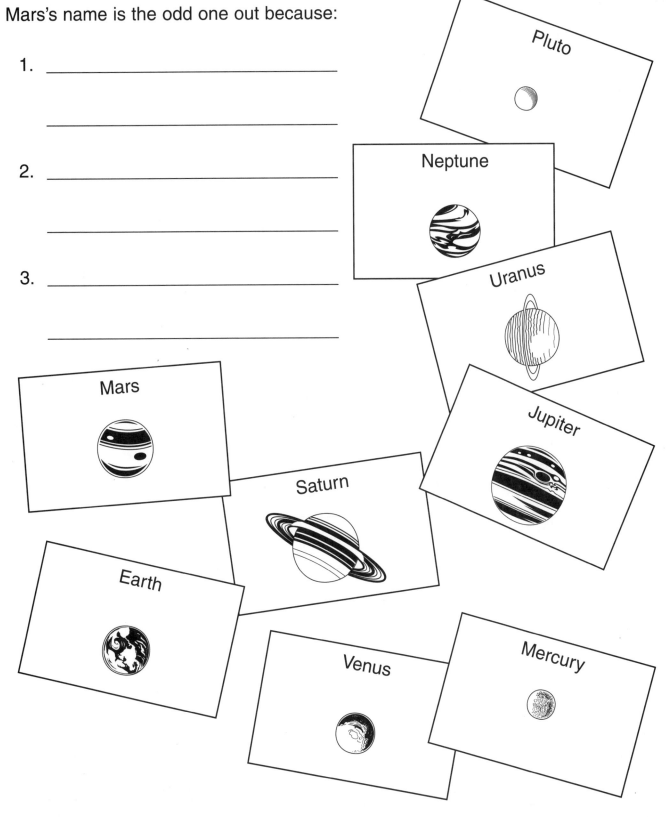

Something Old, Something New

Traditionally, a bride wears something old and something new. Can you turn old into new in nine tries by changing one letter at a time? Only use the clues if you really have to!

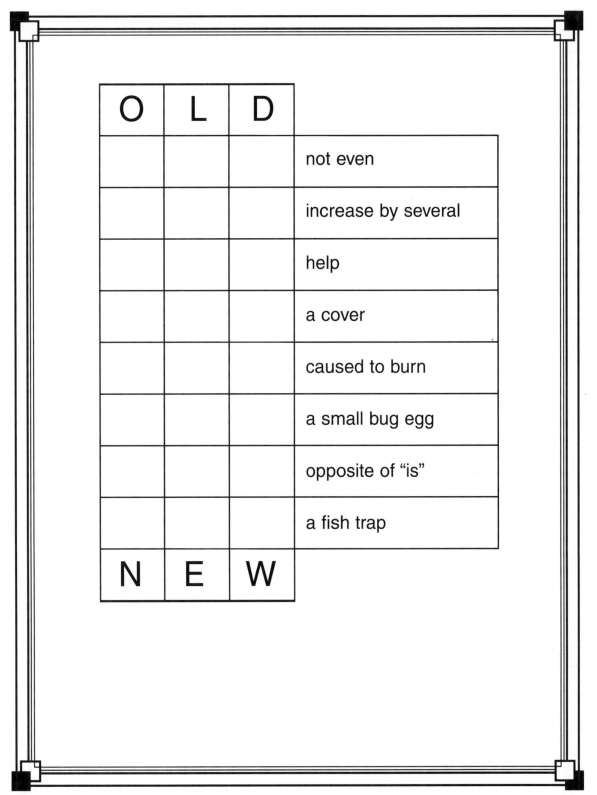

O	L	D	
			not even
			increase by several
			help
			a cover
			caused to burn
			a small bug egg
			opposite of "is"
			a fish trap
N	E	W	

Inside the Hindenberg

How many words of four or more letters can you make from the word Hindenberg?

HINDENBERG

Four-letter words:

Five-letter words:

Six-letter words:

Seven-letter words:

Eight-letter words:

Spot the Sea Monster!

If you are going to survive on the seven seas, you'll need to be able to identify and name these creatures (mythical and real) of the deep. You may need to do some research to solve this puzzle.

1. common fast-moving ten-armed mollusk
2. the largest mythical monster
3. a carnivorous marine fish with tough skin
4. a burrowing marine mollusk
5. home of the mythical Scottish sea serpent
6. large venomous ray with barbed spines
7. a snake-like sea creature
8. eight-legged sea creature
9. huge marine mammal
10. mythical Norwegian sea-monster

End with a Nap

Can you make a bed? Into a cot? Then end with a nap? Just change one letter at a time to make the next word. Use the clues to help.

B	E	D	
			a wager
			a striking implement
			feline
C	O	T	
			policeman
			type of hat
N	A	P	

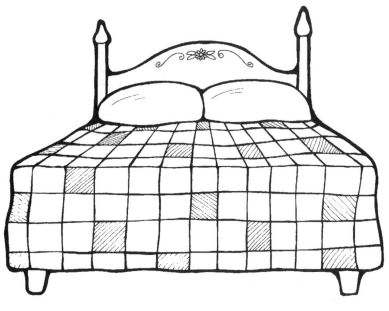

Bikinis!

Bikini has an unusual pattern of letters:
consonant-vowel-consonant-vowel-consonant-vowel.

Even more uncommon is the reverse pattern:
vowel-consonant-vowel-consonant-vowel-consonant.

Here are some words based on those patterns. Can you identify them all?

	a		a		a	Mexican musical instrument
	a		a		a	large desert
	a		a		a	tropical fruit
	a		a		a	a type of hat; a canal
	e		e		e	erase
	e		e		e	calm
	o		o		o	part of a pirate chant
e		e		e		a number
e		e		e		a metal ring for lining a small hole

Library Find-a-Word

Find the words below. The unused letters will spell out a place where family or institutional records are kept.

author, book, catalogue, Dewey, dictionary, due, file, index, lend, librarian, library, overdue, Q (found on the spine of the Quarto books), reference, shelf, stacks, tome, volume.

```
F  E  L  I  F  D  E  W  E  Y
L  M  S  K  C  A  T  S  R  R
E  U  G  O  L  A  T  A  C  A
H  L  D  U  E  O  N  A  R  R
S  O  C  H  M  O  K  O  O  B
I  V  V  E  I  X  E  D  N  I
L  A  U  T  H  O  R  Q  E  L
E  E  C  N  E  R  E  F  E  R
N  I  S  O  V  E  R  D  U  E
D  L  I  B  R  A  R  I  A  N
```

Family or institutional records are kept in _____.

It's Not That Easy Being Green

Each of the words or phrases starts with green. Work them all out and your friends will be green with envy!

GREEN	F	L	Y				greenish pest on garden plants
	B	E	A	N			a long thin vegetable
							a large cold island to the north
							American slang for paper money
							a building with glass walls
							a signal to proceed
							a special ability to make plants grow
							a vegetable that is hollow inside
							a merchant who sells fresh foodstuffs
							someone in charge of lawns and grounds

International Police

Police forces exist in almost every country of the world, and it's handy to know who to ask for when you're traveling. So here are the names of six police forces. Take away the extra letters and unjumble them to find out what nationality the force is. Get on the beat!

polizel: manger = _____

politie: touched – oe = _____

polizia: mail train – mr = _____

policia: happiness – ep = _____

gendarme: arch-felon – alo = _____

mounties: ball and chain – bhll = _____

Coats

What kind of coat goes on best when it's wet—and stays on best when its dry? Find each of these coats in the word search grid. Then rearrange the missing letters.

anorak	jacket	sport coat
blazer	mackintosh	topcoat
bolero	overcoat	tuxedo
bomber	parka	windbreaker
fur	ski	wrap

```
A  R  U  F  C              O  P  A  T  S

S  P  O  R  T  C  O  A  T  O  F  A  P  K

A  R  E  K  A  E  R  B  D  N  I  W  R  I

H  S  O  T  N  I  K  C  A  M  O  I  N  W

      T  T  T  A  B  O  R  V

      U  A  E  N  L  R  E  E

      X  O  K  O  A  E  B  R

      E  C  C  R  Z  L  M  C

      D  P  A  A  E  O  O  O

      O  O  J  K  R  B  B  A

      T  T  P  A  R  K  A  T
```

Answer: _____

More Proverbial Codes

Use the code in the box to crack the code below and finish the sentences.

Letter	m	n	o	p	q	r	s	t	u	v	w	x	y
Code	A	B	C	D	E	F	G	H	I	J	K	L	M

Letter	z	a	b	c	d	e	f	g	h	i	j	k	l
Code	N	O	P	Q	R	S	T	U	V	W	X	Y	Z

1. Don't (oagzf) _____ your (otuowqze) _____ before

   they (tmfot) _____.

2. Birds of a (rqmftqd) _____ flock (fasqftqd) _____.

3. A (efufot) _____ in (fuyq) _____ saves

   (zuzq) _____.

4. A (bqzzk) _____ saved is a (bqzzk)_____

   (qmdzqp) _____.

5. Two (idazse)_____ don't make a (dustf) _____.

6. Where there is a (iuxx) _____, there is a (imk) _____.

7. (efduwq) _____ while the (udaz) _____ is hot.

8. A (imfotqp) _____ pot never (nauxe) _____.

Frontier Words

Frontier living generated many new words that were commonly used by the pioneers. Figure out these words by reading the clues first. Then find the coordinates on the grid below.

Write the letter that is in that space on the proper lines. (To find the coordinates, go across the first number of spaces. From there, count up the second number of spaces.)

4	l	d	s	i	g	e	m	c	p	s	u	g	l	a	t
3	f	e	a	n	r	o	i	u	i	h	e	u	o	n	d
2	p	o	h	e	m	a	s	f	c	y	m	t	p	r	s
1	c	a	e	y	l	t	g	r	o	n	d	o	a	f	s
0	1	2	3	4	5	6	7	8	9	10	11	12	13	14	15

1. ___ ___ ___ ___ ___ is a prairie sod house.
   3,4 13,3 2,4 11,1 10,2

2. ___ ___ ___ ___ ___ ___ ___ ___ ___ ___ ___ are also known as johnnycakes.
   8,4 9,1 5,3 4,3 15,3 2,2 2,4 5,4 6,4 14,2 7,2

3. ___ ___ ___ ___ ___ - ___ ___ ___ ___ ___ ___ rushed to California to find gold.
   8,2 12,1 8,1 15,4 4,1   4,3 7,3 10,1 3,1 5,3 10,4

4. ___ ___ ___ ___ ___ are dried buffalo manure used for fires.
   8,4 3,2 9,3 13,2 3,4

5. ___ ___ ___ ___ ___ ___ ___ ___ ___ are settlers of the western frontier.
   4,2 7,4 4,4 7,1 5,3 2,1 14,3 6,1 7,2

6. ___ ___ ___ ___ is a disease now known as malaria.
   6,2 12,4 8,3 11,3

7. ___ ___ ___ ___ ___ ___ ___ ___ are thieves who stole cattle.
   5,3 11,4 15,2 6,1 13,4 2,3 8,1 15,1

8. prairie ___ ___ ___ ___ ___ ___ ___ ___ is a nickname for a covered wagon.
   7,2 1,1 10,3 2,2 9,1 14,3 3,1 5,3

Palindromes

Palindromes are words, phrases, sentences, or numbers that read the same forward and backward. Write a palindrome that relates to each word or phrase below. An example has been done for you.

> **12 o'clock = noon**

1. distress call _____

2. organ to see with _____

3. quiet _____

4. by yourselves _____

5. dad _____

6. amazing _____

7. little child _____

8. radio tracker _____

9. a joke _____

10. female parent _____

11. short for Robert _____

12. woman's name _____

13. term of respect for a woman _____

14. The paper that says you own property _____

15. female sheep _____

Meteorite Mix-Up

It's amazing what you can find hidden inside a meteorite. What can you find in the letters of the word "meteorite"? The black squares are the letters not used in the answer. Unscramble the remaining ones for the answer.

Row labels (top to bottom): E T E O R I T E M

Column clues:
- Woody plant with trunk and branches
- To remove the edges
- Mysterious
- Deserve
- 100 cm
- Aquatic mammal with gnawing teeth
- Clock that measures a time interval
- A section of a school year
- Far away
- Whitish insect that feeds on wood

Publishing Sports

Write a plan to show how you would make a book on a sport. Include the following in your plan:

- where you would get photos, etc.
- whom you would interview for first hand knowledge about the sport
- the style of the book

Safari

Imagine you have been given the task of organizing an African safari. Plan your advertising campaign to attract people to join you.

My Favorite Animal

If you could choose to be one animal that lives in the African jungle, which animal would you choose, and why?

_____

_____

_____

_____

_____

_____

_____

_____

_____

_____

_____

_____

_____

_____

_____

_____

_____

Fairy Tales

What might the cow have seen when she jumped over the moon? _____

_____

_____

_____

Brainstorm all the possible ways that Little Bo Peep could locate her sheep. _____

_____

_____

What are 10 other unusual names instead of Rumpelstiltskin? _____

_____

_____

_____

_____

_____

_____

_____

_____

_____

What are some of the dreams that Sleeping Beauty could have had? _____

_____

_____

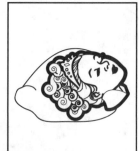

Brainstorm questions you would like to ask the Magic Mirror. _____

_____

_____

Funny Conversations

Make up a play about a conversation between:

Pinnochio and Humpty Dumpty
or
The Ugly Duckling and Snow White's Stepmother
or
Baby Bear and the Pied Piper

_____

_____

_____

_____

_____

_____

_____

_____

_____

_____

_____

_____

_____

_____

_____

_____

Letter of Complaint

Write a letter from Papa Bear to Goldilocks' mother complaining of her daughter's behavior, and in the letter list the damage she has caused.

_____ ,

_____

_____

_____

_____

_____

_____

_____

_____

_____ ,

_____

Redesign Your Classroom

Improve your classroom so that it becomes more unusual and an exciting place to be. Begin by listing what you do not like about the room and then think creatively about the changes that you can make.

Things I do not like:

_____

_____

_____

_____

_____

_____

Changes I would make:

_____

_____

_____

_____

_____

_____

Communicating in Code

Different kinds of languages and codes have also been created to help people who can't see or hear well to communicate. Here is what the Braille alphabet would look like if it were printed in black and white instead of raised dots on a page which a blind person would read by touch.

A B C D E F G H I J

K L M N O P Q R S T

U V W X Y Z

If you couldn't speak or hear, you would still be able to read, but how would you talk to your friends or family?   One way would be to use your hands. Here is the Sign Language Manual Alphabet.

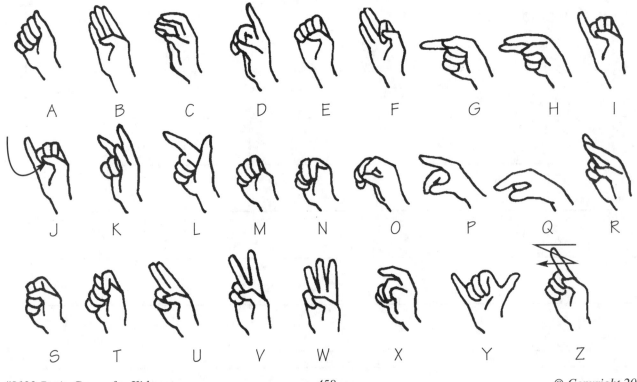

Communicating in Code *(cont.)*

Make a code that you could use to write a paragraph about yourself. Use the space below to create your code. The symbols you use can be art or geometric forms, numbers, letters, dots and dashes, or any combination. Include things like where you were born, how many brothers or sisters you have, your favorite subject, food, sport, etc. Write the paragraph on the lines below.

My Code

A	B	C	D	E	F	G	H	I	J	K	L	M	N	O	P	Q	R

S	T	U	V	W	X	Y	Z	1	2	3	4	5	6	7	8	9	10

_____

_____

_____

_____

_____

_____

Your Senses

How do your senses help you to learn?

Write about each one:

sight _____

hearing _____

smell _____

taste _____

touch _____

Which sense do you think we depend upon most? Why?

_____

_____

_____

_____

More Senses

Why do some people love the taste of a particular food, while other people don't like it at all?

_____

_____

_____

_____

Why does a bump on the nose hurt more than a similar bump on your arm or leg?

_____

_____

_____

_____

Why does a minute particle of grit cause real pain when it is in your eye, but doesn't bother you if it is in your hair?

_____

_____

_____

_____

A New Game

Prepare a storyboard to advertise the new basketball game you have invented. Use the boxes to draw your cartoons, and put any dialogue, directions, special effects, or music in the lines below. These boxes will be used to develop the script for the promotional commercial of your new game.

I have called my new version of basketball:_____.

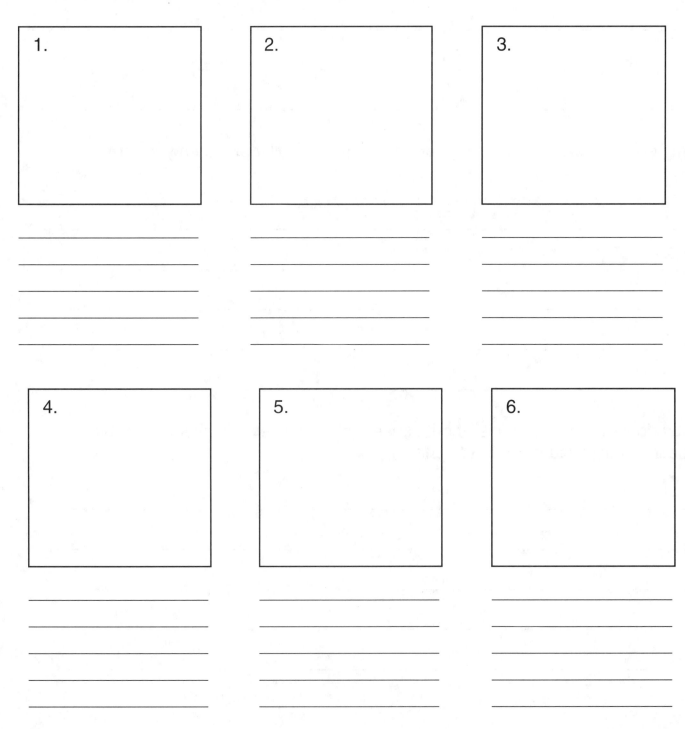

1.

2.

3.

_____

_____

_____

_____

_____

4.

5.

6.

_____

_____

_____

_____

Clean Up!

Create a "clean up the garden" machine. Draw it and explain how it works.

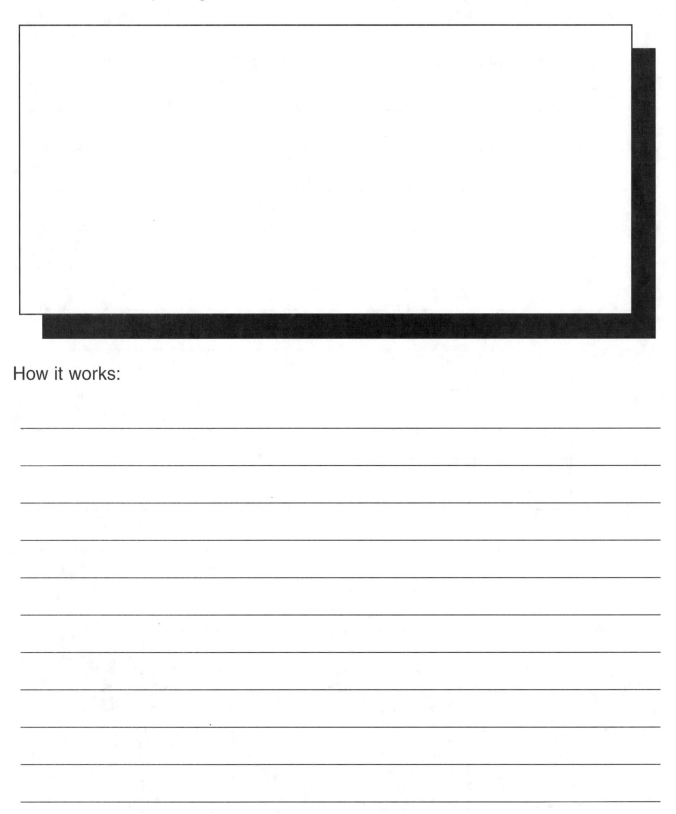

How it works:

_____

_____

_____

_____

_____

_____

_____

_____

_____

_____

Dinosaur Expedition

You are heading an expedition to capture the last living dinosaur in a remote part of the world.

1. Describe it and explain how it managed to survive.

_____

_____

_____

_____

2. Devise a plan to capture it.

_____

_____

_____

_____

3. How would you look after it until experts arrived?

_____

_____

_____

_____

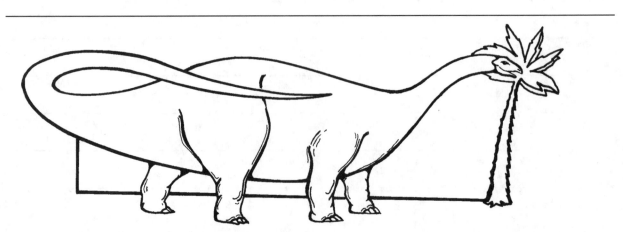

Extinction

The answer is "extinction."

Write ten questions for this answer.

1. _____

2. _____

3. _____

4. _____

5. _____

6. _____

7. _____

8. _____

9. _____

10. _____

A Brand New Pastime

Imagine that you are not able to do any of your favorite activities (no television, computer, CD's, radio, games, or books) for a whole week! Devise a new hobby to occupy your time.

_____

_____

_____

_____

_____

_____

_____

_____

_____

Popular Hobbies

Can you name five hobbies that would be suitable for older people? _____

_____   _____   _____   _____

Why do you think they would be suitable?

_____

_____

_____

_____

Can you name five hobbies that would be suitable for children aged 10 and under?

_____

_____

_____

Why do you think they would be suitable?

_____

_____

_____

_____

Patterns

Design the school's new sports uniform.

You may only use two colors and you must include three connecting shapes. The pattern is to be repeated over the whole uniform.

The colors I have chosen are _____ and _____.

Draw the three shapes you will use here.

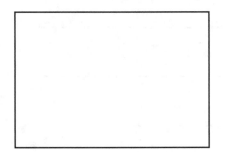 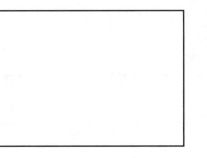 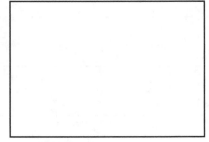

My pattern will look like this:

Now choose a new pattern of your own.

I have decided to use _____ colors.

These will be: _____

I have decided to use _____ connecting shapes.

These will be:

My pattern will look like this:

Communication Types

Fill in the table below. In column two, check if you use the communication methods listed. In columns three and four, write down who would or would not use the communication methods listed. Give as many answers as you can.

1. Method	2. You	3. Would use	4. Would not use
Speech			
Letters			
Telephone			
Radio			
Television			
Art			
Music			
Books/Stories			
Computer			
Drums			
Smoke			
Dance			
Telegraph			

Imagine

1. Imagine you were to step back in time. Explain how you would have communicated with other people.

---

2. Now imagine you step forward in time. Explain what you think your relatives will be using to communicate with people in another city 100 years from now. Write a description and draw a picture below.

Signs and Logos

What are some of the most common signs and logos that you see every day in your community? Illustrate your favorite ones. (Remember that correct color is often the most important part of the plan.)

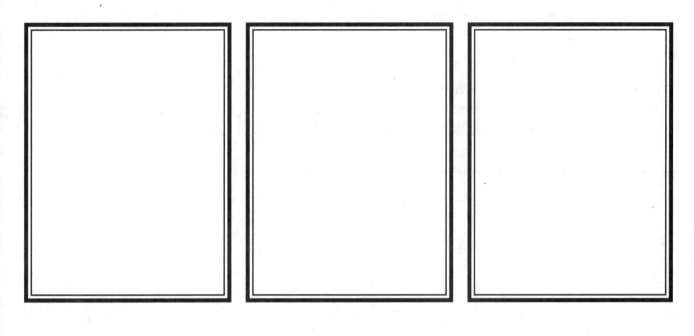

Game Plan

Invent a new game that requires players to . . .

- run, hop, and jump

- touch, catch, and throw

- twist, stretch, and bend

- use one piece of equipment.

The area of play must not be larger than half a basketball court.

Math Mystery

Fred's father is a lawyer who carries a briefcase. On the morning of Fred's birthday, Fred's father left his briefcase at home. While Fred was getting ready for school, he found a note his father left him about solving the math mystery. It was related to the birthday present left inside the briefcase. Fred must solve the math mystery to unlock his father's briefcase to get his birthday present. Here are the clues that Fred's father left behind.

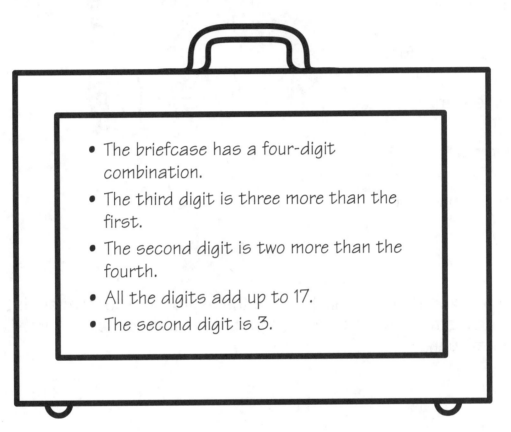

- The briefcase has a four-digit combination.
- The third digit is three more than the first.
- The second digit is two more than the fourth.
- All the digits add up to 17.
- The second digit is 3.

Here's a hint that you might find useful to solve the mystery.

- Use algebraic equations and assign each digit with a different unknown variable. For example, the first digit of the four-digit combination could be *a*, the second digit could be *b*, etc. By applying this hint, you already know that $b = 3$ because this information is given to you.

Use the clues above along with this hint to solve the math mystery.

What is the four-digit combination for the briefcase?

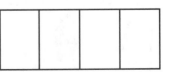

                   #8122 Brain Games for Kids

Dance Diagrams

You might not find people waltzing in a disco, but the waltz is certainly danced in many other places! Read the instructions while you follow the diagram.

1. left foot forward

2. right foot to side

3. left foot up to right foot

4. right foot forward

5. left foot to side

6. right foot up to left foot

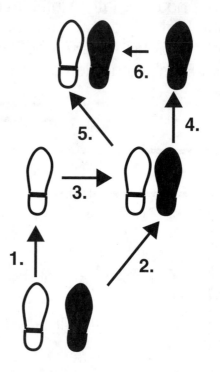

Now you are an expert on the waltz! Write the instructions for the tango by following the diagram. Use the dance diagrams and try the steps yourself. For fun, invent a new dance!

1. _____

2. _____

3. _____

4. _____

5. _____

Investigative Journalist

Kelly Sly has given this story to her editor, who finds new mistakes—seven to be precise! Can you find them all?

I visited the harbor on Saturday, September 31. I was after a gang of smugglers operating out of a four-engine sailboat docked at pier 3. A quick view of the vessel showed the anchor safely pulled up. I walked up the gangplank onto the deck and looked for somewhere to hide. A barrel full of ropes seemed ideal, so I climbed in and waited. It wasn't long before some men appeared. "We share the loot three ways, like we always do," said one. The others nodded sullenly. Unfortunately, I chose that moment to sneeze. They were onto me immediately, dragging me from the tight funnel. "A spy! Throw her overboard!" cried the one with the black long-sleeved shirt and the tattoos on his back. "Look behind you!" I screamed, and as they turned, I dove into the murky river. Unfortunately, the smugglers spotted me and finished me with a fatal shot.

1. _____

2. _____

3. _____

4. _____

5. _____

6 _____

7. _____

On the Farm

Farmer Kelly has very kindly donated 1/4 of his land to the local school for a new playground. He's also given the school a long roll of barbed wire and some rules.

1. Each of his three prize cows must have her own separate paddock.

2. The three paddocks and the playground must be exactly the same size and shape.

3. Each of the cows must be able to lean over her fence and look into the playground.

How did the school do it?

_____

_____

_____

_____

Solar System Mnemonics

It is difficult to explore the frontiers of space if you don't even know the planets of your own solar system. There are nine of them and its easy to mix them up, so what you need is a mnemonic. A mnemonic is a memory aid.

For example, Many Various Elephants Munch Jam So Underwater Numbats Purr. Confused? Each initial letter represents the initial letter of a planet. So: Many = Mercury, Various = Venus, and so on.

If you don't think much of munching elephants, make up your own! Here are the planets (in order):

Mercury, Venus, Earth, Mars, Jupiter, Saturn, Uranus, Neptune, Pluto.

The sillier the better, so go for it!

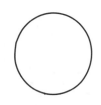

Questions and Answers

Match the question with the answer.

1. _____   2. _____   3. _____   4. _____

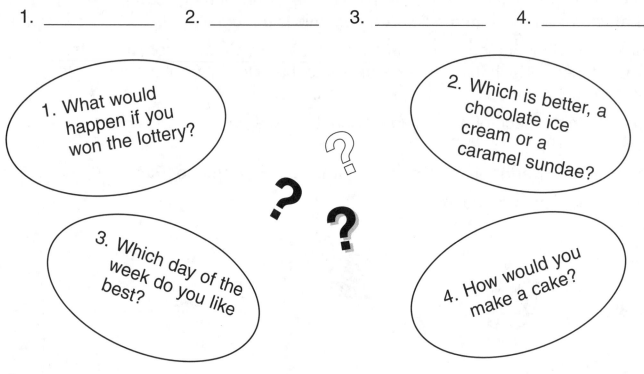

Answers:

A. A sundae is better because you can have nuts on top.

B. Turn on the oven, then put all the ingredients in a bowl, mix them, and put them in the oven to cook.

C. Sunday is best because I go out with Mom and Dad.

D. I would be able to buy lots of different things for my family.

Choose one of the above questions and write down five different answers.

Question: _____

Answers:

1. _____

2. _____

3. _____

4. _____

5. _____

fairy Tale Questions

What if a fairy godmother had a chance to restock Old Mother Hubbard's shelves? What would she put inside?

How could you redesign the house of the old woman who lived in a shoe, so that she and her children could live underwater?

Helicopters

1. Draw a helicopter and label it.   Draw an airplane and label it.

2. List ways in which helicopters and planes are used to help people.

Helicopters	**Planes**
_____	_____
_____	_____
_____	_____
_____	_____

3. Describe how helicopters take off. What is the main difference between helicopters and planes in their take-off procedures?

4. Which aircraft would be more suitable in these situations?
   Explain why you think so.

• Transporting workers to an off-shore oil rig	• Taking a concert group to another state to perform
• Herding cattle in the outback	• Taking people in a parachuting contest to the drop off point

Hobbies That Earn Money

How many hobbies can you think of that could earn money?

The Environment

Record the changes in our environment by studying each of the listed areas. The first one has been done for you as an example.

Place	Description	Habitat For	Threatened By	If Lost	Can Be Protected By
Beach	sand, water, shells	crabs, fish, birds	people leaving their garbage lying around	nowhere to swim or sail	people picking up their own garbage
School Yard					
Park					
Rain Forest					
Wet Lands					

Listing Ideas

List objects that have a handle.

_____

_____

_____

_____

List words that have to do with feeling happy.

_____

_____

_____

_____

List three syllable words (for example ex-cite-ment).

_____

_____

_____

_____

List as many rhyming-word pairs as you can (for example a black sack, a big pig).

_____

_____

_____

_____

What a Ladder!

Example:

1. Dog kennel.

2. Make it Bigger. This will give the dog more room.

3. Add bedding and windows for greater comfort.

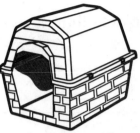

4. Replace the simple wooden walls with brick for better insulation against the cold.

Now you try it!

Redesign the stepladder using the BAR strategy (explained below). Draw and explain each change.	**B** Make it **b**igger Reasons: _____ _____
A **A**dd something Reasons: _____ _____	**R** **R**eplace, change, or rearrange Reasons: _____ _____

A New Body

If you had the imaginative task of redesigning the human body, think about the changes you could make. Draw the changed body and list the advantages of the new design.

Create a New Cage

Help redesign this monkey's cage. Draw and explain each change.

A Time Capsule

Imagine that you have to choose 10 personal items to fit in a time capsule. You have been asked to choose items that would use each of the senses. What would you include? Explain the reasons for each choice.

Choice	Reasons
1. _____	_____
2. _____	_____
3. _____	_____
4. _____	_____
5. _____	_____
6. _____	_____
7. _____	_____
8. _____	_____
9. _____	_____
10. _____	_____

Think carefully about what you could include in a 30-word message to go in your time capsule. What would you like people to know about this time and the way you live?

_____

_____

_____

Finding Attributes

List the attributes of each of the objects below.
An example has been done for you. Choose some
attributes to link together to form a new object.
Describe this new object and draw it below.

(cat: playful, purrs, affectionate, furry, independent, scratches, cuddles, warm)

(child: playful)

(daffodil)

Description of new object:	Drawing:
_____	
_____	
_____	
_____	
_____	

Make Them Interesting!

Turn these shapes into different, creative, and interesting objects or people. While drawing, you can turn the page to face any direction.

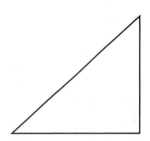

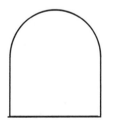

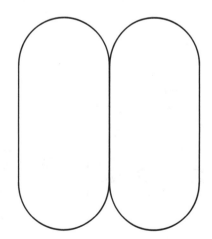

Hidden Meanings

Explain the meaning of each box.

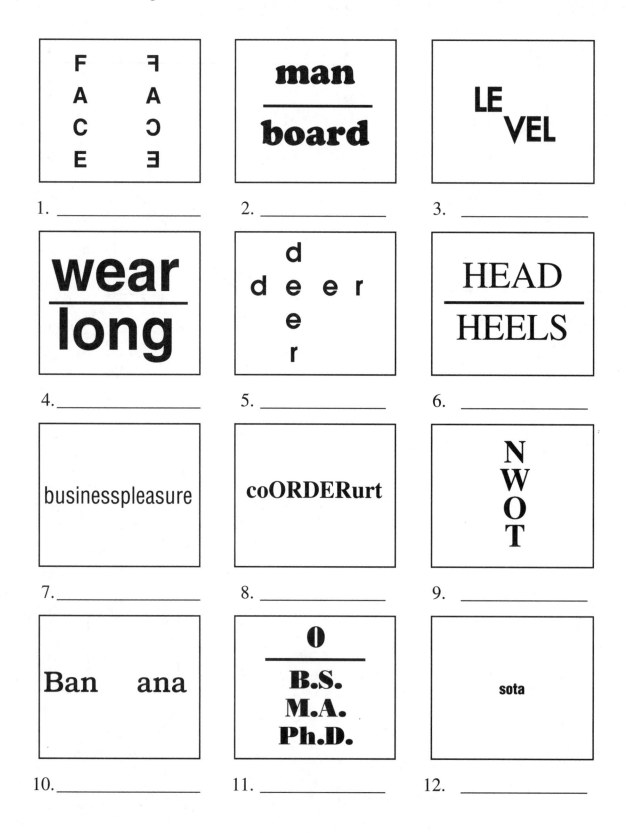

F Ⅎ A A C Ɔ E Ǝ	**man** ――――― **board**	LE VEL
1. _____	2. _____	3. _____

wear
―――――
long
	d
	d e e r
	   e
	   r
		HEAD
		―――――
		HEELS

4. _____	5. _____	6. _____
businesspleasure	coORDERurt	N W O T
7. _____	8. _____	9. _____
Ban ana	0 ――――― B.S. M.A. Ph.D.	sota
10. _____	11. _____	12. _____

Brain Challenges

#8122 Brain Games for Kids

Scrambled Math

Can you unscramble the following words to find the math terms? Write the correct word on the line after each scrambled word.

1. dad _____

2. mus _____

3. roze _____

4. lahf _____

5. slup _____

6. sinum _____

7. nitodida _____

8. geanevit _____

9. gidit _____

10. citsaamthem _____

11. trasucbt _____

12. simet _____

13. viddie _____

14. tracifon _____

15. bumner _____

How Many?

1. sides in a dodecagon? _____

2. items in a baker's dozen? _____

3. rings on the Olympic flag? _____

4. years in a century? _____

5. original colonies in the United States? _____

6. sides does a pentagon have? _____

7. wheels on a unicycle? _____

8. hours in a week? _____

9. days in a leap year? _____

10. years in a millennium? _____

11. cards in a standard deck? _____

12. centimeters in a meter? _____

13. degrees in a right angle? _____

14. planets in our solar system? _____

15 eyes on a Cyclops? _____

16. keys on a piano? _____

17. bones in a human body? _____

18. degrees in a circle? _____

19. events are in a decathlon? _____

20. squares on a checkerboard? _____

Choices

The following exercises are taken from real-life examples. The answer to each is found in how often you intend to buy or use the product or service. Answer the question by showing your work on each.

A Mexican restaurant sells tacos for $1.50. As part of their special "Taco Thursday" promotion, if you wear a T-shirt printed with the restaurant logo that advertises "Taco Thursday," you can buy the tacos for $1.25 each. The shirt costs $12.99. Should you buy a shirt? Will you really save money on the tacos? What other factors are there?

_____

_____

_____

Your friend's mother has a car and is willing to drive you to school for $25 a month or 10 cents a mile. Suppose you live 2.7 miles from the school. Calculate which deal you should take. Consider your other options.

_____

_____

_____

Writing Numbers

The numbers we use are called Arabic numbers. They were first developed in India and introduced to the rest of the world by Arab traders. This system gained popularity because it was far easier to use than most of the previous number systems. One of the most important concepts that the Arabs helped to introduce was zero. Without zero, our decimal system would not be possible. The following table shows the first 11 numbers in five other systems. Note that the ancient Mayans also discovered and used a symbol for zero.

Arabic	1	2	3	4	5	6	7	8	9	10	11
Babylonian	▼	▼▼	▼▼▼	▼▼▼▼	▼▼▼ ▼▼	▼▼▼ ▼▼▼	▼▼▼▼ ▼▼▼	▼▼▼▼ ▼▼▼▼	▼▼▼ ▼▼▼ ▼▼▼	<	<▼
Egyptian	I	II	III	IIII	II III	III III	III IIII	IIII IIII	IIII IIIII	Ω	Ω I
Roman	I	II	III	IV	V	VI	VII	VIII	IX	X	XI
Mayan	○	○○	○○○	○○○○	___	___○	___○○	___○○○	___○○○○	═══	═══○
Base 2	1	10	11	100	101	110	111	1000	1001	1010	1011

Use the patterns above to extend each system to show the numbers 12 to 20.

Arabic	12	13	14	15	16	17	18	19	20
Babylonian									
Egyptian									
Roman									
Mayan									
Base 2									

"Sum" Triangle

Arrange the numbers 1–6 with one in each circle so the sum along each side of the triangle is the same. If done correctly, each triangle will have a different answer. Write the answer for each triangle in the center circle. One number for each sum is given. **Hint:** The four sums are consecutive numbers.

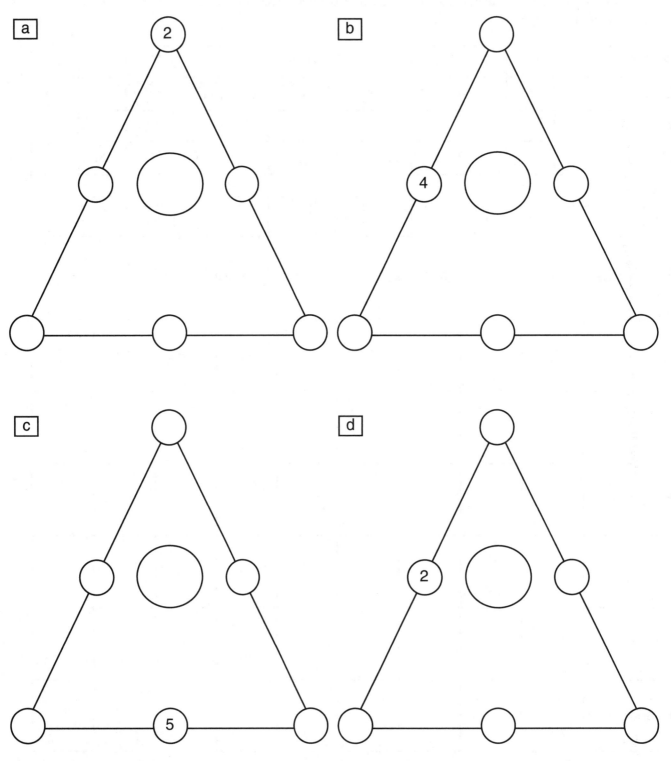

Estimation

1. Estimate how many jelly beans would fit into a one-gallon container.

_____

_____

_____

_____

How many candies are in this jar?

2. How could you check your answer without actually counting the jelly beans?

_____

_____

_____

_____

3. Would this be a reliable method?

_____

_____

_____

_____

4. Give reasons for your answer.

_____

_____

_____

_____

Math Fair

Your school is going to have a math fair. Design a poster to advertise your presentation stating why it is the best topic to be presented at the fair.

Math Names

What is the correct name for the objects described below?

Description	Name	Description	Name
500 sheets of paper		200th anniversary	
Dinosaur with three horns on its head		Married to two people at the same time	
Four babies at the same time to one mother		Roman officer in charge of 100 soldiers	
Six-pointed star		10-event athletic competition	
Three-sided figure		5-event athletic competition	

Credit Card Capers

Credit cards have a 16 digit number, such as 4567 6002 0762 3535. What's unusual about each of these credit card numbers?

1. 2884 4646 2228 8422

_____

2. 1009 8423 3248 9001

```
    ==== Credit Card ====

    John Smith
    4567 6002 0762 3535
```

_____

3. 0537 1074 2148 4296

_____

4. 1991 3357 9113 9711

_____

5. 5238 1654 9858 1234

_____

6. 1113 2317 3719 2931

_____

7. 1248 1632 6412 8256

_____

8. 1500 2534 4104 8138

_____

9. 0088 5489 3774 0648

_____

10. 0003 1854 9203 1184 (c = 3, r=18, etc.)

_____

Number Challenge

Use the numbers below to total 100, without rearranging the order. You can add, subtract, multiply or divide.

1 2 3 4 5 6 7 8 9

Can you think of a way to make them total 50?

Consecutive Numbers

Consecutive numbers are those which follow each other in counting order, for example: 2, 3, 4.

Many numbers can be made by adding consecutive numbers, for example:

9 = 4 + 5 and 10 = 1 + 2 + 3 + 4

Beside each number below, show the consecutive numbers which add up to make that original number. (Do not use zero.)

Are there any you can't do?

1 = _____   16 = _____

2 = _____   17 = _____

3 = _____   18 = _____

4 = _____   19 = _____

5 = _____   20 = _____

6 = _____   21 = _____

7 = _____   22 = _____

8 = _____   23 = _____

9 = _____   24 = _____

10 = _____   25 = _____

11 = _____   26 = _____

12 = _____   27 = _____

13 = _____   28 = _____

14 = _____   29 = _____

15 = _____   30 = _____

Decimal and Binary Numbers

Computer don't work with decimal numbers. Instead, they use binary numbers, or "ons" and "offs." The binary numbers **1** is "on" and **0** is "off." In decimal numbers 11,101 =

1 ten-thousand + 1 thousand + 1 hundred + 0 tens + 1 one.

In binary numbers 11101 =

1 sixteen + 1 eight + 1 four + 0 twos + 1 one. This is the number 29 in decimal.

Can you change these binary numbers into decimal numbers?

1. 100 = (1 four + 0 twos + 0 ones) = _____

2. 110 = _____

3. 1001 = _____

4. 10101 = _____

5. 11111 = _____

Now change these decimal numbers into binary numbers:

6. 19 _____

7. 7 _____

8. 25 _____

9. 10 _____

10. 5 _____

Toppling Tree Conundrum

Leonard the lumberjack has to cut down the tall tree on the left. Unfortunately, it's surrounded by smaller trees on each side—and he can't let the big tree drop onto them. How can he discover the height of the tall tree to see if he has enough room?

He knows that:

There are 18 m between the trees.

The small trees are 1.6 m wide.

He is 1.8 m tall.

The small trees are all about 4 m tall.

The small trees' shadows are 1 m long.

The tall tree's shadow is 5 m long.

The drawing is not to scale!

His axe is 1.2 m long.

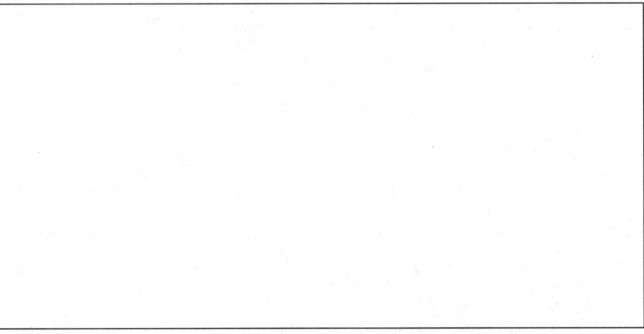

Moons of Saturn

Saturn has about twenty moons, compared to Earth's one. In the puzzle, find these ten moons: Dione, Enceladus, Hyperion, Lapetus, Janus, Mimas, Phoebe, Rhea, Tethys, Titan and this space probe: Pioneer 11.

The letters left over spell out the name of the scientist who first discovered that Saturn's rings were separate from the planet.

p.s.: One moon appears twice—it orbits Saturn in the opposite direction to all the others.

E	P	I	O	N	E	E	R	11
N	N	A	T	I	T	B	C	H
O	O	C	R	I	M	E	S	L
I	I	T	E	I	I	O	A	A
D	R	A	N	L	M	H	J	P
A	E	H	R	H	A	P	A	E
U	P	Y	G	E	S	D	N	T
S	Y	H	T	E	T	N	U	U
P	H	O	E	B	E	S	S	S

The name of the scientist who first discovered that Saturn's rings were separate from the planet: _____

The name of the moon that appears twice: _____

What's in the Bag? #5

Read the words on the next page. Then match the letters with the correct synonyms in the clues. (You will not use all of the letters.) Put the five clues together and discover what's in the bag!

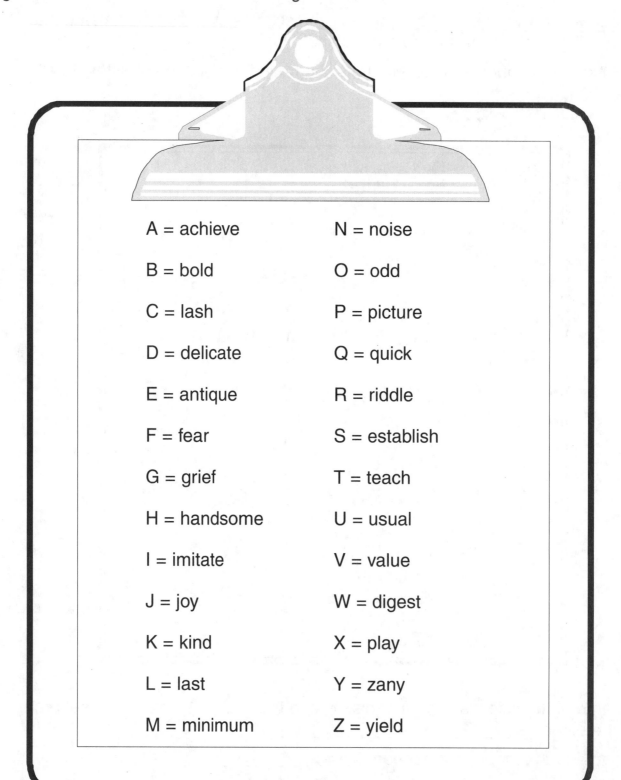

A = achieve

B = bold

C = lash

D = delicate

E = antique

F = fear

G = grief

H = handsome

I = imitate

J = joy

K = kind

L = last

M = minimum

N = noise

O = odd

P = picture

Q = quick

R = riddle

S = establish

T = teach

U = usual

V = value

W = digest

X = play

Y = zany

Z = yield

What's in the Bag? #5 *(cont.)*

Clue 1:

_____   _____   _____   _____   _____   _____

anxiety   final   common   anxiety   anxiety   funny

Clue 2:

_____   _____   _____   _____   _____

eat   lovely   copy   coach   ancient

Clue 3:

_____   _____   _____   _____   _____

form   eat   ancient   ancient   coach

Clue 4:

_____   _____   _____   _____

coach   strange   image   form

Clue 5:

_____   _____   _____   _____   _____

whip   strange   whip   strange   attain

What's in the bag? _____

What's in the Bag? #6

Read the words on the next page. Then match the letters with the correct synonyms in the clues. (You will not use all of the letters.) Put the five clues together and discover what's in the bag!

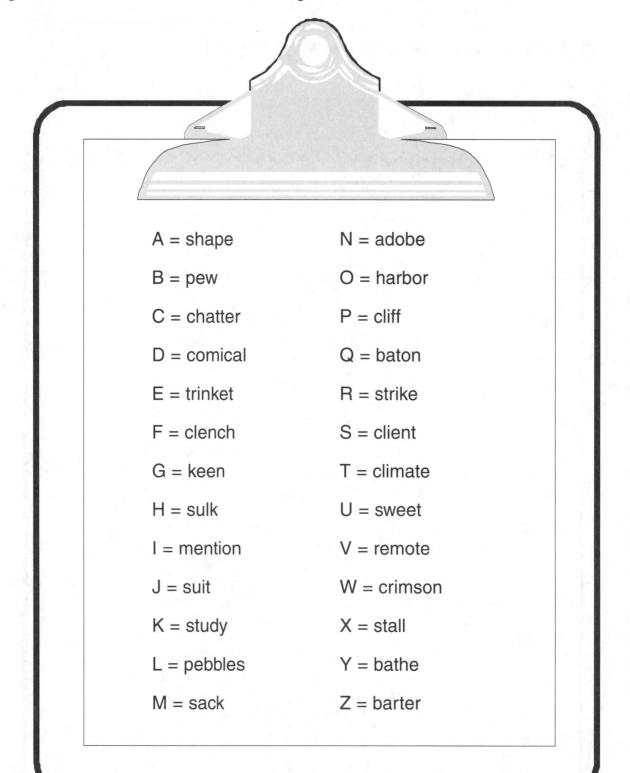

A = shape

B = pew

C = chatter

D = comical

E = trinket

F = clench

G = keen

H = sulk

I = mention

J = suit

K = study

L = pebbles

M = sack

N = adobe

O = harbor

P = cliff

Q = baton

R = strike

S = client

T = climate

U = sweet

V = remote

W = crimson

X = stall

Y = bathe

Z = barter

What's in the Bag? #6 *(cont.)*

Clue 1:

_____   _____   _____
gravel   form   bench

Clue 2:

_____   _____   _____   _____
weather   cove   cove   gravel

Clue 3:

_____ _____ _____ _____ _____ _____ _____
charm   clay   gravel   form   hit   clever   charm

Clue 4:

_____   _____   _____   _____   _____
grip   cove   jabber   sugary   customer

Clue 5:

_____   _____   _____   _____
gravel   charm   clay   customer

What's in the bag? _____

What's in the Bag? #7

Read the words on the next page. Then match the letters with the correct synonyms in the clues. (You will not use all of the letters.) Put the five clues together and discover what's in the bag!

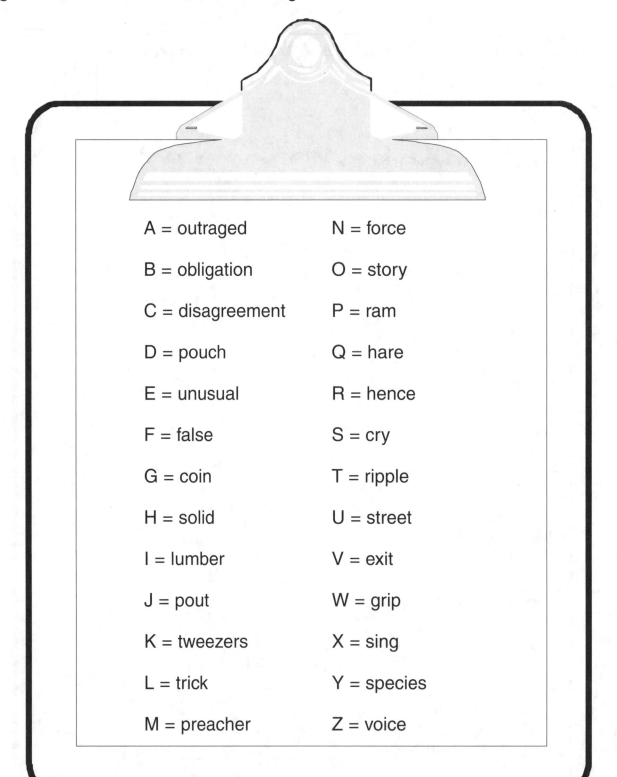

A = outraged

B = obligation

C = disagreement

D = pouch

E = unusual

F = false

G = coin

H = solid

I = lumber

J = pout

K = tweezers

L = trick

M = preacher

N = force

O = story

P = ram

Q = hare

R = hence

S = cry

T = ripple

U = street

V = exit

W = grip

X = sing

Y = species

Z = voice

What's in the Bag? #7 (cont.)

Clue 1:

_____ _____ _____ _____ _____ _____ _____

conflict   tale   tale   tongs   wood   power   token

Clue 2:

_____ _____ _____ _____

firm   unique   thus   duty

Clue 3:

_____ _____ _____ _____ _____ _____

howl   wave   thus   tale   power   token

Clue 4:

_____ _____ _____ _____ _____

grab   firm   wood   wave   unique

Clue 5:

_____ _____ _____ _____

duty   road   prank   duty

What's in the bag? _____

What's in the Bag? #8

Read the words on the next page. Then match the letters with the correct synonyms in the clues. (You will not use all of the letters.) Put the five clues together and discover what's in the bag!

A = fare

B = lane

C = lake

D = landmark

E = graph

F = gown

G = mark

H = gossip

I = gobble

J = clown

K = double

L = duct

M = silent

N = soil

O = lantern

P = speck

Q = clog

R = opening

S = donkey

T = courage

U = region

V = struggle

W = content

X = fling

Y = pig

Z = bottle

What's in the Bag? #8 *(cont.)*

Clue 1:

____ ____ ____ ____ ____ ____

lamp   dress   dress   gulp   pond   chart

Clue 2:

____ ____ ____ ____

valor   lamp   lamp   pipe

Clue 3:

____ ____ ____ ____ ____ ____ ____

burro   chart   pond   district   door   chart   burro

Clue 4:

____ ____ ____ ____ ____

pipe   lamp   lamp   spot   burro

Clue 5:

____ ____ ____ ____

satisfied   gulp   door   chart

What's in the bag? _____

            #8122 Brain Games for Kids

Occupation Word Puzzle

If Handel had struck out at being a composer, maybe one of these other jobs in opera may have suited him:

1. a player of a violin shaped instrument with a spike

2. a player of a particular wind instrument

3. a person who plays music

4. a person who ensures pianos are in tune

5. a player of an air-operated keyboard with pipes

6. a female singer with a high voice

7. a person who entertains

8. a wooden flute with a mouthpiece like a whistle.

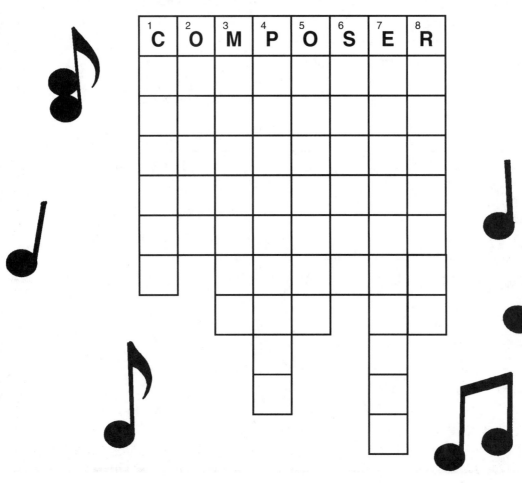

Fast or Slow?

Can you change SLOW into FAST in five tries? You can only change one letter of a word at a time.

S	L	O	W	
				A small slit
				A thin strip
				Level
				Italian car
				Clenched fingers
F	A	S	T	

In the Middle

It's the middle of the year, and the temperatures are in the mid-teens. You're feeling fair to middling when you get dropped right in the middle of—all these middles.

	Clue:	**Answer:**
M	between youth and old age	
	the period in history between the Roman Empire and the Renaissance	
	the note on the first ledger line below the staff	
I	not rich or poor	
D	a cavity essential to hearing	
D	the area from Turkey to North Africa	
L	a person who buys goods and sells them to shops rather than customers	
E	views on issues that are not extreme	
+	not large or small	
	a wrestler who weighs 171–192 pounds	

Totem Poles

Can you complete this totem pole puzzle?

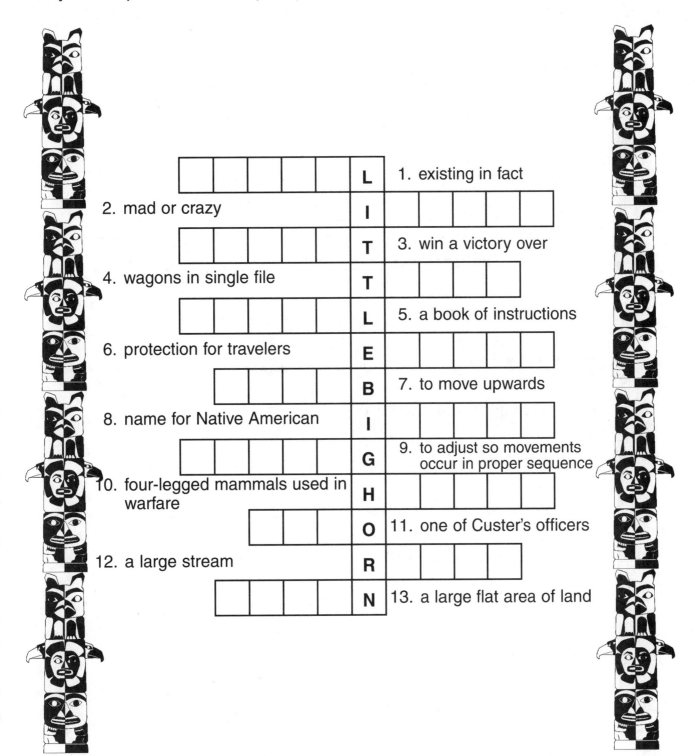

| | | | | | **L** | 1. existing in fact |

2. mad or crazy **I**

| | | | | | **T** | 3. win a victory over |

4. wagons in single file **T**

| | | | | | **L** | 5. a book of instructions |

6. protection for travelers **E**

| | | | | **B** | 7. to move upwards |

8. name for Native American **I**

| | | | | | **G** | 9. to adjust so movements occur in proper sequence |

10. four-legged mammals used in warfare **H**

| | | | | **O** | 11. one of Custer's officers |

12. a large stream **R**

| | | | | **N** | 13. a large flat area of land |

517   #8122 Brain Games for Kids

Corn-Fed Words

Each phrase below is a clue for a word or phrase that contains the letters CORN.

1. A horn of plenty_____

2. Something of fundamental importance _____

3. Where two streets meet _____

4. A type of sandwich meat _____

5. The center part of an ear of corn _____

6. A building for storing corn _____

7. A position in football_____

8. A product used in cooking and salads_____

9. An instrument that looks like a trumpet _____

10. The kind of joke that makes people groan _____

11. The outer covering of the eyeball _____

12. A way to save money, time, or effort (two words) _____

13. A thickening agent in gravy_____

14. An ornamental molding along the top of a wall _____

15. A breakfast cereal _____

Which Word?

Words that sound or look alike often have meanings that are not alike at all. Decide which of the two word choices on the right is the correct one to correspond with the word or phrase on the left, and then circle it.

1. Dry land   desert/dessert

2. Washington, D.C.   capital/capitol

3. Complete   through/thorough

4. In any case   any way/anyway

5. A result   affect/effect

6. To hint or suggest   imply/infer

7. Second in a series of two   later/latter

8. A heavenly body   angel/angle

9. Unlawful   illicit/elicit

10. To prove something is false   disapprove/disprove

11. Writing paper   stationary/stationery

12. To take that which is offered   accept/except

13. To go forward   precede/proceed

14. A part of speech   preposition/proposition

15. To stop   quit/quite

Telephone Trivia

Use the letters that correspond to the numbers on a real telephone to decode the other cities spelled by these imaginary telephone numbers. The state where each city is located is in parentheses.

1. 639-9675 _NEW YORK_____ (New York)

2. 244-2246 _CHICAGO_____ (Illinois)

3. 468-7866 _HOUSTON_____ (Texas)

4. 522-5766 _JACKSON_____ (Mississippi)

5. 746-3649 _PHOENIX_____ (Arizona)

6. 338-7648 _DETROIT_____ (Michigan)

7. 667-3655 _NORFOLK_____ (Virginia)

8. 873-6866 _TRENTON_____ (New Jersey)

9. 285-2682 _ATLANTA_____ (Georgia)

10. 636-7447 _MEMPHIS_____ (Tennessee)

11. 732-8853 _SEATTLE_____ (Washington)

12. 726-8233 _SANTA FE_____ (New Mexico)

One Word Plus Another

Add one word to another word to make a third word. The first one has been done for you.

1. A water barrier plus a writing utensil equals a verb that means "to make slightly wet."

   dam + pen = dampen

2. A large body of water plus a male child make a period of time.

   _____ + _____ = _____

3. A lightweight bed of canvas plus 2,000 pounds make a type of fabric.

   _____ + _____ = _____

4. A vegetable plus an edible kernel make a seed that ripens underground and is usually roasted before being eaten.

   _____ + _____ = _____

5. The nearest star plus the antonym of *wet* make an adjective meaning "various" or "several."

   _____ + _____ = _____

6. A male offspring plus something used to catch fish make a form of poetry.

   _____ + _____ = _____

7. The antonym of *on* plus frozen water make a place for business.

   _____ + _____ = _____

8. A rodent plus a shade of brown make a plant used to make furniture.

   _____ + _____ = _____

9. Male adults plus the highest playing card make a threat.

   _____ + _____ = _____

10. A man's name plus a male child make the name of a former U.S. president.

    _____ + _____ = _____

How Many?

Answer each question with a number. How many . . .

1. Eyes did Cyclops have?_____

2. Planets in our solar system have no moons?_____

3. Sides does a pentagon have? _____

4. Teeth does an adult have? _____

5. Degrees are in a right angle?_____

6. Centimeters are in a meter?_____

7. Faces are carved on Mt. Rushmore? _____

8. Musical instruments are played in an *a cappella* performance?_____

9. Stories are in the Sears Tower? _____

10. Degrees are in a circle? _____

11. Bones are in the body? _____

12. Items are in a gross? _____

13. Lines of verse in a sonnet? _____

14. Cards are in a deck?_____

15. Squares are on a checkerboard? _____

16. Years are in a century?_____

17. Days are in a leap year?_____

18. Sheets of paper are in a ream?_____

19. Keys are on a piano? _____

20. People are on a soccer team?_____

All Five Vowels

Make a list of words that have all five vowels within them.

_____

_____

_____

_____

_____

_____

_____

_____

_____

_____

_____

_____

Inventive Analogies

Use a reference book or an appropriate Web site to help you complete each analogy below.

Example: Washington is to president as George III is to king.

1. _____ is to telephone as
   Guglielmo Marconi is to radio.

2. Henry Ford is to _____ as
   George Eastman is to cameras.

3. Cyrus McCormick is to the reaper as Eli Whitney is to the _____.

4. Light bulb and phonograph are to _____ as bifocals and lightning rod
   are to Benjamin Franklin.

5. _____ is to steam engine as Orville and Wilbur Wright are to airplane.

6. Elias Howe is to sewing machine as _____ is to telegraph.

7. Abner Doubleday is to baseball as Levi Strauss is to _____.

8. Reaper is to crops as _____ is to seeds.

9. Baseball is to _____ as blue jeans are to clothing.

10. _____ is to photograph as Howe is to garment.

11. _____ is to telegram
    as Bell is to phone call.

12. Telephone is to ear as bifocal is to
    _____.

Animal Families and Groups

Fill in the blanks in the chart.

Animal	Male	Female	Young	Group
fox	dog	_____	_____	skulk
_____	rooster	hen	_____	_____
lion	_____	lioness	_____	pride
cattle	bull	_____	calf	_____
whale	_____	cow	calf	_____
seal	bull	_____	pup	_____
ostrich	cock	hen	_____	flock
sheep	_____	ewe	_____	flock
goose	gander	_____	gosling	gaggle
kangaroo	_____	doe	_____	_____
hog	_____	sow	_____	herd
_____	billy	nanny	kid	herd

From Traitor To Patriot

A Traitor is only one letter away from a Patriot. Use the clues to work out these words.

Traitor	−	R	+	P	=	one who loves and defends his or her country	Patriot
		T		P		an airfield with control tower and hangers	
		I		C		a vehicle with large wheels used in farming	
		O		E		more worn and torn	
		T,R		C,P		orange-colored fruit	
		T,R		Y,P		trimming shrubs or trees into shapes	

George Giraffe

By the time you complete this word puzzle (George has filled in some letters for you), you'll know all about giraffes! You may need to do some research to complete this puzzle.

1. Giraffes have an excellent sense of…
2. Number of neck vertebrae
3. The giraffe's chief predator
4. Giraffes live south of this desert.
5. The giraffe's _____ is long and flexible.
6. Captive giraffes can live up to 36 _____.
7. Giraffes may need to _____ if their food source depletes.
8. The giraffe's favorite tree
9. Older giraffes are a darker _____.
10. The giraffe belongs to this group of animals.
11. Giraffes bear only one _____ at a time.
12. Male giraffes use their long necks to _____.
13. Giraffes live in groups called _____.

Zip It Up!

Put zip in your day—and your vocabulary. All the following words have a "zip" in them somewhere. Use the clues to work out the whole word.

1. A type of monkey _____

2. Conduct as a citizen _____

3. A city in east central Germany_____

4. A sweet made with almond paste _____

5. Spectacles clipped to the nose by a spring_____

6. Italian open pie _____

7. Method of playing a stringed instrument by plucking_____

8. Award for victory in a contest_____

9. A mystery, or bewildering_____

10. A quadrilateral with only one pair of opposite sides parallel _____

11. A large dirigible balloon _____

12. An American post-code _____

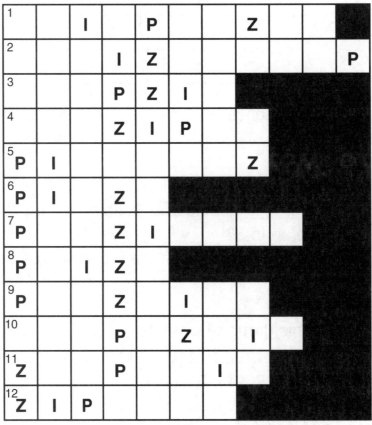

Bridge Word Search

Find these bridges in the word search below. The leftover letters spell out the name of an unusual bridge in the United States.

Akashi Kaikyo	movable bridge
arch	pontoon
cantilever	span
Clifton	support
Commonwealth Bridge	suspension
Golden Gate	Sydney Harbour Bridge
Humber	Tasman
London Bridge	Tower Bridge
Mackinac	Victoria Bridge

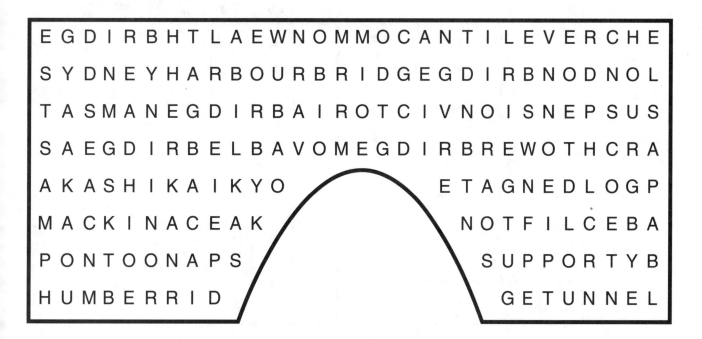

```
E G D I R B H T L A E W N O M M O C A N T I L E V E R C H E
S Y D N E Y H A R B O U R B R I D G E G D I R B N O D N O L
T A S M A N E G D I R B A I R O T C I V N O I S N E P S U S
S A E G D I R B E L B A V O M E G D I R B R E W O T H C R A
A K A S H I K A I K Y O              E T A G N E D L O G P
M A C K I N A C E A K                N O T F I L C E B A
P O N T O O N A P S                  S U P P O R T Y B
H U M B E R R I D                    G E T U N N E L
```

The name of the unusual bridge in the United States:

_____.

Jumbo Elephants

Test your "jumbo" knowledge here! When you've completed all the horizontal words, the central vertical word spells out an alternative name for an elephant.

1. The largest land animal

2. Smaller of the two types of elephants

3. Larger of the two types of elephants—its ears look like a map of its home

4. The elephant's ancient hairy ancestor

5. Flesh-eating mammal that preys on elephant calves (baby elephants)

6. An extinct type of elephant

7. To search for food

8. A group of elephants

9. The elephant is this type of animal

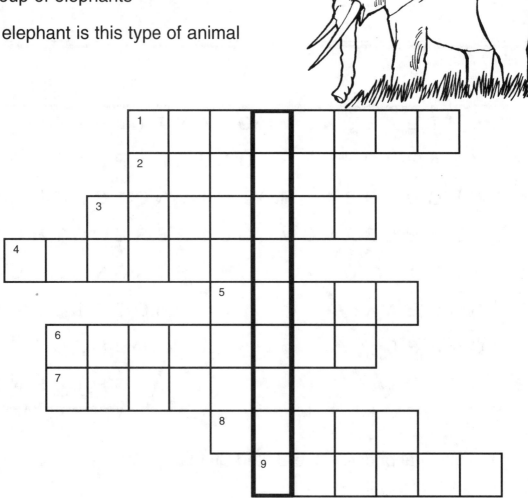

Rods

Here are seven words with "rod" in them—can you find what they are?

R O D + _____ =

to poke	
stepped	
a car modified for speed	
a rod inside an engine	
a rod for finding water	
a rod that protects a building from lightning	
a rod between 1 cm and 10 cm used in math	

Jules Verne Acrostic

The missing words come from titles of Jules Verne's novels, or predictions he made about the future.

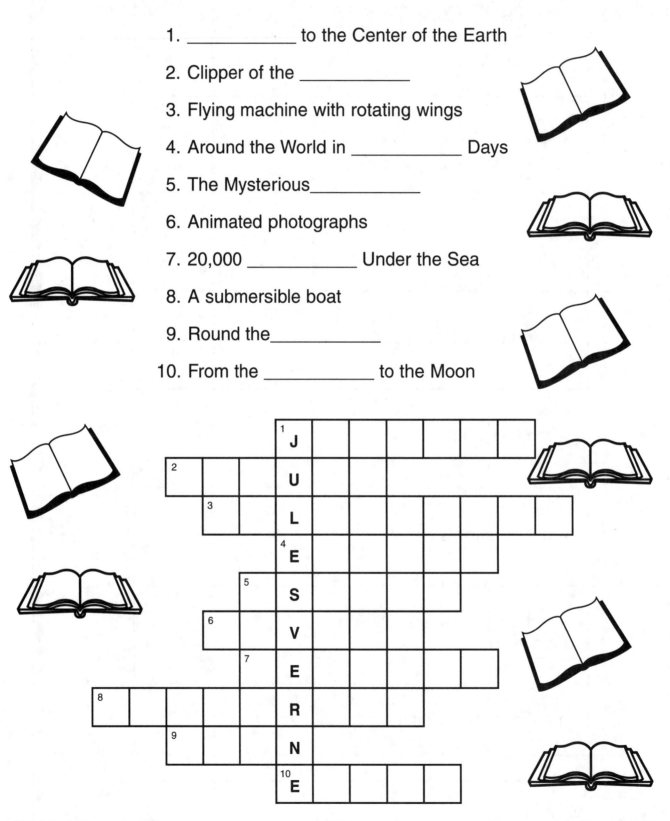

1. _____ to the Center of the Earth

2. Clipper of the _____

3. Flying machine with rotating wings

4. Around the World in _____ Days

5. The Mysterious_____

6. Animated photographs

7. 20,000 _____ Under the Sea

8. A submersible boat

9. Round the_____

10. From the _____ to the Moon

Tammy's Tattoos

Tammy the tattoo artist will only do tattoos of objects that have the word tattoo in them. Her range, to say the least, is limited. What can she draw? Use the letters of the word "tattoo" and combine them with the letters in the second column. Use the clues to help you solve the words.

T A T T O O	+ HOP	A cooked spud	
	+ CILN	Small rabbit	
	+ EHPS	Paste for cleaning teeth	
	+ EEPSW	Type of yam	
	+ HPS	Photocopy	
	+ DDEPS	Amphibian with spots	
	+ EEMR	South American plant that looks like a tomato	

Tipperary

What can you find in Tipperary, the name of a town in Ireland?

How many words of at least four letters can you make from "Tipperary"? Oh, and they have to start with a T . . . .

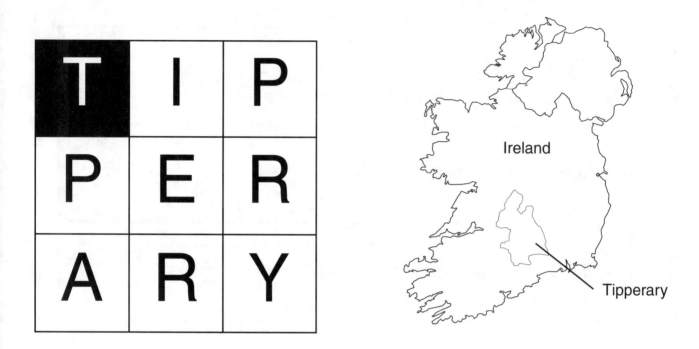

Ireland

Tipperary

_____ _____ _____ _____

_____ _____ _____ _____

_____ _____ _____ _____

_____ _____ _____ _____

_____ _____ _____ _____

E's Front and Back

Use the clues to fill in the blanks in the following words. All the words both begin and end with the letter **e**.

#	Word	Clue
1.	e ___ ___ ___ ___ ___ e	to do
2.	e ___ ___ ___ ___ ___ e	make higher
3.	e ___ ___ e	comfort
4.	e ___ ___ ___ e	national bird
5.	e ___ ___ ___ ___ ___ ___ e	guess
6.	e ___ ___ ___ ___ ___ e	teachers do this
7.	e ___ ___ ___ ___ ___ ___ e	a letter goes in one
8.	e ___ ___ ___ ___ ___ ___ e	data or proof
9.	e ___ ___ ___ e	send away
10.	e ___ e	female sheep
11.	e ___ ___ ___ ___ ___ ___ e	leave
12.	e ___ ___ ___ ___ ___ e	to check
13.	e ___ ___ ___ ___ ___ ___ ___ e	disappear
14.	e ___ ___ ___ ___ ___ ___ e	workout
15.	e ___ ___ ___ ___ ___ ___ ___ e	cheer up or cheer on
16.	e ___ ___ ___ ___ ___ ___ ___ e	administrator
17.	e ___ ___ ___ ___ e	breathe out
18.	e ___ ___ ___ ___ e	get free
19.	e ___ ___ ___ ___ e	lure
20.	e ___ ___ ___ ___ ___ ___ ___ ___ e	to free from oppression

Letter Answers

Use one or two letters of the alphabet to respond to each of the clues. The first one has been done for you.

1. Not difficult   **EZ**

2. Cold

3. Goodbye

4. Vegetable

5. Body of water

6. Girl's name

7. Exclamation

8. Organ used for sight

9. Pronoun

10. Tent home

11. Plant or vine

12. Question

13. Something to drink

14. Insect

15. Radio announcer

Rhyming Word Pairs

Find an adjective that rhymes with a noun so that the two words together have about the same meaning as the phrase that is given. An example has been done for you.

Example: girl from Switzerland = Swiss miss

1. ailing William =
2. mischievous boy =
3. unhappy friend =
4. bashful insect =
5. fiesty primate =
6. overweight referee =
7. soft young dog =
8. unhappy father =
9. soaked dog =
10. watered-down red juice =
11. reliable Theodore =
12. flower that is messy =
13. tiny bug =
14. ill hen =
15. smart instrument =

Word Chains

To make a word chain, each new word must begin with the last letter of the previous word. For example, if the category is Famous Americans, a possible word chain would be the following: George Bush—Herbert Hoover—Ronald Reagan, etc. This can be adapted to any area of study or played in teams, each team taking turns adding to the chain.

Countries	Proper Nouns	Foods
Chile	Betsy Ross	hot dog
England	Salt Lake City	green bean

Coded Message

Circle the correct letter for each problem below. Then, take the circled letter and put it in the corresponding blank in order to reveal a famous saying.

```
 __  __  __      __  __  __      __  __      __  __  __
 7   2   6       8   5   3       11  1       7   2   6

 __  __  __  __  __      __  __  __      __  __  __
 9   4   11  3   10      7   2   6        8   5   3
```

1. If man walked on the moon in 1492, circle S. If not, circle F.

2. If a prairie dog is a dog, circle K. If it is a rodent, circle O.

3. _____ If your father's sister is your aunt, circle N. If not, circle A.

4. If 6 x 9 = 55, circle M. If not, circle H.

5. If antonyms are words that mean the opposite of one another, circle A. If not, circle L.

6. _____ If Brazil is a country in Europe, circle K. If not, circle U.

7. If the capital of Illinois is Springfield, circle Y. If not circle, U.

8. If the trumpet is a woodwind instrument, circle Z. If not, circle C.

9. If Charles Dickens wrote David Copperfield, circle T. If not, circle W.

10. If a telescope is used to view things far away, circle K. If not, circle M.

11. If the Statue of Liberty is located in Washington, D.C., circle E. If not, circle I.

The Wheel

1. The wheel was first invented in Sumer about 3500 B.C. By about 3250 B.C., the first wheeled vehicles were used there. How do you think the idea of the wheel might first have come to the Sumerians? Write your thoughts here:

   _____

   _____

2. How might the first wheels have been made?

   _____

   _____

3. List the improvements made by the wheel for these people in the chart below.

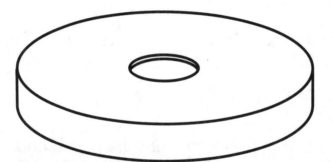

Rulers	Traders	Farmers	(you choose)

Heroes

Brainstorm: What makes a person a hero? List as many ideas as you can think of.

Can you write a definition of a hero?

_____

_____

_____

Are there any particular occupations from which heroes emerge? Why do you think this is so?

_____

_____

_____

_____

_____

More Heroes

List all the ways that people in the following occupations could be heroes:

a. teachers _____

_____

_____

b. plumbers _____

_____

_____

c. bank tellers _____

_____

_____

d. bus drivers _____

_____

_____

e. doctors _____

_____

_____

f. nurses _____

_____

_____

g. students _____

_____

_____

Louis Braille's Code

(Born January 4, 1809)

Louis Braille was a Frenchman who invented a raised dot writing system for the blind. A special typewriter presses against paper to form the different dot sequences.

Use the Braille letter dot code to write and read the messages.

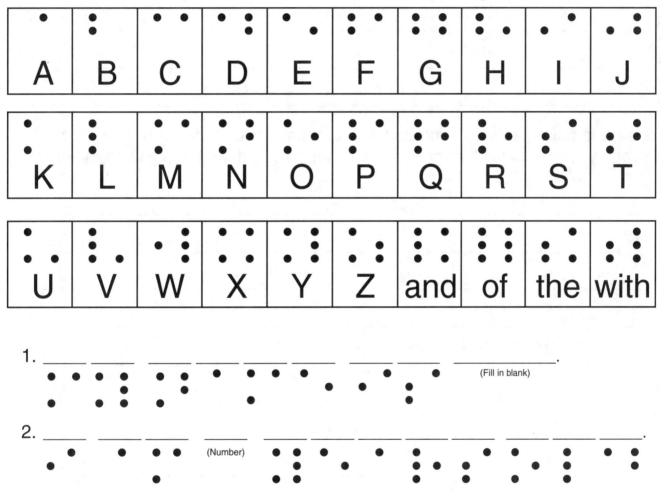

1. _____ _____ _____ _____ _____ _____ _____ _____.
   (Fill in blank)

2. _____ _____ _____ _____ _____ _____ _____.
   (Number)

3. Challenge: Write a message in Braille dots below. Now have a friend tell you what it says!

_____

_____

_____

_____

Famous People

The answer is "fame."

List 5 questions.

1. _____

2. _____

3. _____

4. _____

5. _____

Choose a famous person. If you could talk to him or her, what would be three questions you would ask him or her, and what do you think the answers might be?

1. _____

_____

_____

_____

_____

2. _____

_____

_____

_____

_____

3. _____

_____

_____

_____

_____

Problems and Solutions

Select three major problems facing America today.

1. _____
   _____
   _____

2. _____
   _____
   _____

3. _____
   _____
   _____

What are your solutions?

1. _____
   _____
   _____

2. _____
   _____
   _____

3. _____
   _____
   _____

Great Ideas!

List all the ways you can celebrate a holiday.

_____

_____

_____

_____

_____

Suggest different ways that children can amuse themselves when they feel bored.

_____

_____

_____

_____

How many different reasons can you think of why you might not be able to close the front door?

_____

_____

_____

_____

_____

Greetings!

List all the different ways that you can think of to greet people. You can show your answers with words and pictures.

Koalas

Make the following statements into questions.

───────────────────── **Factual** ═════════════════════

1. Koalas, kangaroos, dolphins, dogs, and humans are all types of mammals.

_____

_____

_____

───────────────────── **Inferential** ═══════════════════

2. With more houses being built and more families moving into the area, more domestic animals will be a part of a koala's habitat.

_____

_____

_____

───────────────────── **Critical** ══════════════════════

3. I think that we need to stop allowing houses to be built in the habitat of koalas.

_____

_____

_____

───────────────────── **Creative** ══════════════════════

4. Sometimes a koala can "fly" from a limb of one tree to a limb of another tree by flapping its front legs very quickly.

_____

_____

_____

Traveling Overseas

1. List the things you would need to organize before leaving your home to go on an overseas trip.

_____

_____

_____

2. Where would you locate information about the length and cost of an overseas trip?

_____

_____

_____

3. What are some of the problems you could encounter? How would you avoid these problems?

Problem	How to avoid it

A Funny Speech

Your favorite funny character has been asked to give a talk at your school. Write out his/her speech.

Future of America

On a seperate sheet of paper, write a brief time line of some of the changes that have taken place in your lifetime.

Illustrate one of the changes in a cartoon strip.

1.	2.	3.
4.	5.	6.
7.	8.	9.

The Importance of Coins

Business has been carried on using a trading or bartering system for many hundreds of years. Coinage was introduced in Persia about 500 B.C. and in China about 220 B.C. How would this have changed the daily activities of the traders and other business people?

_____

_____

_____

_____

_____

_____

_____

_____

_____

_____

_____

_____

Non-Human Hero

Write a story where a non-human becomes a hero.

New-Age Poem

Write a poem depicting life in the year 2500.

Brainstorming About Food

What is food? _____

_____

_____

_____

_____

_____

Who needs food? _____

_____

_____

_____

_____

_____

Why do we need food? _____

_____

_____

_____

_____

_____

What is your favorite food? Describe this food in 20 words.

_____ _____ _____ _____

_____ _____ _____ _____

_____ _____ _____ _____

_____ _____ _____ _____

Food Groups

Give examples of common foods in each group. Combine at least one food from each group to make a balanced meal. Describe this meal and draw a picture of it.

Common foods in each group:

_____

_____

_____

_____

_____

_____

_____

Described a balanced meal:

_____

_____

_____

_____

_____

_____

Draw this meal:

Math Likes

What do you like about mathematics? Why?

_____

_____

_____

_____

Name 10 fun things you can do that use math.

1. _____   6. _____

2. _____   7. _____

3. _____   8. _____

4. _____   9. _____

5. _____   10. _____

Pick one of these things and write about it.

_____

_____

_____

_____

_____

_____

_____

Working Math

List as many different people as you can who use math every day in their professions.

Choose two of these people.

_____   _____

Write down five questions to ask these people about how they use math in their professions.

1. _____

   _____

2. _____

   _____

3. _____

   _____

4. _____

   _____

5. _____

   _____

Survival

What does "survival" mean?

_____

_____

_____

_____

What do I need to survive?

_____

_____

_____

_____

How do I ensure that I have everything I need to survive?

_____

_____

_____

_____

If I had to do without something to survive, what would it be?

_____

If I could add another element to my needs for survival, what would it be?

_____

_____

_____

Calculating

Draw a mathematical calculator like the one you use at school.

Write and practice a short speech explaining how to use the calculator to a younger student at your school.

Designing an Exhibition

You have been asked to design a new exhibit for the local museum containing artifacts found during the excavations of a city believed to be over 2,000 years old. How would you choose what to display and the information provided for visitors? Write down your findings and begin your preliminary sketches of the exhibit. Include some drawings of artifacts that will be on display.

List of artifacts chosen for display	Information about the artifacts

Plan of display

Inventions

1. Choose an invention that you would like to investigate. The invention I will investigate is _____.

2. Write down five things that you already know about this invention.

   a. _____

   b. _____

   c. _____

   d. _____

   e. _____

3. Write down four things that you would like to know about this invention.

   a. _____

   b. _____

   c. _____

   d. _____

4. Change one component in this invention. What effect would this have?

The component I changed . . .	How it will work now . . .
_____ _____ _____ _____	_____ _____ _____ _____
What the new component looks like . . .	Did I improve the invention? . . .
_____ _____ _____	_____ _____ _____

I'm a Hero!

Imagine you have the opportunity to become a hero.

Choose one of these scenarios:
- a fire
- an accident
- a storm

Display your heroic feats in this cartoon strip.

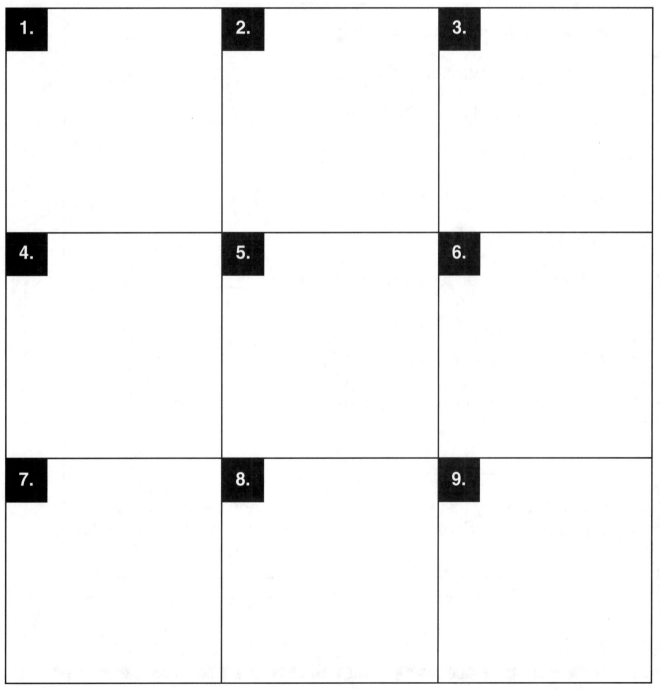

Poem Puzzle

Robinson Crusoe would never have survived without help—from whom?

_____

Use the clues below to answer the question.

1. My first is in maroon but not in lagoon. _____

2. My second is in palm but not helm._____

3. My third is in land and also in sand. _____

4. My fourth is in fir but not elm. _____

5. My fifth is in rifle but nowhere in gun. _____

6. My sixth is in sink but not sunk. _____

7. My seventh's in danger and hazard, not axe! _____

8. My eighth is in water and wax. _____

9. My last is in years, and every and why— _____

My all's a beloved friend. (Spell out the letters from the first three clues.)

_____

I'm named for the day that we met on the beach and the day that the working week ends. (Spell out the letters from clues four through nine.)

_____

Blood Donors

Alan, Chris, and Brad visit the blood bank. They fill out their details and list their professions (not necessarily in order) as scientist, sprinter, and secretary. Their blood types are tested and one is type A, one is type B, and one is type O. If you know that:

1) Brad was ahead of the secretary in the line and behind Chris.

2) Chris has type B blood, but the sprinter has A.

Can you work out each donor's profession and blood type?

	Secretary	Sprinter	Scientist	A	O	B
Alan						
Brad						
Chris						

Alan: _____

Brad: _____

Chris: _____

Hidden Meanings

Explain the meaning of each box.

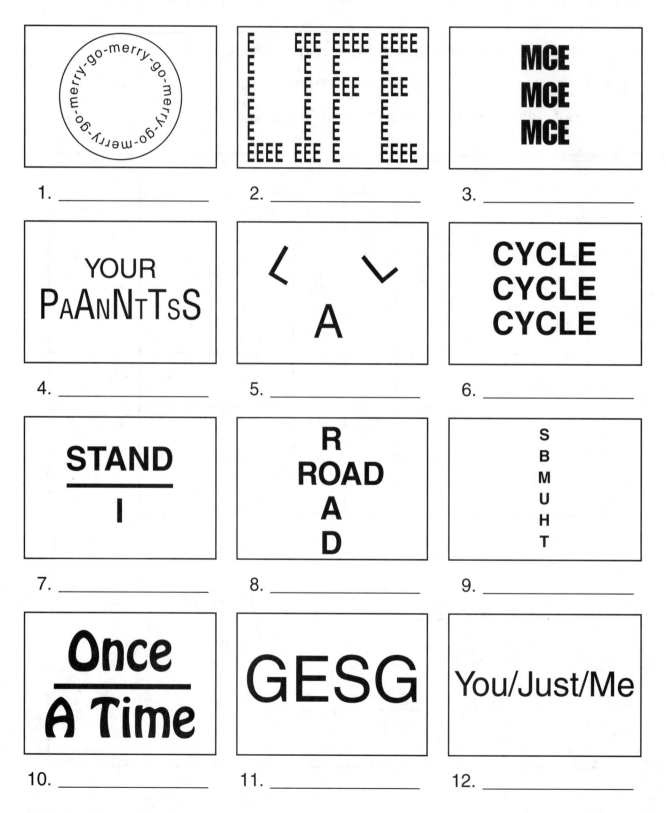

1. _____

2. _____

3. _____

4. _____

5. _____

6. _____

7. _____

8. _____

9. _____

10. _____

11. _____

12. _____

10 Questions

Write a question for each of the following answers.

1. **Question:** _____

   Answer: Saturn

2. **Question:** _____

   Answer: Cat

3. **Question:** _____

   Answer: Train

4. **Question:** _____

   Answer: 18

5. **Question:** _____

   Answer: Mozart

6. **Question:** _____

   Answer: Atlantic Ocean

7. **Question:** _____

   Answer: Earthquake

8. **Question:** _____

   Answer: 22

9. **Question:** _____

   Answer: Thanksgiving

10. **Question:** _____

    Answer: Atlas

Softball Lineup

All nine players on the Tiger softball team are sitting on the bench in their batting order. Using the clues below, find their batting order. Record their batting order by putting an **X** in the correct box.

1. Jane is batting fifth, and Daisy will bat some time before Carrie.

2. Joanne sits between Daisy and Gertie, and Annie is to the right of Jane.

3. Gertie bats after Joanne but before Annie.

4. Penny sits next to Carrie.

5. Carrie and Tammy are at each end of the bench.

	1	2	3	4	5	6	7	8	9
Jane									
Daisy									
Carrie									
Joanne									
Gertie									
Annie									
Penny									
Tammy									
Lindsey									

Six Words

Write as many sentences as you can, using the following words:

gumball, serious, shrieking, follow, happy, day

Can you write a sentence that includes all the words?

Computer Complaints

If computers could talk, what do you think would be the 10 major complaints they would have?

_____

_____

_____

_____

_____

_____

_____

_____

_____

_____

_____

Umbrelon

Choose two unrelated objects, such as a melon and an umbrella, and combine them. Choose a name for the new object, and then list what the qualities of the object are, and what the object could be used for. Draw the new object.

Square Eggs!

Visualize a square egg. Explain in detail how you think this egg could be used, and what might be the advantages and disadvantages of its shape.

_____

_____

_____

_____

_____

_____

_____

_____

_____

_____

_____

_____

_____

_____

_____

_____

Out in Space!

List as many objects as you can think of that you would find in outer space. Think of ways to group or categorize the objects, and give each category or group a label.

List:

Items listed under their categories:

What Do You Expect?

Design a questionnaire to predict what American people expect of the future.

What Could This Be?

List two objects or images that each drawing could be.

Draw one of your own and have a friend guess what it is.

Clean the Graffiti

Your school has a terrible problem with graffiti. Think of ways that you can stop this from happening. Your solution must involve a human, something mechanical, or something that has to be eaten.

How will you stop the graffiti writers and sprayers?

_____

_____

_____

_____

_____

_____

_____

_____

_____

_____

Draw your solution here.

Come and Play

Imagine you are in a junkyard. There are old tires, ladders with missing rungs, empty paint tins, boxes, ropes, old cupboards, etc.

Think about how you might use these items to design a safe playground for a number of students. Think about what other recycled items you would like to add. Write your ideas here.

_____

_____

_____

_____

_____

_____

_____

_____

Draw a map of your new playground in the space below, labeling its different parts.

Brushing Plus . . .

Create an improved toothbrush. Make sure that for each change that is made, there is a clear explanation. You could use the **BAR** strategy to help you consider how different features could be improved.

B = make it **bigger**

A = **add** something

R = **remove** something and **replace** it with something else

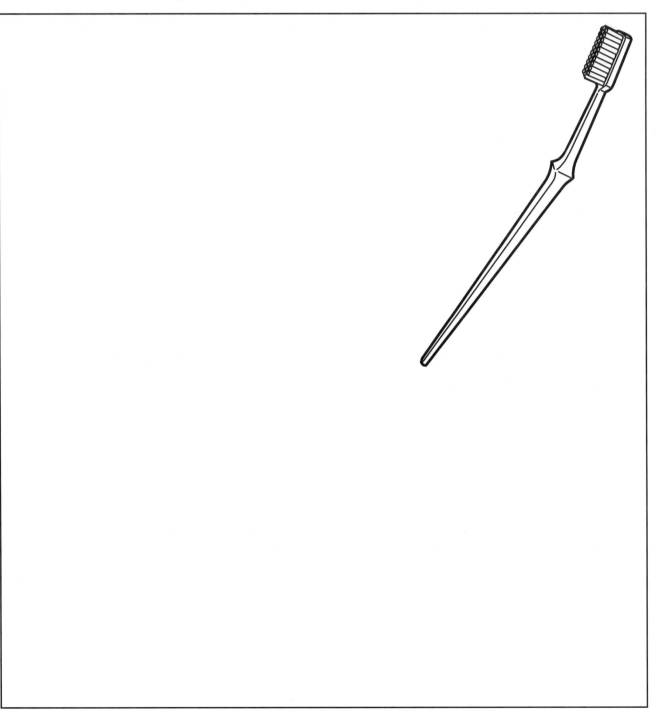

Egyptian Writing

If you visit Egypt you may find some very old writing on some walls. Here is what some of the symbols mean:

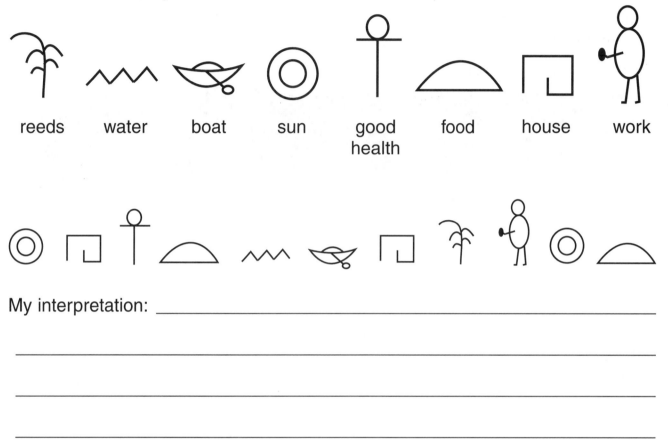

reeds   water   boat   sun   good health   food   house   work

My interpretation: _____

_____

_____

_____

Now design your own picture alphabet which tells a story about life in ancient Egypt and the building of the Great Pyramid.

My Picture Alphabet Symbols

My Story

City of the Future

1. Imagine that you could design a model of a **City of the Future** which will have no pollution problems.

2. Explain how you would solve each of the following potential pollution problems in your city.

My **City of the Future** would be called: _____

Potential Problem	Solution
household waste	
polluted drinking water	
air pollution from cars	
air pollution from factories	
noise pollution from cars and planes	

Pollution

Read each statement below and decide if you agree or disagree. Place a mark on the line to show how you feel. Explain why you made this choice.

1. Pollution is a necessary part of modern life.

   ├───┤

   Agree   Disagree

   Justification: _____

2. Household waste can easily be reduced.

   ├───┤

   Agree   Disagree

   Justification: _____

3. Pollution is not a problem in our local environment.

   ├───┤

   Agree   Disagree

   Justification: _____

4. The media exaggerates pollution problems.

   ├───┤

   Agree   Disagree

   Justification: _____

5. All countries should use nuclear power because it produces cheap electricity.

   ├───┤

   Agree   Disagree

   Justification: _____

Explanations

Bright purple snow is falling! Give five possible explanations for this.

1. _____

   _____

2. _____

   _____

3. _____

   _____

4. _____

   _____

5. _____

   _____

Draw a picture showing how people might react to seeing purple snow.

Survival Skills

You and a friend have been shipwrecked on a deserted island. The ship you were on has sunk in 10 yards of water not far from the shore. All that you could salvage from the ship was:

- a piece of rope

- a sheet from one of the bunks

- a bucket

You must both survive until the next ship passes in 30 days.

Describe what you would do to survive.

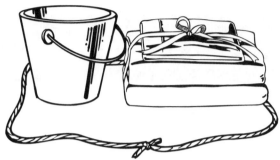

_____

_____

_____

_____

_____

_____

_____

_____

Invent something that would help you to attract the attention of the passing ship. Describe and illustrate how this will help you.

_____

_____

_____

_____

_____

_____

_____

Planning a Dinner Menu

How many of your favorite foods originated in another country? Complete this table. Choose four more countries to add to the table.

Country	Name of Dish	Main Ingredients
Italy		
Spain		
China		
India		
France		
Japan		
Mexico		

Bug Fan Club

First, think of your favorite insect. Write it here: _____

Write five questions that you would ask a bug expert in order to gain more information about this insect.

_____

_____

_____

_____

_____

List all the words you can think of that would describe this insect. Be as creative and thorough as you can.

_____

_____

_____

_____

Draw your insect surrounded by these words.

Solar Systems

On the chart below all the planets in our solar system are listed in order of their proximity to the sun. Fill in the squares with Yes or No. Some of the headings have been filled in for you. Use your own ideas for the rest.

Planet	Small	Round	Has moons		
Mercury					
Venus					
Earth					
Mars					
Jupiter					
Saturn					
Uranus					
Neptune					
Pluto					

What do all the planets have in common? _____

_____

In what ways are the planets different? _____

_____

What do Mercury, Venus, and Pluto have in common? _____

_____

List the planets according to their size. _____

_____

Come to My Party!

Make up a party list of your five favorite humorous characters. Design some party games they might like to play.

Cartoon Hero

Who is your favorite cartoon hero? Draw him/her in action.

Uniforms

What are uniforms? _____

Name six groups of people who wear uniforms.

_____

_____

_____

_____

_____

_____

Why do these people wear uniforms?

_____

_____

_____

_____

_____

_____

If you could design your own uniform, what would it look like? Draw a picture of it below and describe your design.

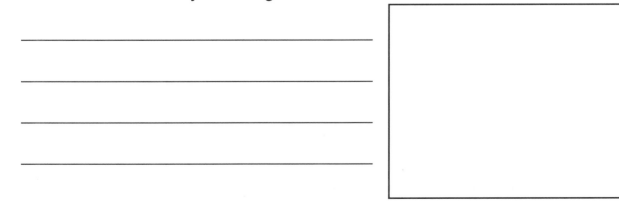

_____

_____

_____

_____

Protective Clothing

Illustrate and label 10 articles of clothing worn as protection in a work situation.
Which occupations require wearing these clothes?

Progress Chart

Page	Title	Date	Completed

Progress Chart *(cont.)*

Page	Title	Date	Completed

Progress Chart *(cont.)*

Page	Title	Date	Completed

#8122 Brain Games for Kids

Progress Chart *(cont.)*

Page	Title	Date	Completed

Answer Key

Page 313

Answers will vary.

Page 314 Patterns

Page 315

Answers will vary.

Page 316

Answers will vary.

Page 317

Start at the arrow. Remember that the nuggets are taken, so they aren't counted on the second round.

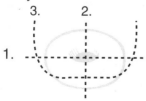

Page 318

C

Page 319

That Jack built.

Page 320

Mars at its closest distance is 51 million km. The martians are 1 million km short.

Page 321

Down the first column, up the second, and down the third.

Page 322

Slice in half across the hole, slice in quarters across the hole, and slice into eighths horizontally to the hole.

Page 323

Cara = A, Lucy = B, Martin = C, Gwen = C-, Donald = D.

Page 324

1. Look before you leap.
2. Never put off until tomorrow what can be done today.
3. A friend in need is a friend indeed.
4. The early bird catches the worm.
5. All that glitters is not gold.
6. Don't cry over spilled milk.
7. You never know what you can do until you try.
8. Make yourself necessary to someone.

Page 325

1. $.94
2. $.84, $.08
3. 2792 pennies

Page 326

4. 30,251 miles
5. 483 marbles
6. 38,404 people

Page 327

7. $3.60
8. $14.35
9. 84 socks
10. 214 rocks

Page 328

Answers will vary.

Page 329

Skippy 5.7m

Page 330

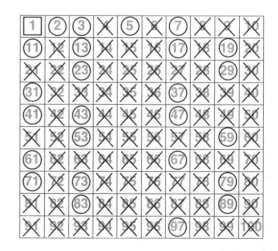

Answer Key *(cont.)*

Page 331

1. eat	6. react	11. mink
2. tow	7. task	12. king
3. wear	8. knife	13. girl
4. road	9. egg	
5. deer	10. germ	

Page 332

How many can you afford?

Page 333

flags, flash, flask

Dvorak keyboard: Andes, audio, aunts, dates, deans, death, donut, duets, hands, hated, haunt, hints, hosed, hunts, ideas, noted, saint, shade, shine, shone, shout, sited, sound, stain, stand, stone, those, unite (to name a few!)

Page 334

1. President
2. as soon as possible
3. adjective
4. pounds
5. maximum
6. et cetera
7. September
8. Master of Arts
9. I owe you
10. post meridian (after noon)
11. collect on delivery
12. respondez sil vous plait (please reply)
13. self-addressed stamped envelope
14. South America
15. building
16. railroad
17. preposition
18. headquarters
19. District Attorney
20. Daylight Saving Time

Page 335

Answers will vary.

Page 336

Chin, chip, chop, Chopin, cinch, coin, con, conch, coop, cop, hip, hoop, hop, icon, inch, nip, phonic, picnic, pin, pinch, Pinocchio, poncho, pooch

Page 337

necklace

Page 338

Aches and pains, again and again, alive and kicking, bacon and eggs, bells and whistles, bits and pieces, crackers and cheese, cut and paste, fair and square, fish and chips, night and day, nuts and bolts, odds and ends, rock and roll, salt and pepper, stars and stripes, thick and thin

Page 339

1. Wol	8. honey	
2. Tigger	9. acre	
3. Kanga	10. piglet	
4. Sanders	11. owl	
5. Rabbit	12. Robin	
6. Eeyore	13. howse	
7. Christopher		

Page 340

Can, car, café, cake, calf, cane, care, clan, coal, cola, cone, core, cork, corn, canoe, carol, clank, clean, clear, clerk, cloak, clone, coral, crane, crank, creak, croak, cornea

Page 341

1. book	9. artist
2. library	10. type
3. read	11. story
4. words	12. plot
5. picture	13. cover
6. print	14. character
7. page	15. illustration
8. author	

Page 342

1. broom	9. music
2. chain	10. number
3. drum	11. potato
4. egg	12. star
5. flower	13. table
6. hand	14. umbrella
7. jar	15. whale
8. letter	16. yellow

Page 343

1. large	6. thief	11. under
2. learn	7. earth	12. allow
3. story	8. price	13. bring
4. right	9. write	14. happy
5. start	10. hurry	15. shout

Answer Key (cont.)

Page 344

Answers will vary.

Page 345

1. huff
2. tar
3. cats
4. nook
5. thick
6. mix
7. tooth/hammer
8. cream
9. fine
10. back
11. scream
12. sticks
13. up
14. dollars
15. peaches
16. law
17. rise
18. war
19. in
20. black
21. prim
22. body/heart
23. silk
24. hook
25. pen/pencil

Page 346

1. south, mouth
2. lake, lane
3. mile, mule
4. explore, explode
5. map, cap
6. west, best
7. land, hand
8. sea, tea
9. mountain, fountain
10. pole, hole
11. state, slate
12. line, lime

Page 347

1. peace
2. seize
3. plain
4. sail
5. world
6. herd
7. site
8. horse
9. strait
10. build
11. fir
12. poor
13. reign
14. tax
15. capitol
16. cede
17. corps
18. route
19. throne
20. war

Page 348–Page 357

Answers will vary.

Page 358

Answers will vary.
1. Three Little Pigs
2. Red Riding Hood
3. Rumpelstiltskin
4. Jack and the Beanstalk
5. The Three Billy Goats Gruff

Page 359–Page 373

Answers will vary.

Page 374

1. turkeys, chickens, ducks, geese
2. because they have webbed feet

Page 375–Page 382

Answers will vary.

Page 383

nails, frame, sky, tree, badge, hair, shirt, expression, freckles, land/water

Page 384

1. railway crossing
2. a train in the station
3. round trip ticket
4. railway line

Page

It comes out at tap two.

Page

Flower pot 1

Page 387

B is attached to D, A is flying free, and Ben is holding onto C.

Page 388

It is a trick puzzle. Try going around the outside.

Page 389

1. red
2. yellow
3. green
4. white
5. black
6. pink
7. red
8. orange

Page 390

A. missing rear-view mirror
B. missing turn signal lights
C. missing windshield wiper
D. no back window
E. no headlights

Page 391

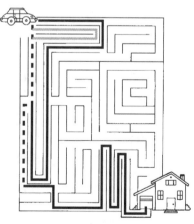

Page 392

1. Marla—pink
2. Pepper—red
3. Rosa—yellow

Page 393

Answers will vary.

Answer Key (cont.)

Page 394

1. June—months that end in -er/or are consecutive
2. glove—footwear
3. notebook—writing tools
4. page—royalty/queen
5. Rich—form of Robert
6. carnation—wood
7. layer cake—cookies
8. nephew—females
9. television—machines for talking into
10. flower—furniture
11. grapefruit—melons
12. strange—noises
13. elephant—large cats
14. lightbulb—tools
15. colon—end punctuation

Page 395

1. types of dance
2. sports
3. flowers
4. large cats
5. desserts/sweets
6. tools
7. moods
8. gemstones
9. dairy products
10. one
11. things that are round
12. air transportation
13. writing tools
14. girls' names starting with H
15. squashes

Page 396

wood	Water	Colors
oak	bay	tan
pencil	sea	red
board	pond	blue
forest	lake	green
walnut	river	scarlet
lumber	ocean	beige
maple	creek	chartreuse
Metals	**Space**	**Furniture**
tin	countdown	lamp
iron	Mars	couch
titanium	moon	mirror
aluminum	orbit	chest
steel	astronaut	rocker
copper	weightless	dresser
platinum	rocket	cabinet

Page 397–Page 404

Answers will vary.

Page 405

1.
144	2
8	1
100	

2. Thailand—Baht   United Kingdom—Pound
   Italy—Lira
   Japan—Yen   India—Rupee

3. 32 carnations, 20 daisies, 80 flowers altogether
4. United States
5.

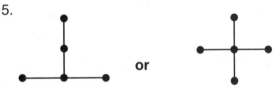

or

Page 406

(There are others, but here is one way.)

(1) 8	(2) 6	(3) 5	(4) 10	(5) 6	(6) 11
9	7	4	5	9	5
1	5	9	3	3	2

Page 407

Answers will vary.

Page 408

Answers will vary.

Page 409

A. 20 B. 14 C. 28 D. 30 E. 32 (highest score possible is 55)

Page 410

Answers will vary.

Page 411

27

Page 412-Page 416

Answers will vary.

Page 417

| 91 x 4 = 364 | 123421 | 988 x 9 + 4 |
| 91 x 5 = 455 | 1234521 | 989 x 9 + 3 |

Page 418

Answer Key *(cont.)*

Page 419

Woodrow Wilson

Page 420

1. Victor-May 7
2. Mary-January 1
3. Marco-April 7
4. Christina-February 21
5. Vicky-August 3
6. Mike-October 30
7. Danielle-July 15
8. Peter-March 25

Page 421

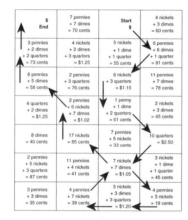

Page 422

1. $9.65
2. $3.53
3. $2.55
4. $2.65
5. $13.00
6. $27.00

Page 423

Answers will vary.

Page 424 and 425

1. warm
2. zipper
3. padded
4. camp
5. bed

a sleeping bag

Page 426 and 427

1. rectangle
2. fabric
3. wave
4. symbol
5. nation

a flag

Page 428 and 429

1. on
2. off
3. portable
4. batteries
5. beam

a flashlight

Page 430 and 431

1. mammal
2. arctic
3. swimmer
4. blubber
5. tusks

a walrus

Page 432

1. alphabetical
2. dictionary
3. fact
4. entry
5. lexicon
6. volume
7. book
8. topic
9. reference
10. index
11. article
12. thesaurus

Page 433

Across:

2. storm
6. kite
7. roads
9. tail
10. all
11. trees

Down:

1. power lines
3. bridle
4. open area
5. park
8. safety

Page 434

Answer Key (cont.)

Page 435

sane, shape, shoe, shone, shoo, shop, snap, snoop, soap, soon, span, spoon

Page 436

deer, me, red, reed, seed, seem, seemed, cede, creed, deem, seer

Page 437

1. It's the only four-letter name.
2. It's the only name with one vowel.
3. All the other names have a "u," even Earth has "you"!

Page 438

OLD, odd, add, aid, lid, lit, nit, not, net, NEW

Page 439

4-letter words: been, bend, bind, bird, deer, dine, ding, Eden, edge, gene, grid, grin, heed, herb, herd, here, hide, hind, hire, need, nerd, nine, reed, rein, ride, rind, ring

5-letter words: begin, beige, being, breed, bride, bring, diner, genie, genre, greed, green, grind, hedge, hinge, hired, inner, neigh, ridge, reign

6-letter words: behind, binder, bridge, dinner, ending, engine, gender, grinned, hinder, hinged, reined

7-letter words: bending, heeding, herding, needing, neighed, reigned

8-letter words: beginner, breeding

Page 440

1. squid
2. leviathan
3. shark
4. clam
5. Loch Ness
6. stingray
7. sea-serpent
8. octopus
9. whale
10. kraken

Page 441

BED, bet, bat, cat, COT, cop, cap, NAP

Page 442

maraca, Sahara, banana, Panama, delete, serene, yo-ho-ho, eleven, eyelet

Page 443

The place where records are kept: Archives

Page 444

green fly
green bean
Greenland
greenback
greenhouse
green light
green thumb
green pepper
greengrocer
green keeper

Page 445

German
Dutch
Italian
Spanish
French
Canadian

Page 446

A coat of paint.

Page 447

1. Don't count your chickens before they hatch.
2. Birds of a feather flock together.
3. A stitch in time saves nine.
4. A penny saved is a penny earned.
5. Two wrongs don't make a right.
6. Where there is a will, there is a way.
7. Strike while the iron is hot.
8. A watched pot never boils.

Page 448

1. soddy
2. corn dodgers
3. forty-niners
4. chips
5. emigrants
6. ague
7. rustlers
8. schooner

Answer Key (cont.)

Page 449

1. SOS
2. eye
3. mum
4. solos
5. pop
6. wow
7. tot
8. radar
9. gag
10. mom
11. Bob
12. Hannah/Eve
13. madam or ma'am
14. deed
15. ewe

Page 450

tree
trim
eerie
merit
meter
otter
timer
term
remote
termite

Page 451–Page 472

Answers will vary.

Page 473

The four-digit combination to the briefcase is 5381.

Page 474

Here's one way to explain it:

1. Left foot forward
2. Right foot forward
3. Left foot forward
4. Right foot swings to side
5. Left foot closes to right foot.

Page 475

1. September has only 30 days.
2. Sailboats don't have engines.
3. If they were docked at the pier, the anchor would be down.
4. You can't climb into a full barrel.
5. The barrel becomes a funnel.
6. You can't see tattoos through a black shirt.
7. If it was a fatal shot, how was the story written?

Page 476

Page 477–Page 489

Answers will vary.

Page 490

1. face to face
2. man overboard
3. split level
4. long underwear
5. deer crossing
6. head over heels
7. business before pleasure
8. order in the court
9. uptown
10. banana split
11. three degrees below zero
12. Minnesota

Answer Key (cont.)

Page 492
1. add
2. sum
3. zero
4. half
5. plus
6. minus
7. addition
8. negative
9. digit
10. mathematics
11. subtract
12. times
13. divide
14. fraction
15. number

Page 493
1. 12 sides
2. 13 items
3. 5 rings
4. 100 years
5. 13 colonies
6. 5 sides
7. 1 wheel
8. 168 hours
9. 366 days
10. 1,000 years
11. 52 cards
12. 100 centimeters
13. 90 degrees
14. 9 planets
15. 1 eye
16. 88 keys
17. 206 bones
18. 360 degrees
19. 10 events
20. 64 squares

Page 494
1. You would need to buy more than 10 tacos on special to equal the cost of the t-shirt.
2. It is cheaper to pay 10 cents a mile.

Page 495

Arabic	12	13	14	15	16	17	18	19	20
Babylonian	<▼▼	<▼▼▼	<▼▼▼▼	<▼▼▼▼▼	<▼▼▼▼▼▼	<▼▼▼▼▼▼▼	<▼▼▼▼▼▼▼▼	<▼▼▼▼▼▼▼▼▼	<<
Egyptian	Ω ||	Ω |||	Ω ||||	Ω || |||	Ω ||| |||	Ω ||| ||||	Ω |||| ||||	Ω |||| |||||	Ω Ω
Roman	XII	XIII	XIV	XV	XVI	XVII	XIII	XIX	XX
Mayan	oo	ooo	oooo	___	o	oo	ooo	oooo	___
Base 2	1100	1101	1110	1111	10000	10001	10010	10011	10100

Page 496
a. 2 + 6 + 1 = 9, 1 + 5 + 3 = 9, 3 + 4 + 2 = 9
b. 5 + 4 + 1 = 10, 1 + 6 + 3 = 10, 3 + 2 + 5 = 10
c. 6 + 1 + 4 = 11, 4 + 5 + 2 = 11, 2 + 3 + 6 = 11
d. 4 + 2 + 6 = 12, 6 + 1 + 5 = 12, 5 + 3 + 4 = 12

Page 497–Page 498
Answers will vary.

Page 499
Ream
Triceratops
Quadruplets
Star of David
Triangle
bicentennial
Bigamy
centurian
decathalon
pentathalon

Page 500
1. contains only even numbers
2. it's a palindrome
3. each four digit number is twice the one before
4. all odd numbers
5. the digits are ordered odd-even-odd-even
6. contains eight two-digit prime numbers
7. double 1 = 2, double 2 = 4, etc.
8. the sum of the first three 4-digit numbers equals the last
9. the sum of the four numbers is 9999
10. when converted to letters of the alphabet they spell credit card (c = 3, r = 18, e = 5, etc.)

Answer Key (cont.)

Page 501

Answers will vary.

Page 502

1. can't do
2. can't do
3. 1 + 2
4. can't do
5. 2 + 3
6. 1 + 2 + 3
7. 3 + 4
8. can't do
9. 4 + 5 or 2 + 3 + 4
10. 1 + 2 + 3 + 4
11. 5 + 6
12. 3 + 4 + 5
13. 6 + 7
14. 2 + 3 + 4 + 5
15. 7 + 8 or 4 + 5 + 6
16. can't do
17. 8 + 9
18. 3 + 4 + 5 + 6 or 5 + 6 + 7
19. 9 + 10
20. 2 + 3 + 4 + 5 + 6
21. 10 + 11 or 6 + 7 + 8
22. 4 + 5 + 6 + 7
23. 11 + 12
24. 7 + 8 + 9
25. 12 + 13
26. 5 + 6 + 7 + 8
27. 13 + 14 or 8 + 9 + 10
28. 1 + 2 + 3 + 4 + 5 + 6 + 7
29. 14 + 15
30. 6 + 7 + 8 + 9

Page 503

1. 4
2. 6
3. 9
4. 21
5. 31
6. 10011
7. 111
8. 11001
9. 1010
10. 101

Page 504

Here's one way: The small trees' shadows (1m) are 1/4 of their height (4m). The tall tree's shadow (5m) must also be 1/4 of its height, which must then be 5 x 4 m = 20 m. Not quite enough room to drop it!

Page 505

Scientist: Christiaan Huygens
Retrograde moon: Phoebe

Page 506–507

1. fluffy
2. white
3. sweet
4. tops
5. cocoa

marshmallows

Page 508–509

1. lab
2. tool
3. enlarge
4. focus
5. lens

a microscope

Page 510–511

1. cooking
2. herb
3. strong
4. white
5. bulb

garlic

Page 512–513

1. office
2. tool
3. secures
4. loops
5. wire

a stapler

Page 514

Cellist
Oboist
Musician
Piano tuner
Organist
Soprano
Entertainer
Recorder

Answer Key *(cont.)*

Page 515

SLOW
slot
slat
flat
fiat
fist
FAST

Page 516

middle age
middle ages
middle C
middle class
middle ear
Middle East
middle man
middle of the road
middle sized
middle weight

Page 517

1. actual
2. insane
3. defeat
4. train
5. manual
6. escort
7. climb
8. Indian
9. timing
10. horses
11. Reno
12. river
13. plain

Page 518

1. cornucopia
2. cornerstone
3. corner
4. corned beef
5. corncob
6. corncrib
7. cornerback
8. corn oil
9. cornet
10. corny
11. cornea
12. cut corners
13. cornstarch
14. cornice
15. cornflakes

Page 519

1. desert
2. capital
3. thorough
4. anyway
5. effect
6. imply
7. latter
8. angel
9. illicit
10. disprove
11. stationery
12. accept
13. proceed
14. preposition
15. quit

Page 520

1. New York, New York
2. Chicago, Illinois
3. Houston, Texas
4. Jackson, Mississippi
5. Phoenix, Arizona
6. Detroit, Michigan
7. Norfolk, Virginia
8. Trenton, New Jersey
9. Atlanta, Georgia
10. Memphis, Tennessee
11. Seattle, Washington
12. Santa Fe, New Mexico

Page 521

2. sea + son = season
3. cot + ton = cotton
4. pea + nut = peanut
5. sun + dry = sundry
6. son + net = sonnet
7. off + ice = office
8. rat + tan = rattan
9. men + ace = menace
10. Jack + son = Jackson

Page 522

1. 1
2. 2
3. 5
4. 32
5. 90
6. 100
7. 4
8. 0
9. 110
10. 360
11. 206
12. 144
13. 14
14. 52
15. 64
16. 100
17. 366
18. 500
19. 88
20. 11

Page 523

Answers will vary. Some possibilities include the following: dialogue, auctioned, housemaid, cautioned, reputation, equation, pneumonia, discourage, ultraviolet, adventitious, and encouraging.

Page 524

1. Alexander Graham Bell
2. automobiles
3. cotton gin
4. Thomas Edison
5. Robert Fulton
6. Samuel Morse
7. blue jeans
8. cotton gin
9. sports
10. Eastman
11. Morse
12. eye

Answer Key (cont.)

Page 525

Animal	Male	Female	Young	Group
fox	dog	vixen	cub	skulk
chicken	rooster	hen	chick	flock
lion	lion	lioness	cub	pride
cattle	bull	cow	calf	herd
whale	bull	cow	calf	herd
seal	bull	cow	pup	herd
ostrich	cock	hen	chick	flock
sheep	ram	ewe	lamb	flock
goose	gander	goose	gosling	gaggle
kangaroo	buck	doe	joey	herd
hog	boar	sow	piglet	herd
goat	billy	nanny	kid	herd

Page 526

airport   tractor
rattier   apricot
topiary

Page 527

1. sight
2. seven
3. lion
4. Sahara
5. tongue
6. years
7. migrate
8. acacia
9. brown
10. mammal
11. calf
12. fight
13. herds

Page 528

1. chimpanzee
2. citizenship
3. Leipzig
4. marzipan
5. pince nez
6. pizza
7. pizzicato
8. prize
9. puzzling
10. trapezoid
11. zeppelin
12. zip code

Page 529

Chesapeake Bay Bridge Tunnel

Page 520

1. elephant
2. Asian
3. African
4. mammoth
5. hyena
6. mastodon
7. forage
8. troop
9. mammal

Bonus Word: pachyderm

Page 531

prod
trod
hot rod
piston rod
divining rod
lightning rod
cuisenaire rod

Page 532

1. journey
2. clouds
3. helicopter
4. eighty
5. island
6. movies
7. leagues
8. submarine
9. moon
10. Earth

#8122 Brain Games for Kids

Answer Key *(cont.)*

Page 533

    hot potato
    cottontail
    toothpaste
    sweet potato
    photostat
    spotted toad
    tree-tomato

Page 534

    tape, tarp, tear, tier, tire, trap, tray, trip, type, taper, teary, tripe, tipper, trapper, tripper

Page 535

1. execute
2. elevate
3. ease
4. eagle
5. estimate
6. educate
7. envelope
8. evidence
9. exile
10. ewe
11. evacuate
12. examine
13. evaporate
14. exercise
15. encourage
16. executive
17. exhale
18. escape
19. entice
20. emancipate

Page 536

1. EZ
2. IC
3. CU
4. P
5. C
6. K, D, or B
7. O
8. I
9. U or I
10. TP
11. IV
12. Y
13. T or OJ
14. B
15. DJ

Page 537

1. ill Bill
2. bad lad
3. glum chum
4. shy fly
5. spunky monkey
6. plump ump
7. fluffy puppy
8. sad dad
9. wet pet
10. pink drink
11. steady Teddy
12. sloppy poppy
13. wee flea
14. sick chick
15. sharp harp

Page 538

    Answers will vary.

Page 539

1. F
2. O
3. N
4. H
5. A
6. U
7. Y
8. C
9. T
10. K
11. I

    famous saying: You can if you think you can.

Page 540–Page 563

    Answers will vary.

Page 564

    Man Friday

Page 565

    Chris, Scientist, B
    Brad, sprinter, A
    Alan, secretary, O

Answer Key (cont.)

Page 566

1. merry-go-round
2. life of ease
3. three blind mice (no i's)
4. ants in your pants
5. all mixed up
6. tricycle
7. I understand
8. cross roads
9. thumbs up
10. once upon a time
11. scrambled eggs
12. just between you and me

Page 567

Answers will vary.

Page 568

Jane 5
Daisy 2
Carrie 9
Joanne 3
Gertie 4
Annie 6
Penny 8
Tammy 1
Lindsey 7

Page 569–Page 590

Answers will vary.

Super Solver Award

To: _____

From: _____

Date: _____

Super Solver Award

To: _____

From: _____

Date: _____